Success at the Heart of Government
Working with Ministers

Also by Pauline Curtis

Quiet Quadrangles and Ivory Towers

Success at the Heart of Government

Working with Ministers

Pauline Curtis

The Courts of the Morning

Published by
The Courts of the Morning, Shooters Hill, Pangbourne, RG8 7EA

email: bookenquiries@pcurtis.com

www.pcurtis.com

ISBN 978-0-9557163-1-7

A share of the proceeds from each copy sold will go to the Association of Senior Members Fund at St Hilda's College, Oxford.

For my mother, my husband Pete and all the friends and colleagues
I worked with during my time working with Ministers

Acknowledgements

These memoirs are published with the permission of Simon Fraser, the Permanent Secretary of the Department for Business Innovation & Skills (formerly the Department for Business, Enterprise and Regulatory Reform and previously the Department of Trade and Industry) and the Cabinet Office.

Throughout the work I had the support of my husband Pete, my most important friend, my soul mate and my partner. I am so lucky to have met him when we were both at Oxford. I believe I was successful in my career because I was able to work very hard, with his encouragement. He was also very successful in his career in the Civil Service. I am proud to dedicate this book to Pete, and to all the friends and colleagues I worked with during my time working with Ministers, especially Alex Williams who went before me to Headquarters, and Peter Adkin, Alan Conway and Dr Keith Shotton who were responsible for my three promotion steps. My thanks to all my colleagues, serving and retired, who read the early manuscript and made useful and encouraging comments.

This book is also dedicated to my mother, still very lively as she celebrates her 95th birthday in 2009. I hope I may inherit her spirit and enthusiasm for life at the same age.

My thanks to the library staff at the Bodleian Library in Oxford who helped me with my research. My special thanks to various members of the Senior Common Room at St Hilda's College, Oxford who encouraged me when progress was slow, especially Elizabeth Llewellyn-Smith and Dr Margaret Rayner.

Contents

Preface

Why should anyone want to read about me and my career? This story is special because it describes a career within the bowels of policy making. Policy work is mainly known by its outputs, whether that is speeches in the Houses of Parliament or elsewhere, the creation of new rules or new organisational structures. My story instead talks about the process of making successful policies. It describes some of what actually happened day by day and week by week, in the real situation of my work with a Conservative Government between 1981 and 1996. I worked hard, yet to the outside world I was just an invisible civil servant.

While I will always have the style and skills of a civil servant I am also an academic. For almost 30 years I have worked for the Open University, in computing, technology and management. My academic colleagues in the OU Business School encouraged me to write about my years in the Civil Service, whereas I received only surprise, curiosity, admiration and occasional criticism from Civil Service friends and colleagues. Now I have completed the description of my career there will be plenty of time for me to stand back and reflect on what happened. At a minimum, I hope my story will provide case studies for teaching, and give examples of particular schemes or interesting anecdotes to illuminate students' understanding of what was really involved when Working with Ministers.

Having been born and educated in a small coal-mining town in the Midlands, I won a place to read Mathematics at St Hilda's College, Oxford, where I gained a First Class Honours degree. At that time I had no thoughts of getting involved with politics or writing. I continued my research at Oxford University, working with the eminent Professor Leslie Fox who was Head of the Computing Laboratory, and gained the degrees of MSc and DPhil in Numerical Analysis using their world-class computer facilities to develop new ways of solving melting and solidification problems. The subject of my thesis meant I was close to being an engineer, yet the actual work was firmly a mixture of programming and numerical analysis. On the basis of this research work I joined the Numerical Analysis Group at the National Physical Laboratory in 1976. I have written about my memoirs of these days as 'Quiet Quadrangles and Ivory Towers' (ISBN 978-0-9557163-0-0).

The National Physical Laboratory, abbreviated to NPL, was a research establishment of the Department of Industry and after my first promotion I was invited to move within the wider Department, joining the Policy and Perspectives Unit in London in 1981. I found I liked policy work and working with Ministers, and settled into 'Whitehall' for the rest of my career. Unlike other scientists plucked out of their comfortable research establishments, I never had any interest in going back to the NPL. As a young scientist I had written a number of research papers which were published, then turned that skill towards writing letters and speeches for Ministers. I was good at taking complicated technical issues and describing them so that 'even a Minister' could understand. The sketches in the two BBC TV series at that time, 'Yes Minister' and 'Yes Prime Minister', give an insight into what the work involved. Success at policy work involves giving good advice too, and my advice was soon trusted by senior officials and Ministers. In a few short years I moved from being a scientist who was searching for consultancy work and funding, to instead being one of the managers who controlled and prioritised budgets.

Even in the 1990s there were only a few dozen women in the Senior Civil Service when I became Assistant Secretary in 1994. In those times male members of the Senior Civil Service were described as 'mandarins', and so I considered myself to be a 'mandarine'. It was a rare and colourful species, still under threat today.

Looking back now, I can see that following a scientific route into policy making was a disadvantage. I know of ambitious senior colleagues who have hidden their research qualifications, and this seems wrong. In my case, I soon found that scientists took longer to get promotion compared with their fast-stream colleagues. The Civil Service is a good employer in terms of equal opportunities, but young scientists were forced to jump more promotion fences. The career routes only meet at Assistant Secretary, and there is a diagram of the various grades at Appendix A at the end of the book. In the normal world where a secretary is a secretary, my ambition to become an Assistant Secretary has to be explained. I hope the diagram in Appendix A helps. If I had stayed until the normal retirement age and continued to work effectively then I hope I might have been promoted one step further, and that would be to Under Secretary. Beyond that was Deputy Secretary, and the top of the tree is the Permanent Secretary.

The Civil Service world is full of acronyms and abbreviations, so to help readers I have provided a list at the end of the book.

Unlike Ministers and Prime Ministers, who always seem to be expected to publish their memoirs, I did not write a diary while I was working. Fortunately, having initially worked in the Department of Industry (DOI), which then became the Department of Trade and Industry (DTI), I have been able to refer to published pamphlets and brochures as well as academic publications. I believe that everything which is described here is already in the public domain, although it may be difficult to find original material . There are many real people who are mentioned by name in the story, and each has added their special ingredient to my career. Political biographies and autobiographies, by convention, do not usually mention civil servants by name and I have been careful to include names only of those colleagues who are listed in the Civil Service Yearbooks. My secretary, Barbara, will recognise much of my story and I hope she will enjoy a journey with me back into the past.

Alongside my career in the Civil Service I also made a parallel career teaching in the Open University, tolerated if not encouraged by my various bosses. The OU is not just any University. It is special in many ways and is open to people, places, methods and ideas. I always called it my charity work because it was not paid very well compared with the Civil Service; teaching one course just paid for a two week package holiday overseas. Being a tutor for the Open University was paid at the same rate as the very bottom of the scale of University teaching staff, which is not unreasonable, yet the tutor had to provide many of the resources which a traditional University provides automatically to staff – for example easy access to necessary books and journals, and their own computer and stationery. In this respect I envied the permanent academic staff who were based in Milton Keynes and had all these facilities on site and benefited from the traditional academic career progression from Lecturer to Senior Lecturer and then in theory to Reader and Professor. An OU tutor was always only an Associate Lecturer and could never aspire to becoming an Associate Professor, even if he or she was a full Professor within their main job in a traditional University. One feature of OU tutoring was that it involved working unsocial hours because all the work was done in evenings or at weekends. Students always seem to ring for help just as we sat down to eat a nice romantic meal. Fortunately I had an answering machine on my telephone and could ring back later at a more convenient time. Now it is all done by email.

Because of my Open University lecturing I had preserved some published material during my DTI days which I used for examples and case studies. It illuminated my teaching on the OU MBA course on Performance Measurement and Evaluation, as well as my contributions to courses on technology policy and innovation. The papers filled two filing cabinets and the time finally came to either use it or donate it all to the library of my old College at Oxford.

Nevertheless, this book might never have been written except that I read an article in 2002 about a new DTI scheme called the Manufacturing Advisory Service (MAS). In 1977 there had been a similar scheme, with exactly the same name, and with very similar policy objectives. I recall because in 1982 I started a scheme called the Small Firms Technical Enquiry Service, and it was my first policy creation, so has always been very special to me. It was based on the MAS. It is perhaps worth noting that the first MAS was set up under a Labour Government, then there was a Conservative Government in power from 1979 to 1997, replaced by a Labour Government, yet each is trying to do exactly the same policy actions. Helping small and medium sized companies solve their technical and manufacturing problems is still a major problem.

In this Internet world, I found no evidence that the old MAS had ever existed, and then I started to search for information about other policy tools which were in common use in the 1980s and early 1990s. Where had all the information gone? I went to visit the DTI library in 1 Victoria Street, London and found there was no longer a library. Everyone is now supposed to get their information from the Internet, with all the known risks of factual content and longevity. This may be reasonable for recent information, but does not go back before 1996. Many of the old traditional paper files have been archived or destroyed, in line with the default instructions officials like me had marked on the files, or the papers are difficult to find. In addition, material found on the Internet can disappear over time; even while preparing this book some of my Internet references have disappeared.

Fortunately the Bodleian library at Oxford University is one of the Legal Deposit Libraries and contains a complete set of all printed publications. Their Official Papers collection is comprehensive and they hold the vast majority of material published in this subject area. The Official Papers section is located in the Radcliffe Camera, which is the beautiful 18th century circular iconic building in central Oxford. As an Oxford graduate I have free access to the libraries and have spent a lot of time since 2002 doing my research there. In spite of having access to information, and lots of time, writing this has been a long and slow journey. Unlike writing a romantic novel, I needed to be scrupulously careful that my information was based on correct facts. Even with the best intentions after many years the memory can play tricks and invent false 'facts'. I would therefore be pleased to hear from anyone who has more information, extra insights or corrections to the text.

If you are one of many people who have an interesting story to tell and would like to write and publish then it is not difficult to follow my journey. For those who want to look at some of the content before deciding to purchase the book, selected Chapters as well as my diary as an author can be found at www.pcurtis.com/author.htm

Pauline E. M. Curtis
20th September 2009

Success at the Heart of Government
Working with Ministers

Introduction

As you read this book then reflect on the following questions :

> Why would anyone want to leave a nice comfortable research job in the quiet countryside of a government laboratory in leafy Teddington in order to join the rough and tumble commute to London?

> Why leave a career in a technical area in which you are an expert to move into a new world where past skills are only slightly relevant?

> Why does anyone want to do something different with their life?

> How do you measure success in your work, career, life? Here you can read about my work, my career, my ideas on achieving the quality of life.

I was invited to move from research into policy work, and it was suggested at such a senior level that I had to consider the move very seriously. The timing was right for me; I was looking for challenges elsewhere and eventually I would have moved, most probably into academia. My first policy job was as the most junior member of a small policy team and the first part of my story is in Part One: Managing Myself. Success here led to promotion and I progressed to manage my own small teams which is described in Part Two: Managing Others. The transition between managing oneself and managing others is a crucial step in a career in any organisation. I found I enjoyed the challenges of policy work, and having succeeded as a manager I became impatient to take more responsibility. This led to a series of short postings, as was the fashion for career development in those days, including a secondment to set up a marketing plan in a small innovative software company. This breadth of experience eventually led to further career success, as described in Part Three: Leadership and Management. My final posting was Director of SME Technology, responsible for encouraging every aspect of the use of technology by small and medium sized enterprises. I achieved my goal of becoming a member of the Senior Civil Service.

If I had to live my life again, I would do exactly the same.

PART ONE: MANAGING MYSELF

New skills:

      managing my time

      writing elegant briefing

      delivering to deadlines

      making meetings work

1 Starting work in the Corridors of Power

It was a sharp bright day in November 1981 when I started doing the daily commute by train from home to London Paddington and onwards by Bakerloo Underground to Victoria. The Department of Industry (DOI) was not based in Whitehall but inhabited several buildings scattered around within walking distance of Victoria station. For one wonderful winter season British Rail provided us with an early morning 125 High Speed Train which was comfortable and fast. Everyone wondered where they had found the train. Had it been accidentally left in the sidings at Oxford one evening and then stopped specially for us as it made its way back to London? All too soon the summer came, the timetable changed, and it was back to the nasty crowded diesel units. Fortunately I was always able to get a seat, so I could catch up with reading journals and planning my day. In the evening I got to know the different fast trains to Reading, so that I could leave London later and change at Reading and still arrive at home at the same time. There was no concept of flexible working. I aimed to be in my office each day between 08.45 and 09.00 and left at 17.30 to catch the 18.15 train home. On Friday I finished a little earlier.

My annual second class season ticket was expensive, and in November 1981 I had to pay the full cost myself. When it came to be renewed in November 1982 it was possible to get an advance from the Civil Service to pay for the season ticket, refunded monthly, and I took advantage of that. My pay checks show that it cost almost £100 per month when my standard pay before tax was only £10,738 per year. I now earned slightly more than I had at the National Physical Laboratory (NPL) because I was eligible for what was called the Inner London weighting, whereas the NPL was only in the Outer London area. My benchmark was whether I earned more than a Co-op milkman because one of my Oxford DPhil friends had chosen that as his initial career. Now I had finally overtaken him, and I hoped to do even better in future.

My first job was in the Policy and Perspectives Unit, which was part of the Research and Technology Requirements and Perspectives Division (RTP) of the DOI. My office was at Room 313 in Abell House in John Islip Street. It was a long way from Whitehall and Westminster but not far from Millbank, and I was soon invited to join my colleagues as a member of the Millbank lunch club which used the canteen in Millbank Tower. I hated being trapped inside the lift but the food and the company made it worthwhile. Millbank Tower is a very tall building, with 32 floors and was said to be the tallest building in London when it was built in 1963.

Usually someone like me who was only a Senior Scientific Officer would work in a team for a Principal Scientific Officer, as had been the case at the NPL. The Civil Service was and is a strongly hierarchical structure and staff usually work for people just one grade above them. In my case my boss was one grade higher than that. Dr Grant Lewison was a Senior Principal Scientific Officer, at Grade 6, whereas a Principal Scientific Office equated to Grade 7. Above him there was Dr Barry Copestake at Grade 5 and then Mr Alex Williams at Grade 3; as the numbers get smaller the person is more senior. I had to get used to the numbering system, which was different to the grades at the NPL. The Senior Civil Service was defined as officials at Grade 5 and above. To join this select group had been my ambition since I joined the NPL. From Appendix A it is clear that Deputy Chief Scientific Officer (DCSO) at the NPL was the same as Grade 5 for a scientist in London, and was equivalent to the grade of Assistant Secretary for administrators.

My immediate boss, Dr Lewison, was a character and I enjoyed working with him. He wore a deer stalker hat and came to work on a bicycle, then changed into a suit. In the summer he would wear shorts, which was very practical for cycling. Headquarters had a formal dress code, quite different to the NPL with its tweed jackets and woolly jumpers. I found that Dr Copestake lived near me, in Caversham on the outskirts of Reading, and we sometimes travelled on the same train between Reading and London. Of course, I knew Alex Williams well from my days commuting by car from Farnborough to the NPL, although I had never worked directly for him before. There were no problems because we had little direct professional contact, as would be expected because in London I was four levels his junior.

Dr Duncan Davies was Alex Williams' boss, as Chief Engineer and Scientist, or Chief Scientist and Engineer depending on which you think is most important. It is interesting that Dr Davies put the Engineer first whereas Mr Williams put the Scientist first. The previous Heads of Profession had been scientists whereas Dr Davies, having joined us from the ICI, was definitely an engineer. I heard interesting lectures from him, including some amazing and valid ideas on what later became known as micro-engineering and micro-machining, using machinery of very small size, which were way ahead of our time. Above Dr Davies in the hierarchy there was the Permanent Secretary, Sir Peter Carey.

I had been a tutor in numerical analysis for the Open University since February 1979 and wanted to continue. This had to be formally approved quickly so that I could continue teaching. My contract was for the lifetime of the course, and new students would be allocated to me in December. It was agreed that I could continue, as long as it only involved lecturing and marking scripts outside official working hours and mainly at weekends. There was no conflict of interest because I saw no project proposals from the Open University in this job, although I had to be careful later.

When I was studying Combinatorial Theory as part of my Mathematics degree at Oxford University my tutor had been Dr Robin Wilson of Jesus

College. His father, the Prime Minister Harold Wilson, had been responsible for the decision to set up the Open University in 1969. Eventually Robin moved from Oxford to become a lecturer at the Open University, based at the new town of Milton Keynes, and one of his first courses for them was a third level mathematics course: 'Graphs, Networks and Design'. It was all very similar to the course material that I knew from Oxford, and based on his classic book 'An Introduction to Graph Theory' which was published in 1972. The first undergraduate presentation was to be in February 1982, and I got involved in 1981 and wrote the Study Guides for students. It was the first of a series of consultancy work I did for the OU. I also became a tutor for this course, so I was now teaching two courses. After paying tax, it all still only paid enough for one nice holiday abroad. Fortunately my journeys commuting to London gave lots of opportunity to mark the scripts while sitting on the train.

I had much to learn about working in a policy area, and there were lots of books to read, as well as a range of courses to attend. I had to do these before I was allowed to draft replies to Parliamentary Questions and Ministers Cases, and draft Speaking notes for Ministers. I also had to spend some effort upgrading my wardrobe. The sort of informal working clothes at a laboratory are not suitable for a professional civil servant. It is not jeans and jumper country! I quickly discovered the Army and Navy Department store in Victoria Street, which had a good selection of nice business suits and posh frocks. Wearing a Jacques Vert suit, carrying my Filofax in my new Samsonite briefcase, and with a drop of Ma Griffe perfume behind my ears and a quick squirt of Gold Spot on my tongue I was ready for anything. The Samsonite briefcase was even strong enough to sit on when there were no seats left on the train home from Paddington.

There is a learning curve to be climbed when moving from a scientific post to that of policy work. Much of my research work had been done alone or contributing to the work of a small team, whereas policy work involved knowing your way around the DOI telephone book and knowing who could contribute a paragraph for a speech, or act as a sounding board for a new idea. It is a mutual arrangement and I had to be ready to help colleagues when they asked me for briefing or advice. I soon learned which colleagues were most helpful and to whom I could turn to for sound advice in an emergency. Not everyone responded well to short deadlines for information.

As soon as it was possible I was sent off to do the compulsory basic courses. 'Brief Writing' was the first course which I attended, and was an important basic skill in my new job. The title relates to the writing of 'Briefs', and does not imply that the writing skills taught will be how to be brief, or short, or to-the-point. Unfortunately I did not keep my notes or the handouts. However I do recall that it was a boring and tedious course where I was required to take a number of different situations and prepare briefing. It was like being back at school with the tutor, a retired civil servant, taking my essay efforts at the end of each day and returning them covered in red ink the following morning. The work was corrected but the basic reasons for the corrections were not explained. I didn't learn very much, and found the best way to improve was to keep writing and use other people's efforts as role models. I was fortunate that there are formal guidelines for writing briefs, with standard headings. Unlike being a scientist, the general idea is to explain something simply, not overwhelm the reader with your own obscure expertise.

As Dr Andrew Wallard, one of my colleagues then, recently pointed out, to do well in policy work you needed to gain a quick appreciation of topics about which you often knew relatively little. Here you needed to ask the right questions and be able to put over a technical concept to the non-specialist, always tough challenges. I used to give presentations to visitors at the NPL and reckoned that if I could explain something to my mother then I could explain it to my Minister, and on just the one sheet of paper. Scientists usually write too much, whereas my approach has always been towards simplification. Soon Dr Copestake encouraged me to go beyond the explanation of the concept and the technical discussions. In many situations you have to provide realistic policy advice, so the aim is to describe the alternative options, make a recommendation and explain why you have chosen that option. It was a skill which I soon developed.

The next useful skill for a policy maker is being effective in meetings, so I asked to attend the course on Making Meetings Work. This was a three day course; mine started on 15 December 1981. The idea was to explore the role of Chairman and individual members at meetings, and how their respective contributions can be directed to achieve maximum effectiveness, or otherwise. It was the second time I had seen a John Cleese film, and we all sat and watched 'Meetings Bloody Meetings'. John is well known for his training material, which I have always found to be excellent.

We had been asked to bring some examples from our present work along. It was too early for me to find an example from my job in London, so I invented an example from when I was working at the NPL. My last task had been to organise the launch of the new NPL Data Approximation Subroutine Library (DASL - pronounced dazzle) at a tutorial Conference at Robinson College, Cambridge which would be held in the Easter vacation of 1982. I had been told that I could not move from the NPL until after Christmas 1981, but had managed to escape earlier, on condition that I continued to spend two days each work organising the conference and contributing to the lectures. The conference applications had closed on 11 December, with 82 conference applications, which was just enough for the NPL to make a small profit. I pretended that a meeting had to be held to decide on the Conference

Dinner arrangements, given there were several options with the constraint to keep within a budget of £12 per person. There was also the issue of whether to provide 'free' sherry and wine.

Several case studies had been prepared and each of our performances was recorded on CCTV during our simulated meetings. It was not a new experience for me to take part in Role Playing exercises, but it was the first time I had seen myself on CCTV. For one of the sessions I was Chairman, which was good experience. This all helped me later with my task as Secretary of the Standards Accreditation Working Party. Yes, being a Chairman is quite different to being a Secretary, but I believe it is easier to be a good Secretary if you can appreciate what the Chairman needs. A good Secretary working with a good Chairman can have an enormous influence on the results of a meeting.

Finally it was going to be inevitable that I would, at some time in the near future, have to deal with Parliamentary Questions which are always abbreviated to PQs. No-one is allowed to draft an answer to a PQ unless they have attended the formal course, which gives an introduction to the history and the rules, as well as allowing practice in looking at examples from the past. Now that proceedings of the House of Commons are available on the television it is clear what is involved, but in those days this part of the machinery of Government was an unknown entity to me. I found that there are two basic types of questions: Oral Questions and Written Questions. Written PQs are part of the process by which MPs gather information from the Government and the objective is to provide Ministers with a draft written answer that is essentially factual, to the point, and as helpful as reasonably possible. Oral Questions are more difficult, and require an answer which can be spoken with conviction. It is a form of theatre. As well as writing the reply to the PQ, notes have to be provided for a range of supplementary questions and the identification of the most likely supplementary is a real skill. The MP who has asked the Oral PQ is able to ask a supplementary and it can be about almost anything, although it must be related to the original question. The only exception to this rule is for Prime Minister's Question Time when anything goes. Background notes have to be provided too, for both Oral and Written Questions.

The arrival of a PQ generally means that everything else has to stop while the PQ is dealt with, and it must, definitely must, be dealt with within the stated deadline. Whoever drafts the answer to a PQ, it has to be approved by senior officers and cleared by an Assistant Secretary (Grade 5) or equivalent. Usually several people are involved in drafting the answer, and agreeing a draft can take some time. Text is faxed or carried by hand from office to office until it is finalised. If the appropriate Assistant Secretary is not available then someone else of the same rank, or higher, has to be found. Ministers would rightly get very angry if they have not received the answer to a PQ in time to perform in the House of

Commons or the House of Lords. Even after the performance, the work is not over. PQs and their answers are published in the journal Hansard, an edited verbatim report of proceedings in both the Houses. It was important to finally check that the answer printed there was correct. Mistakes or mis-spellings can sometimes happen. Everyone breathes a sigh of relief when it is all over without any mishaps.

These three courses were an essential starting point for my new career and I was soon dealing with PQs, drafting replies to Minister's Cases and drafting Speaking Notes.

Once I had settled into my new duties I was invited to go and meet the Permanent Secretary, Sir Peter Carey. I suppose I was somewhat of a novelty because there were only a handful of bright women scientists in the Civil Service, and many of the scientists seconded to Headquarters did not want to be there and were counting the days until they could get back to their laboratories. I was different and was enjoying my new duties. Sir Peter Carey's office was in the main building, which was then in Ashdown House, a modern glass building in the middle of Victoria Street, and next to the Westminster Roman Catholic cathedral. I was located ten minutes walk away, on the very edge of his empire. The most important people and the most important parts of Government were always closest to the Houses of Parliament. Ashdown House was still 10 minutes walk away from Whitehall and the Houses of Parliament.

In 1980, just before my promotion to Senior Scientific Officer, I had been asked by Dr Ron Coleman, then Deputy Director of the NPL, how I saw my future career and whether I would consider spending some time working at the DOI Headquarters in London. He said that there was the possibility of a vacancy in a Private Office, and I was asked whether I would be interested in the opportunity. I expressed interest, without having the faintest idea what happened in a Private Office. I did not even know how many Private Offices there were. I wanted a move, something which looked like a career move, and away from the NPL. I found out later that I was supposed to go and work as part of the team in Sir Peter Carey's Private Office. I wondered whether the invitation to meet him was because there was still an idea that I might move.

When I arrived I found Sir Peter Carey had an enormous room and was seated behind a large prestigious desk. For one moment the room reminded me of Pete's flat in Oxford in Bardwell Road, when he was a graduate student. It also was very large and spacious. I approached the desk nervously, and sat down when invited. I have no idea what we spoke about, except it must have been generally about joining the Department. I think I managed without making any serious mistakes, but if it was intended as an interview with the possibility of my working in his Private Office in future then it was not a success because that opportunity never came around. I went back to my desk in my little office in Abell House, and its in-tray exercise.

I soon discovered there were no structured training arrangements for scientists who had moved to Headquarters from the DOI research establishments, and I enquired about whether the training incorporated in the Senior Professional Administrative Training Scheme (SPATS was a training scheme for scientists with potential) might contain elements of appropriate training for me. One of my ex-NPL colleagues was on SPATS, and had mentioned the scheme to me else I would not have been aware of it. In those early days I wanted to learn the new skills and take advantage of every relevant training opportunity. I was told it was too late for me to benefit from SPATS because by then I had too much work experience. I wondered if it was also because I was only an SSO whereas my colleague who was on SPATS was older and one grade more senior.

On searching the literature in 2006 I discovered that the SPATS scheme, which began some 30 years previously, has like many things been re-invented. The Government is, yet again, committed to increasing the number of trained and experienced professionals throughout the Civil Service and, as part of this commitment, the SPATS programme has been entirely redesigned to make it more flexible and responsive to the needs of participants and their departments or agencies. To quote from the Internet 'SPATS in 2006 aims to equip professionals, in areas as diverse as accountancy, medicine and engineering, to operate more effectively in higher management roles, either within a particular function, or more broadly'. The scheme is said to most benefit those in middle management with the potential to progress to advanced levels in the Civil Service. The total cost (spread over two years) was stated as £5,345, which is not expensive. While there are benefits in a course which is focussed precisely on the needs of civil servants there are also benefits in more general management training, as found for example in the post-graduate degree of Master of Business Administration (MBA), although that is a more serious commitment and much more expensive. An MBA is also more general and likely to be valued outside the Civil Service.

To fill one of the gaps in my knowledge, I found time to fit in the course on The Cabinet System. This was a one day course, in my case on 5 April 1982, which had a useful suggested reading list including The Governance of Britain by Sir Harold Wilson, and The Diaries of a Cabinet Minister by Richard Crossman. The course began with an introduction to the machinery of government by the famous Sir Robert Armstrong, Secretary of the Cabinet, Joint Head of the Home Civil Service and Permanent Secretary. In those days the Cabinet machinery was still classified information, and The Economist had decided to publish a list of the names of the Cabinet Committees and their Chairmen on 6 February 1982. Discussions about Open Government were just starting to appear. On 24 May 1979 the Prime Minister, then Margaret Thatcher, had answered a Written PQ about the membership and terms of reference of Cabinet Committees, which announced that there were four standing committees of the Cabinet, and naming the Chairman of each. This had never before been public information. Only other civil servants and historians will be interested in the details of these Committees of some thirty years ago; the information about current Cabinet Committees is freely available. The course was not directly relevant to me except for general information about the workings of the Cabinet Office, but it would be useful background for interviews if I moved into the Cabinet Office later, as part of my career. Most high-flying civil servants would expect to have a posting to either the Cabinet Office or the Treasury, and scientists usually went to the Cabinet Office.

To complement this formal training, the BBC had just started the TV sitcom series 'Yes Minister' which was then followed by 'Yes Prime Minister'. They were set in the Private Office in Whitehall of a British government Cabinet Minister who later became Prime Minister, and followed the fictitious career of James Hacker MP. It was compulsory viewing for everyone who worked as a civil servant, and was very authentic. It was based on the recently published Richard Crossman diaries, so in that sense had a sound pedigree. Many of us smiled at the accuracy of the situations encountered by the lead actors, and wondered which Permanent Secretary had been the model for the fictitious Sir Humphrey. Later his name was further immortalised when the cat at Number 10 Downing Street was named Humphrey.

So, as well as attending lots of courses and reading books, what was I actually doing? The output of a junior policy maker is advice – usually words on paper because I was too junior to be allowed to meet or talk to a Minister, or attend policy meetings myself. One of my early responsibilities was to assemble the briefing material for when Mr Williams and Dr Copestake attended meetings of the Science and Engineering Research Council and its Engineering Board respectively. These are important and prestigious gatherings of eminent scientists and are the means by which grants for research work are allocated. Papers which first went through the Engineering Board often surfaced later at the Science and Engineering Research Council, so some briefing could be repeated and updated. Other topics, not to do with science or engineering, were more challenging - a Civil Service euphemism for difficult and sometimes downright impossible to deal with thoroughly within the deadlines. Dates for the meetings for the year were already etched into everyone's diaries, so I was ready on the due day for the arrival of the papers. As soon as the papers for a meeting arrived it was necessary to make lots of copies and then assemble the official DOI view. Some papers could be dealt with in my own area or down my corridor, whereas others needed the input of colleagues. Many of the technical committees which underpinned the Engineering Board had Assessors from the DOI, staff usually at Principal level and often scientists or engineers who had special responsibilities for the subject area, and their advice had to be sought too. So I quickly got to know a number of colleagues, and they got to know me, even if we were in different buildings with different responsibilities and only met over the telephone or fax machine. Much of success in policy work involves knowing colleagues, helping each other with briefing for meetings, and making sure that you work together.

Abell House was an old building which was well due to be refurbished and I was pleased when we all had to move out, to a new office building at 29 Bressenden Place. Our ground floor entry there was enclosed by the surrounding Hotel, and the DOI offices were on the floors on top of the Hotel Reception. My new office was on the 8th floor, and I was forced to take the lift. It was a better location than Abell House, closer to Victoria Station and within easy walking distance of other DOI buildings down Victoria Street. Instead of eating at Millbank Tower we quickly discovered there was a canteen at the main building, Ashdown House, just 5 minutes walk away, although that part of London is full of little sandwich bars and cafés. The Tavola Calda in Bressenden Place, one of many Italian eating places in the Spaghetti House chain, became a favourite place for us all to meet for lunch on Friday.

I was also within walking distance of the United Oxford and Cambridge University Club (UOCUC), in 71-77 Pall Mall, of which I became a Lady Associate. In 1982 proper full Membership was restricted to men only, although women who had been to either Oxford or Cambridge University, or were married to Members, could join at roughly half the normal rate as Lady Associates. At this grade I was unable to work in the libraries upstairs, or go into the Smoking Room, but I still had access to the restaurants, squash courts and comfortable lounges. It was not until February 1996, under pressure from the two Universities and with the change in climate towards equality, that women were finally allowed to become Members, and the grade of Lady Associate became closed to new applicants. I am still a Lady Associate and pay the lower membership subscription.

The building is an amalgamation of houses, and 77 Pall Mall was the main building used by ladies. The downstairs rooms include the ladies powder room, and the Club cat was often found curled up on a sofa. Upstairs was the most delightful drawing room looking out over Pall Mall, and on the south side was the Princess Marie Louise Room which was used for meetings and banquets. It quickly became my base in London and I usually managed to escape there for lunch once or twice each week. Many other civil servants were Members, and I noticed Sir Peter Carey having dinner there one evening. Occasionally politicians went there too. One evening I think I spotted Patrick Jenkins, then Secretary of State for Industry, having dinner with a large group in the Coffee Room.

2 Setting up the Small Firms Technical Enquiry Service

As well as assembling briefing material, another activity of a junior policy maker is to work with senior colleagues to make policy happen. This sounds vague so let me use my early experience as an example. My boss, Dr Lewison, had arrived in London some few months before my arrival. When I arrived he was thinking about what to do to help small firms with their technical problems. In 1977 a Manufacturing Advisory Service (MAS) had been established, funded by the DOI and operated by the Production Engineering Research Association (PERA) at Melton Mowbray, which aimed to help small and medium companies to increase productivity by applying more efficient methods, systems and equipment in manufacturing processes. The service was available to factories employing between 60 and 1,000 employees in particular sectors of manufacturing industry. The MAS covered help with manufacturing techniques and equipment, manufacturing management, systems services, materials, energy consumption, value engineering and many other activities which directly or indirectly affect production efficiency, including the selection and use of computers for all business purposes.

There was a limit to the amount of free help from the MAS, which was paid for by the DOI. Firstly there was an advisory project involving up to fifteen man-days work by specialist advisors. Secondly there were answers on up to three technical enquiries on any subject related directly or indirectly to efficiency or competitiveness. Thirdly there was assistance with training. In addition it was possible to commission a second advisory project involving up to fifteen man-days work. For this second project the MAS paid half the cost and the company paid the balance.

The scheme operated by arranging for a MAS senior industrialist accompanied by a MAS field officer to visit the factory to explain what help was available from the MAS. After an opening discussion a tour was made of the factory to determine how best the service could meet the company's needs. When a suitable subject for an advisory project was agreed, the most appropriate specialist organisation to undertake the work was selected, and the terms of reference agreed.

The specialists were drawn from 300 consultants, research associations and technical centres which were registered with the MAS. The MAS senior industrialists had long experience of senior executive responsibilities in industry and therefore knew the kinds of problems and pressures faced every day in industry. Many of them were recently retired. When I made contact with the MAS the specialist organisations had several years experience of working in close harmony with factory managements and employees in overcoming production problems and in seizing opportunities to cut costs and increase efficiency. Advice from the MAS aimed to be practical, down-to-earth and financially realistic, and to make the most effective use of the skills and experience of all concerned. Set up during a Labour Government, in 1981 the MAS was deemed a success and had been continued after the change of administration.

One obvious side-effect of using the MAS was that the firms often began to appreciate the expertise at PERA, and decided to pay to become members. They could then get regular access to PERA staff. In those day the Research Associations, of which PERA was one, were dedicated to helping their members, but only in exchange for subscription memberships.

At the same time, the Ministry of Agriculture, Fisheries and Food (MAFF) had a well respected advisory service for farmers, ADAS, which had been established in 1971. Its principal advisory function was to provide scientific, technical and business management advice to the agricultural and horticultural industries. The aim was to help farmers develop technically efficient and financially sound farm businesses. It had a network of offices throughout England and Wales, co-located usually with MAFF's network of local offices. It was in order to better understand ADAS that I found myself accompanying Dr Lewison on a visit to a farmer, and then donning protective clothing in order to be shown around his turkey farm. It was approaching Christmas and I remember being overwhelmed by all the turkeys. This sort of experience is not suitable when wearing a traditional ladies business suit, and I was glad I had decided to wear trousers. We also visited a dairy farm, where the farmer proudly showed us his personal computer, and demonstrated how he could monitor the feed and milk yield of each of his cows individually. In those days it was very rare for anyone to have their own PC, and we were impressed by the role of ADAS in providing technical advice and support to farmers.

We also wanted to find out what services small firms had access to and we went to visit Slough Industrial Estates to see their way of working with small firms. The Slough Trading Estate was set up in the 1920s and covered a large site with hundreds of small firms. Unfortunately the visit was not very helpful because we found that the firms there had few central services provided, except for the obvious infrastructures. It did not give any new ideas for dealing with technical queries from small firms, but did reinforce the need for something to be provided. There was indeed a gap.

There was one problem. My part of the DOI was responsible for research and technology policy, not for helping small firms. There were two Branches which were responsible for policy for small firms; one was led by Brian Hilton as Assistant Secretary and the other with Martin Stanley as Principal. Both men went on to have distinguished careers in the Civil Service. Their responsibilities included the Small Firms Service which operated as a collection of drop-in Centres for small firms as well as running a telephone help service on general management or financial problems. There were Small Firms Counsellors who were themselves experienced businessmen and were expected to give advice on marketing, sales and finance for example. They did not give any help to small firms with technical problems, so there was no duplication. It was nevertheless essential to discuss our new ideas with these colleagues and to make sure that our new technical enquiry service had their support. And it was not just a one-way discussion. They had experience working with small firms whereas we did not, and so their practical advice was very valuable. One impact they had was in suggesting we use a normal telephone number for the SFTES, rather than a Freephone number as was used by the Small Firms Service. It also made a clear distinction between the successful and well-established Small Firms Service, and what eventually became known as the Small Firms Technical Enquiry Service (SFTES).

So weeks passed and the rules for the new SFTES began to be firmed up. Much of the existing Manufacturing Advisory Service was used as a model, for example the SFTES would also be run from PERA. The benefits were that there was an existing system in place for dealing with the MAS, and this could be used in a slightly modified way for SFTES. Also the small firms who had over 60 employees were eligible in theory for help from both MAS and SFTES, whereas we wanted to limit their eligibility so that they could only get help from one scheme, not both. This meant that SFTES administrators had to be able to check the MAS database. I had to work closely with my colleague, Gordon, who ran the MAS project, and with his contractors at PERA.

But all this planning and the negotiations were a waste of time if Ministers did not like the idea of a SFTES. That is where a clear understanding of Government policy and a good relationship between senior officials and politicians is essential. I drafted the papers which described the new scheme and they were re-drafted and polished until they were good enough to be sent up to Ministers. Mr John MacGregor MP, Parliamentary Under Secretary of State for Industry and the Small Firms Minister approved the new scheme, and we could move on to the next stage of its launch.

Once the idea for the new scheme had been concretised, and Ministers had agreed the expenditure, within existing budgets of course, then the next step was to announce the scheme. There are many ways to announce a new scheme. One is to use a PQ as the vehicle, and for a friendly MP to ask the Minister a question. As an artificial example here, the PQ may take the form 'How many firms in Hampshire have used the Manufacturing Advisory Service, and if the Minister will make a statement'. Then the Minister can report that, say, 67 firms have used MAS, and that there is a need for a technical help service for smaller firms and that he has today allocated £2.2m for the setting up of such a service etc. In this case it seemed best to launch the scheme by the asking of 'The First Technical Enquiry' so where would I find a small firm who would be prepared to do this? In practical terms there were two choices. The one option is to find a firm in a town the Minister is already planning to visit, not necessarily his own constituency although this is often a desirable possibility. The second option is to find somewhere within an easy drive of the Houses of Parliament. I was tasked with finding the firm, and organising the visit.

The DOI had a number of Regional Offices and I approached the one responsible for the South East and London and asked for their advice. I was given a list of possible small firms within an hour drive from the Houses of Parliament, from which I made a short list and found out more information. I visited three of them. It was planned that the Press and photographers would be invited too, so the company had to be easy to reach and also be an interesting company visually. SFTES was a telephone help line, so the small company had to have a neat office area for asking their Technical Enquiry.

Of the three firms which I visited, I recommended the choice of Frema (Combustions) Ltd, at Mile End in East London, although it was only just close enough to Central London for the constraint of being within one hour for driving. The Managing Director, John Whatmore, was keen to make sure that the company site was tidy in preparation for the visit and the extra Press and their photographers. He also had to think up a question to ask, and it had to be something relevant to his business but which also showed the type of typical question which other small companies might need help with. Meanwhile I had to agree the design of the advertising leaflet, and work with the Press Office to write the Press Notice, which included a number of extracts from the short speech which I had written for the Minister for the launch event.

The SFTES was launched on 10 June 1982, by John MacGregor. It was an important milestone in my career and I had come a long way from my work at the NPL just over six months earlier. I travelled from his office at Ashdown House in his car, and as is typical with a busy Minister, we left London later than planned and were then unfortunate with the traffic. It did give time to outline the scheme, check on the details for the launch, and then sit back while the Minister continued with his other work and dealt with more papers. For my first interaction with a Minister I was very impressed with John MacGregor, and he had a flair and enthusiasm for what the DOI was trying to achieve. We eventually arrived at the company, the speeches were made, the photographs were taken, the Press asked a few simple questions, and John Whatmore asked 'The First Technical Enquiry' which was about avoiding porosity problems caused during welding. With a pre-planned question, it was not surprising that he got an instant answer.

In parallel with the choreography of the launch of the scheme it was vital to have the administrative systems in place at PERA for dealing with what was expected to be a flood of technical questions from small firms. PERA printed thousands of leaflets, in the same house style as the other Small Firms Service leaflets, so it was green and black, and they were distributed widely. The same cartoon imagery was used as for the Small Firms Service, with a senior manager on the telephone, then meeting a specialist advisor, and finally filling in an assessment form. Assessment was an important part of measuring the success of any scheme which helped industry.

The eligibility criteria were that any manufacturing firm with not more than 200 employees could have up to four technical queries answered within an overall limit of five man-days. There were some little rules about dealing with companies who had already used MAS, but generally users of SFTES were new to asking for technical help. Some small companies wanted one problem solved using the five days limit, with a specialist expert visiting their site. Other small companies only needed to ask a few short questions which could be solved over the telephone. Enquiries were logged at PERA who then directed the enquiry to the organisation most suitable to deal with the problem. After the work had been done, an assessment form was used to make sure that the companies did get a good service from whichever organisation was allocated to help them.

Some enquiries were dealt with by PERA's own Technical Enquiry Department which had many years experience in dealing with this type of service. Other enquiries were answered by other Research Associations, Government Research Laboratories including those of the DOI, the Council For Small Industries in Rural Areas (CoSIRA), Universities and other higher education establishments, and a few private consulting organisations. I had never before had any contact with the Research Associations, who were funded by industry subscription, and provided research and technology services. I visited a selection, including the Machine Tool Industry Research Association (MTIRA), the Cutlery and Allied Trades Research Association (CATRA), the Furniture Industry Research Association (FIRA), the Paint Research Association (PRA) and the Spring Research and Manufacturers' Association (SRAMA).

The advertising leaflet gave a long list of examples of the type of enquiries which could be answered:

> Where can particular materials or goods be obtained?
>
> What is the best material for the job?
>
> Can the existing methods of manufacture be improved?
>
> What measuring instruments are available to monitor a product or process?
>
> Is there technical information on a particular subject?
>
> How can sudden snags in a product or process be overcome?
>
> Which is the most suitable small computer to buy or rent?

How can production be better controlled?

What is the best layout for a factory?

Can savings be made in energy costs?

How can higher quality standards be met?

We had made the list long so that it gave ideas to companies for the sort of question which they might ask. In addition, it made managing the scheme easier if we had already agreed what sort of help was eligible. Sometimes there were unusual enquiries and then PERA rang me and I had to decide whether they were eligible or not. It had already been agreed that enquiries about general management or financial problems were not eligible and were forwarded to the Small Firms Service on Freefone 2444.

I made regular visits by train to Melton Mowbray planning their side of the launch, meeting with the PERA Director, Ron Armstrong, and working with the project officer, Philip Sowden, who was responsible for the team of experts at the end of the telephones. I was very proud of the project, and felt the responsibility of managing a significant budget. I had been allocated £2.2 million over three years. I seemed to visit PERA every week to check on progress, and quickly got tired of the journey from home via London by train. It was quicker and easier to drive and it saved the need for staying in a hotel because I could just do the return journey in one day. My normal routine was to leave home soon after 6.30 in the morning, then drive up to Melton Mowbray for a 9.00 start, work through the day and into the early afternoon, and then drive home.

In early September 1982 I made a mistake one afternoon, taking a bend on one of the country lanes on my way back home near Melton Mowbray too fast, and then losing control of the resulting skid. The car was a wreck and ended up in a ditch, under a tree, and written off. Fortunately it was an Austin Maxi and was a solid car, and I walked away. I think I had to climb out of the window to escape, but I was in shock and really have no idea how I got out of the car with the doors still shut. A passing motorist helped me get to a nearby house and ring for an ambulance which took me to the Leicester Royal Infirmary. I was told that I would have been dead if I had been going faster than 50 mph, yet there were no special speed limits on the road. I had a few minor scratches, but glass from the window had cut the palm of my right hand and severed the tendons. I was so worried about the car that I hadn't noticed that the fourth (ring) finger on my right hand wouldn't move any more. The A & E staff at the hospital had noticed, and I was offered the choice of going home or staying in Leicester and getting the tendon repaired. I was still suffering from the shock of it all and decided to stay put. They operated the next day, and fortunately they tried to join up the tendons so I would still be able to play the piano. Initially they were just going to fix the finger bent and rigid. The problem was to get all the glass out, because you can't see it on an X-Ray and I discovered many years later that some had been left inside. The stitching was also very rough, presumed done by some young doctor who hadn't been taught how to sew, and from later problems he or she was not very good at finding glass either. Next time I would think more seriously about getting a taxi back home and finding a hospital which I knew, but I was in shock and couldn't think straight. PERA soon found out about the accident and Philip Sowden dropped by with flowers and asked if there was anything they could do to help.

The car was deemed a write-off by the insurance company, which was no surprise given all the damage. Pete borrowed a car from a friend and I was soon back home but with my arm in a sling, and with a string through a hole drilled in the end of the finger. These first few days were OK because I was on sick leave, although I got some strange looks when we went to the Farnborough Air Show on 9 - 12 September. From when he was a student at Oxford, Pete had flown gliders. This had developed into more than just a hobby when he and two friends imported the first Astir glider made by Grob at its own airfield at Mattsies near Mindelheim in West Germany, and then set up Soaring Oxford Ltd to import Grob gliders. As the business expanded and the range of gliders, motor gliders and power aircraft increased Grob always displayed their newest model at the Farnborough Air Show. I helped with the stand over the weekend, when there was general admission and glider pilots and their families came to see what new gliders were on offer and arrange for demonstration flights. There were lots of jokes as to what I had done with the aircraft. It was assumed that my accident had taken place while flying.

Being right-handed, and having the right hand immobilised while it was hoped the tendon would join up, was a problem when my job involved such a lot of writing. Dr Copestake came and visited me, was very supportive, and suggested ways in which I might be able to use a keyboard with one hand instead of writing. He said he had a similar accident in the past. I knew I was going to be off work for several weeks and eventually learned how to write left-handed after a fashion. Playing the piano had made me reasonably ambidextrous. The problem was that as well as my main job with the policy work in London I also had a lot of marking to do for the Open University. My undergraduate students had their exams in early October, and their last piece of written work was submitted to me in mid-September. Fortunately I was only tutoring two courses, both third level mathematics, so much of my marking was just ticking the work, not writing long essays. The students understood that my writing was going to be irregular, but would be still just legible. Someone else gave the final revision Day School in my place, because writing with my left hand on a blackboard was too difficult.

I was going to be on sick leave for some time, and I was not going to be driving for many months, so action had to be taken to find someone else to manage the SFTES. Even when I was allowed back to work I had to go to the Royal Berkshire Hospital in Reading to join the physiotherapy classes one afternoon each week. Once the hand came out of plaster then it was pretty immobilised and had to be exercised. The physiotherapy began with immersing the hand in warm wax to loosen the stiffness, and then it was pushed and stretched. Initially the hand was totally rigid but eventually I was able to move the finger under my own control. I was so pleased that the tendon had grown back. Working in London it was not convenient to go to the Royal Berks and after a few months my GP arranged that I should continue physiotherapy at St Mary's Paddington, on my way to work in the mornings. I spent many weeks walking around with a soft tennis ball in my pocket, squeezing it to exercise and lengthen the repaired tendons. This was all under the NHS and then we remembered that BUPA would cover individual physiotherapy which was paid privately. I started having sessions with May Antschel in Reading and she made a spectacular improvement by loosening all the scar tissue around the tendon and enabling me to have much more movement. Now it is only just possible to notice that the grip of my right hand is less than normal. Over the years I had three more minor operations to take out pieces of glass.

3 Expanding the Teaching Company Scheme

So, in November 1982 I was finally well enough to go back to work and was given new responsibilities, working directly with Dr Copestake to expand and raise the profile of something called the Teaching Company Scheme.

I had never heard of the Teaching Company Scheme (TCS) but soon found out more. Funded under the Science and Technology Act 1965, the TCS was devised in 1974/75 by a working party appointed jointly by the then Science Research Council, which was the predecessor of the Science and Engineering Research Council, and the DOI. The background to the TCS was that the Universities and Polytechnics contained much scientific and technological expertise which was useful to industry. The difficulty was to ensure that this expertise flowed as easily and directly as possible to the right places in industry. The TCS idea was based upon the familiar idea of the 'teaching hospital' where there was learning by doing. Under the TCS academic staff and companies collaborated together. This was done by setting up a partnership, which was called a Teaching Company Programme. A Review in 1981, when there were 46 Teaching Company Programmes, had recommended further expansion of the Scheme to over 200 programmes by 1985. I was going to be responsible for achieving that expansion. Now, in 2006/07, there are over 1000 partnerships and the scheme has expanded to cover most business sectors. The scheme has also been copied overseas, for example in Hong Kong.

The management of the TCS and the approval of funding for new programmes were carried out by the Teaching Company Management Committee, and administration was done by a small group at the Teaching Company Directorate in the Science and Engineering Research Council offices in Swindon. The Director of the TCS was Professor Derek Saunders from the Cranfield Institute of Technology, and he steered the Teaching Company Management Committee. When the Science Research Council had expanded to become the Science and Engineering Research Council the staff had moved into new modern offices at Polaris House next to Swindon railway station. I had no staff in London, only in Swindon, where I had an allocated desk and worked alongside my opposite number Dr David Jones. I was still responsible for briefing for various Research Council meetings, so this new task fitted well. I soon found that I spent a lot of time travelling by train, with meetings in Swindon each week as well as attending management meetings on site at some of the existing Teaching Company Programmes.

To expand the scheme it was important to encourage new applicants. The key academics were easy to find and encourage to be involved. It was much harder to get to the extra companies who might benefit from taking part. I updated the old leaflet about the scheme, adding a lot of bright pictures of academics and industrialists working together. It was the first time I had done any design work and I collected interesting photographs of work being carried out in industry and of traditional engineering buildings in Universities and Polytechnics. These were then made into a collage for the front cover of the leaflet, and the objectives of the scheme were listed inside, as well as details of how to apply.

The TCS is one of the few DOI/DTI schemes to celebrate its 30th birthday although its name has now been changed to the more fashionable Knowledge Transfer Partnerships, but the aims have stayed broadly constant. In my leaflet in 1984 the aims were:

> to raise the level of industrial performance by effective use of academic resources;
>
> to improve the manufacturing and industrial methods by the effective implementation of advanced technology;
>
> to train able graduates for careers in industry;
>
> to develop and retrain existing company and academic staff;
>
> to give academic staff broad and direct involvement with industry to benefit research and enhance the relevance of teaching.

The original emphasis was on batch manufacturing in the mechanical and electrical engineering sectors, and only using University expertise. As time passed the academic base expanded to include the Polytechnics, which are now all renamed Universities. The logic of limiting the academic partner to being a University or Polytechnic was that they were eligible for funding from the Science and Engineering Research Councils, whereas other institutions of Further and Higher Education and Government Laboratories were not, in those times. I remember the discussions when the first application came from a good academic group at the Dorset Institute, which was then only a College of Higher Education although it is now the University of Bournemouth. By coincidence I had a contact there who was a colleague as a mathematics tutor with the Open University, so I knew at first hand that there were some good academics in some Colleges of Higher Education. In the climate of an expanding scheme, possible prejudices about academic excellence being based exclusively in the Universities were not a serious obstacle, and the Dorset Institute programme was eventually approved. It was a success and opened the door for other academic groups.

Each partnership typically involved a company being partnered by a nearby academic group, to work on a defined project. Being within one hours drive had been shown to be a key to getting the partners to work closely together. Another key to the success of the partnership was the enthusiasm of the Associates. These were high quality young graduates who were appointed by the academic Department and were paid full industrial salaries to work on the specified projects. It was a good option for the Associates, who worked in industry, for industry, but with the backing of the expertise and facilities of the academic. In theory the company could be of any size, but generally in the early days they were large or medium size. There were clear opportunities to benefit small firms using the same approach and there were several club groupings where one academic Department managed a group of several Associates who were shared across a club of small firms. Now there are many partnerships where the companies are small firms.

The matchmaking process between academics and industry was facilitated by the Teaching Company Directorate which included a group of senior engineers. I remember going to visit companies with Tony Coppen, Stan Gent and Donald Entwhistle. They were each experienced industrialists who helped the academic and the company decide on their project and write their proposal for funding. Many projects involved the use of computers and I was encouraged to build on my own qualifications and become a Member of the British Computer Society. I am sure it helped to have a doctorate and belong to a professional engineering institution when dealing with academics. However I was not a mechanical engineer by training, although I told people that my Oxford DPhil was about welding, which was true.

Because the TCS was about getting firms to implement new technology, many of the new programmes for approval were for Computer Aided Design (CAD) or CADCAM (CAD and Computer Aided Manufacturing). Dr Copestake was not an expert in these technologies either, and he arranged with UMIST that we would both spend a few days being trained at Manchester on the use of CAD software. It improved my 'street credibility' with the Regional Consultants, and my background in computing and drawing tools meant that I grasped the principles of CAD very quickly. The TCS continued to expand as planned, and there started to be partnerships in the service industries and into management. I spent more of my time attending quarterly meetings of a variety of programmes, and meeting Professors and Managing Directors of companies. It was all very useful in establishing a network of contacts for the future.

During the summer of 1983 my name was put forward by the Chief Engineer and Scientist, now Oscar Roith who had replaced Dr Duncan Davies, for the filling of vacancies in the ACARD Secretariat. ACARD was the Advisory Council for Applied Research and Development, based in the centre of Government in the Cabinet Office in Whitehall. ACARD members were a mixture of senior academics and industrialists, chosen to be the best in the UK. The Secretariat had to be able to work with them and for them, and to sharp deadlines.

ACARD's terms of reference were to advise the Government and publish reports as necessary on:

> applied research, design and development in the UK;
>
> the application of research and technology, developed in the UK and elsewhere, for the benefit of both public and private sectors in accordance with national economic needs;
>
> the co-ordination, in collaboration with the Advisory Board for the Research councils, of these activities, with research supported through the Department of Education and Science;
>
> the role of the UK in international collaboration in the fields of applied research, design and development related to technology.

I went to the Cabinet Office building in Whitehall to be interviewed by Dr (later Sir) Robin Nicholson. I was not selected but the feedback from my interview was that I had created 'a very favourable impression' and that my lack of success was only because of my shorter experience in Headquarters work. I heard later that a female colleague from the DOI had got the job, and she had much more experience then I had of working in Whitehall. Recall that the initial impetus for greater efficiency after 1979 came from the programme of Rayner Scrutinies, which were named after the head of the Government's Efficiency Unit, Sir Derek (later Lord) Rayner from Marks and Spencer. These were one-off quick reviews of selected policy areas or activities within a Department, carried out by bright young high-flying civil servants, with the aim of achieving savings and increasing efficiency. She had been chosen as one of these high-flyers, and had already shown that she could perform well in the busy atmosphere of the Cabinet Office, whereas I was untested and untried.

4 Celebrating Professor Fox's Contribution to Numerical Analysis

Professor Leslie Fox had been my DPhil supervisor at Oxford University, and was Head of the Computing Laboratory. Following health problems in 1981, he had decided to retire when he reached 65 years old, and the Institute of Mathematics and its Applications (IMA) organised a special one day meeting on 'The Contributions of Leslie Fox to Numerical Analysis', held at The Royal Society in London. The date planned was 14 September 1983, just before his 65th birthday, and although I was no longer an active numerical analyst I was one of six 'fox cubs' invited to give a talk. During his career Professor Fox had supervised 19 DPhil students, and the Chair of Numerical Analysis had been established for him in 1963. The meeting had a politically correct mix of speakers, with three women and three men selected.

I was honoured to be invited, and lost no time in accepting the invitation. Until recently I had been an Associate Fellow of the IMA; it was the professional body for numerical analysts. The provisional invitation had been sent out fifteen months before the event, so there was plenty of time to make sure that I and the other speakers could keep the date free. I had to send in a title for my talk by April 1983, and then an abstract by the end of July 1983. Sitting in my office in the DOI in Bressenden Place I wondered what to talk about. In what way was my career now able to be described as part of his contribution to numerical analysis? I decided on my title 'Computing without Numerical Analysis', because I could see that many ordinary people were now using computers without any basic understanding of the pitfalls of numerical computation.

I had originally suggested that speakers at the conference might like to meet at the United Oxford and Cambridge University Club (UOCUC) for dinner, after the proceedings. I was happy to organise a table, and the UOCUC in Pall Mall was only a short walk around the corner from the Royal Society. I enquired about possibilities and was offered a small room which could hold eighteen people. This was barely going to be large enough; most speakers had brought their spouse and a quick count of likely numbers soon got beyond the magic eighteen. There was some discussion, and I found out that an informal farewell dinner was also being organised in Hertford College on 27 September, for his friends in Oxford and elsewhere. I did not know about it simply because I was not in Oxford any more.

While thinking what could be done to celebrate in London I suddenly had an appointment to go back into the Royal Berkshire Hospital in Reading for another attempt at removing glass fragments from my hand. Most had been removed after my car crash in 1982, but some more had surfaced. Apparently it is not unusual for glass to work its way to the surface later. I went into hospital, had the pre-med injection, and was then sent home because they ran out of time to perform the operation and was told it had to be re-scheduled later. Bless the National Health Service. At the time I was very angry. I was left feeling sedated from the pre-med but at least able to use my right hand, for which I was grateful. Contingency plans had been made so that I had help with giving my presentation, just in case the hand was still bandaged and immobile. The idea of organising a dinner in London for the speakers after the conference was abandoned; it was just too much effort for me.

There were six invited papers, and Professor Fox was to give the final paper at the end of the day, introduced by his friend and ex-NPL colleague Jim Wilkinson. Dr J H Wilkinson was almost exactly one year the younger, but had already retired from the NPL and was a Professor at Stanford University in the USA. In alphabetical order, the six speakers were P E M Curtis, M O Nicholas (AERE Harwell), N Nichols (University of Reading), J K Reid (AERE Harwell), F H Ris (IBM Yorktown Heights) and J E Walsh (University of Manchester). It was a popular event and 82 people attended, including many friends from Oxford and the NPL and eminent academic colleagues from the UK and overseas.

I was given the graveyard slot, the first talk after lunch. I began by speaking mainly about the problems. Every computer is different. In my short career I had used eleven different computers, often using two or three at the same time. In 1982 the market for home computers was said to be 459,000 and they were priced under £200. Home computing was becoming a consumer product and this had consequences as well as special requirements. Yet there are many sources of potential error in numerical work, and it is important to ask several questions. How good is the result? Can you check it? And if so How? I was a firm believer in thinking before coding and then documenting what is done. I mentioned the problems of software transportability, and used the NPL Data Fitting Library and the NAG software library at Oxford to indicate good practice. It was not a contentious talk, only lightly technical, and I referred to the two examples from my research at the NPL which I knew well: (i) the analysis of aircraft engine performance and (ii) the production of alcohol tables. I hope a Minister would have understood what I was saying, although I didn't practice the talk on one to find out. At the end there was polite clapping, but I think it would have been exactly the same response if I had spoken about the problems of technology transfer between Universities and industry, and with hindsight perhaps that would have been a more interesting and controversial subject. There was still the expectation that every 'fox-cub' should automatically become an academic computer expert, and success in another field of endeavour, for example as a manager, was of less merit.

Following the celebration event, a capital fund was established for the award of an annual prize to a promising young numerical analyst. This was in recognition that Leslie had inspired many talented scholars to enter the field of numerical analysis and had done much to develop educational and research opportunities for students of the computing sciences. The Institute of Mathematics and its Applications wanted to show their appreciation of his devotion and to continue his work of encouragement to others with these awards. The first winner of the prize, on 30 August 1985, was L. N. Trefethen of MIT in the USA; he became Professor of Numerical Analysis and Head of the Numerical Analysis Group at Oxford. He is also a Fellow of the Royal Society whereas sadly Professor Fox never achieved the distinction of being FRS. After his death in 1992 the prize continued to be awarded, and many able young scholars applied; the competition was not limited to those studying and working in the UK.

The NPL, the NAG and the Argonne National Laboratory in the USA also sponsored a prize for numerical software in honour of the outstanding contributions of my NPL colleague Dr J H Wilkinson. He died in October 1986.

5 Three weeks of meetings with French civil servants

Over the last two years my French language skills had been steadily improving. I had begun with French at roughly A-level standard at the NPL, having studied at school and then spoken the language in Geneva while working at CERN in the summer vacation of 1973. Then at DOI Headquarters I had regular lessons with the French teacher Nicole, mostly on my own but sometimes shared. So I was ready for the three weeks residential course in December 1983 run by the Civil Service College to hone my skills. Nicole said that I was good enough, and I applied for the course and was duly accepted. The format involved two weeks in Paris followed by one week somewhere in the provinces; in my course we would be visiting the area around Bordeaux. In Paris we had each booked our Hotel separately and so everyone was scattered around the 5ème arrondissement. I had chosen the Hotel Claude Bernard in the Rue des Écoles, which was the cheapest of the 3* Hotels in the area. Our daily allowance was set for a typical 2* Hotel, but the Claude Bernard was a very similar price. I recall my little single room was very simple but the Hotel had a breakfast room and was in a good central location. When we all met together on the first day we were a small select group, maybe ten or eleven people, and we could get around easily in a little minibus. The disadvantage of the course was that every day was full of French classes and meetings with French civil servants, and even in the evening we English students were instructed that we had to only speak French between ourselves. In spite of there being no-one watching to make sure we obeyed the rules, we did all try very hard. It was a true immersion in the language.

I also learned a lot about current French Government policy work. I was able to meet some of my opposite numbers in the Research and Technology Ministry in the Rue Descartes in Paris, which was useful for the future. One of the main reasons to attend the course had been to identify my opposite numbers in the French administration, with a view to having regular discussion meetings. Our group was treated very well, and most days there were receptions and long French lunches with the inevitable glasses of Champagne, and everyone toasted Anglo-French collaboration and we took turns to thank our hosts in French. It was all part of developing confidence in speaking French in an official capacity.

By the end of the two weeks in Paris I was getting homesick for plain English food. We had been eating the most wonderful French meals but there were a lot of cream sauces and rich meats and pâtés, and tempting glorious smelly cheeses. I remember buying a lump of cheddar cheese and a bag of English Cox's apples in the Marks and Spencer's Food Hall in Paris. Most other customers were French, buying specialist British Christmas delicacies like smoked Scottish salmon, Stilton, Plum Pudding and Iced Christmas cake. But all I wanted was the plain and simple flavour of cheese and apples.

My colleagues went home for the weekend but I stayed and enjoyed my two days as a tourist. I had been to Paris several times before but it had been when I was much younger and there had not been the freedom to explore. Paris is a nice small town for walking, and the Métro system is good. I went up the Eiffel Tower and the Arc de Triomphe again, spent too long in the Louvre and also visited the Madeleine.

Each year we had a holiday visiting Pete's sister and her husband in Guernsey and on our last visit we had purchased an old dinner service from an antiques shop in St Peter Port which was a mixture of modern Coalport Elite Gold bone china and old Limoges porcelain. Guernsey people, living between England and France, were well placed to have both French porcelain and English bone china. Both patterns had a gold edge with a thin gold line and another thin gold line midway, on a white background. The Limoges gold edge pattern was holly leaves whereas the Coalport was geometric. It had taken us many years to find a dinner pattern which we both liked, and second-hand it was not expensive. It was under £100 for a set of three enormous oval serving platters, a tureen and a gravy boat, and six sets of plates of four different sizes, including crescent shaped side plates for vegetables. We could not carry it all back on the aircraft, it was too heavy and fragile, and had to wait until the summer when the family came over with their car. The Coalport Elite Gold was then a current pattern, and the small plates must have been purchased by the previous owner as the best and closest match to the original old Limoges. To contrast prices, we then ordered two new Coalport Elite Gold coffee cups and saucers from Harrods in London which cost almost £50, and when they eventually arrived the two handles were gilded slightly differently. They had been decorated to order, but not at the same time. The shop admitted that when the first two cups arrived one had been broken and a new cup had to be made, hence the slight difference and the delay in receiving them.

As is usual, the Limoges porcelain had been decorated in Paris, not in Limoges, and we had taken a photograph of the design to try and find the name of the pattern and the date of manufacture. I was unlucky. The plate was marked with an address in the Boulevard Malesherbes, and the shop still existed but the staff were too young to remember the design, and there was no book of old patterns. They could only say it was before the Second World War, which we had already guessed from the condition.

My visit to France was at the time of the Grand Décentralisation policy. Our course had begun with visits to several Ministries in Paris, and would then continue with visits to the regions to observe policies on the ground. We were going to spend a week in Bordeaux to see how implementation of the Grand Décentralisation was working. On Monday morning we were all reunited and set off together on the train from Paris to Bordeaux. This part of the trip was more organised and we all stayed at the same Hotel.

There has always been a special relationship between Bordeaux and England, so we were made especially welcome by our French friends. Obviously we were introduced to their most famous export, fine Bordeaux wine. One special evening we were taken to visit Château Ausone to taste the new wines from the barrels. Before leaving Paris I had taken the precaution of buying a large and heavy reference book which described the wines and vineyards of the Crus Classé Bordelais. The intention was to use the book as a souvenir of the course and also in case I found any interesting wine to take back home as a souvenir. Château Ausone is in the area of Saint Émilion and is classed as a Premier Grand Cru Classé, so its wine is very expensive and well beyond the salary of a humble civil servant. Even only tasting the young wine straight from the barrel it was obviously going to develop into something very, very special.

Another day we were taken to visit the nearby port of Arcachon, famous for its oysters. We were met at the Mairie, the Town Hall, for yet another typical gastronomic lunch with the compulsory glasses of Champagne. It was the time when the oyster industry was angry about the damage to their shellfish caused by pollution from the old-fashioned lead-based anti-fouling on boats. In the afternoon we were all dressed in yellow oilskins and taken out by boat to visit the oyster beds. I was glad that I had changed into trousers. I had not eaten oysters before, and once I was forced to admit this, a special large one was found for me to taste. They certainly taste nice when fresh straight out of the water. The idea was open mouth, swallow oyster, smile, and think of England. I wondered whether I should take acting lessons. At least I managed to swallow it whole, in spite of its size, and I did not have to eat anything which was alive and wiggled, unlike some of my senior colleagues who had business trips to Japan.

When we flew back with British Airways from Bordeaux to London my new Samsonite suitcase weighed 33 kilos at the check-in because of all the books, papers and pamphlets we had been given during the three weeks. That was in addition to other papers which had gone back through the British Embassy and the diplomatic bag. Fortunately we had been booked into Club Class and this was within the luggage allowance. I could only just lift the suitcase, so was pleased the suitcase had wheels. Everyone else in the group had exactly the same problem.

6 DTI is given its Central Aims by Norman Tebbit

I returned to my desk, keen to use my new language skills, but without any new opportunity. In 1983 Norman Tebbit had arrived as Secretary of State and the Department of Trade and Industry had been created, joining together the separate Department of Industry and the Board of Trade. Initially there were two Permanent Secretaries: Sir Brian Hayes from the Industry side and Sir Anthony Rawlinson from Trade although eventually Sir Anthony Rawlinson took early retirement. One Department did not need two Permanent Secretaries. There had been just under ten years with the two Departments of Trade and Industry separated.

A booklet was published in January 1984 which explained that the merger was intended to facilitate clearer and more consistent policies, and result in simpler and clearer access to officials and Ministers. I welcomed the change, but for different reasons. In theory it was going to be possible for officials to move between the old Industry and Trade areas, for career development, and this would give more opportunities for me to look for a promotion to Principal or its scientific equivalent. In practice I quickly found that the two groups kept separate, except at the highest policy levels.

One of the early activities after Norman Tebbit's arrival had been to draw up and publish a statement of Aims for the new combined Department. It was a good management concept to make a consolidated statement, as part of bringing together the two distinct cultures. I had never seen a published set of Aims before, and everyone had to know what they were. Previously I, and other colleagues at my level, just got on with our work. We had budgets to manage and approved programmes of work to implement. The views of Ministers were sought by more senior officials on new activities, and then these new activities were carried forward if approved. I was lucky to have had direct contact with a Minister, and was generally treated as if I was already promoted to the next grade. Principals and their scientific equivalents were the key administrative policy workers, with the crucial job of being responsible for actually doing policy work.

Not every new programme of expenditure had to be approved by the Secretary of State. Approval for small new activities could be by junior Ministers, depending on the costs and political sensitivities. The size and type of activity which had delegated approval was known, and new activities were often limited to match, typically defined as a pilot for a more general programme. This was not unusual and had been the case in 1982 with the SFTES. There were always a few large or unusual programmes, which did need the approval of the Secretary of State and sometimes in addition the approval of the Treasury, but in my small corner I did not get involved with those.

The new formal Central Aim of the DTI was: 'To encourage, assist, and ensure the proper regulation of, British Trade, industry and commerce: to increase the growth of world trade and the national production of wealth'. It was to be the key to the Department's future policy work. The simple view was that only the people who worked in industry and commerce could create wealth. Government could not. What the Government could do was help by ensuring that the conditions were right, that the framework was right, and that the tools were available to enable industry and commerce to get on with the job.

The Central Aim had three main sub-headings – Climate, International Competitiveness and Innovation. It was all drawn out onto a single sheet of A4 paper, and looked like a dart board. For reference, the details are given below.

1 <u>Climate</u>

1.1 A financial and fiscal climate which encourages enterprise, investment and growth and minimises Government burdens on business.

1.2 A wider understanding of the value of productive activity, enterprise and profit.

1.3 European Community and international agreements, laws and commercial relations working to the advantage of UK trade and investment.

1.4 A regulatory framework which promotes fair competition and the efficient use of resources and safeguards the interests of customers.

1.5 Standards which strengthen the international competitiveness of British trade, industry and commerce.

1.6 Reduced regional disparities.

2 <u>International Competitiveness</u>

2.1 Improved management and other skills throughout UK industry and commerce, targeting smaller firms in particular.

2.2 Market information and support for UK firms competing in overseas markets.

2.3 Increased efficiency in state owned enterprises through privatisation, exposure to competition, target setting and monitoring.

2.4 Inward investment and collaboration with foreign companies yielding advantages to the UK.

2.5 Measures to increase UK output, improve performance and encourage the formation of new businesses.

3 Innovation

3.1 Increase civil R&D in industry.

3.2 Effective exploitation of UK and foreign science and technology.

3.3 Awareness and rapid adoption of key technologies.

3.4 Levels of quality and design to highest world standards.

3.5 Closer co-operation on new products between UK producers and customers, for example through public purchasing.

The short and sharp DTI Management Task was 'To use Departmental resources efficiently to pursue these aims'.

Like many of my colleagues, I looked at the pretty picture and wondered where my work fitted into all of this. Naively, it must fit in somewhere else the new Secretary of State might decide we should not be doing it. It was obviously an important part of this new heading of Innovation. Both the Small Firms Technical Enquiry Service and the Teaching Company Scheme had focussed on improving skills throughout UK industry and commerce, and targeting smaller firms was essential to SFTES but was barely part of the TCS. At the time I read down each heading in the list and idly wondered whether my TCS work could also be labelled as part of International Competitiveness within the Central Aims.

I remember thinking it was the first time I had met the word 'innovation' and wondered what exactly it meant. The classic definitions are about the introduction of something new, whether that is an idea, a method, or a device. There is an implicit expectation that innovation is linked to a process of improvements. The official DTI definition was that innovation was the successful exploitation of new ideas, and it may refer to both radical and incremental changes to products, processes or services. It was a good definition which has stood the test of time.

I don't remember innovation being defined earlier although I later found references to it in academic articles written back in the 1970s. Certainly there had been lots of interest in the process of 'invention' and how new products became successful in the marketplace. There had been a simplistic linear model which began with a perception that the UK was good at invention but then criticised UK industry for not getting these wonderful ideas into the market place. Now it was recognised that developing successful products was not that simple, and technology-push was not sufficient. Companies needed innovation.

Previous Government programmes to support research and development had at their core an implicit appreciation that some strategic areas needed special support, for example microelectronics development and applications had been supported under two programmes, MISP and MAP. Then there was the PPDS, a scheme to develop products and processes, and there had been a scheme to support pre-production orders whereby Government purchased early versions of equipment to place into companies. Now innovation had suddenly become a new and important policy area and I knew it was useful if you were ambitious to be working in fashionable areas. I did not realise it then but contributing to innovation was going to be the key for the rest of my work, and indeed for the rest of my career.

Within the Central Aim's heading of Innovation I identified three headings that were relevant to my current responsibilities with the TCS: increased R&D in industry, effective exploitation of UK and foreign science and technology, and the awareness and rapid adoption of key technologies. Not only did that confirm that the TCS was an important part of DTI policy to support the Central Aim, but it meant that future continuation programmes should be eligible for funding too. Everyone in my area would have been surprised if that was not the case, but it was good to have it spelled out so clearly. At the time, I did not fully appreciate the strategic importance of the new emphasis on key technologies, and on the exploitation of science and technology wherever it was developed. What were these Key Technologies? I was too busy to go and find out more. It was an important question that I was only able to really address much later.

Looking inwards within the DTI, a new approach to managing staff was indicated, with a new emphasis on ordering activities and setting priorities. Departmental resources were now going to be used efficiently to pursue the aims of Climate, International Competitiveness and Innovation within the Central Aim. Exactly how that efficiency was going to be measured and achieved was still to become evident. Inevitably, as always, it meant being seen to be doing more with less resource, not only by eventually removing one of the two Permanent Secretaries and two out of eleven Deputy Secretaries but also at lower levels. Reducing staffing levels was an easy way to seem to be increasing efficiency, but not very useful when instead trying to measure effectiveness. I would much rather have staff that were effective, not simply efficient.

In parallel, work programmes had to be defined for the coming six months and twelve months, setting objectives where appropriate and dates by which they would be achieved. While initially seen as a fun academic exercise, there came the time when it was necessary to report on whether these objectives were indeed being achieved on time or not. The Secretary of State thought this was a useful discipline, so we became accustomed to the idea too, and worked harder each year on setting sensible objectives.

By July 1984 I had moved my office from 29 Bressenden Place to Ashdown House, still doing the same job. Ashdown House was the main DTI building, and my office was in Room 244 on the second floor. It was very convenient for the Army & Navy Department store next door and only a short pleasant stroll through St James's Park for lunch at the United Oxford and Cambridge University Club. I seemed to be moving office even more often than jobs! I hoped that being in the most important DTI building, the one closest to the Houses of Parliament, must mean that my area of work was becoming more important. It had been over 3 years since my last promotion and I had discovered that getting promoted at Headquarters was a different process to that at the NPL. Jobs had grades and the only way to get promoted was to successfully apply for a job which was vacant. It was usually essential that you had first passed a Promotion Board, so that you were considered suitable for promotion, but you still had to compete with everyone else to capture a specific job. I started to go hunting.

I applied for a job working for Dr Andrew Wallard and Derek Howarth in the Long Term Studies Group (LTSG), which would have been a promotion and a move to a different area but still within the Research and Technology Policy Division. In 1983 one of my duties had been to provide support to the LTSG. This had included briefing for the annual meeting of senior DTI officials at the Civil Service College at Sunningdale in Berkshire, when the carving up of budgets between key budget holders was agreed. So I knew something of the work involved in the job. The competition was stiff - there were six of us invited for interview and everyone had a PhD or DPhil. Two of the others were already at Principal Scientific Officer/Grade 7 while the rest, myself included, were hoping to get promoted. I was not successful, but felt that the experience of going for a job interview had been useful.

The Farnborough Air Show happens only every two years, and so after September 1982, when I had my car accident, the next one was scheduled for September 1984. Soaring Oxford Ltd continued importing Grob Astir gliders from Mindelheim-Mattsies, in West Germany, and our summer weekends were often spent demonstrating the glider while evenings were spent replying to requests for brochures, information and prices. Then suddenly, in March 1984, the senior partner in the business, Peter Pratelli, died. He had been a good friend of Pete for over fifteen years, and his sudden illness and death in hospital while we were away abroad for two weeks on holiday was a shock to us. He had always taken a more active role in the company, and the immediate choice for Pete was either to go full-time, or find someone else to take over the business. Meanwhile that left the problem of running the company and I had to ask special permission from my line management in the DTI to become Company Secretary and the second Director of the company, as a temporary measure while everything was sorted out. Fortunately there are rules in the Staff Manual to cover this situation and within 24 hours I had asked for the permissions and received a positive formal reply. What had previously been a hobby and a sideline suddenly started to devour all our spare time. It meant an extra burden for us both, and soon afterwards another friend and experienced pilot, John Adams, took over Soaring Oxford Ltd. We helped him in the transition, and again worked with him at the Farnborough Air Show in 1984, talking to people about the Astir gliders.

Then at the Conservative Party Conference in the Autumn of 1984 everything changed for the DTI for a short time when Norman Tebbit was seriously injured by the bomb which wrecked the Grand Hotel at Brighton. I watched with shock as the extent of the damage was shown on TV. Fortunately there were no immediate changes in policy direction, although eventually in September 1985 he made the move to Central Office as Chairman of the Conservative Party and Chancellor of the Duchy of Lancaster. Perhaps he would have stayed longer at the DTI under different circumstances. He was replaced by Leon Brittan, who only stayed for 4 months until he in turn was replaced by Paul Channon.

PART TWO: MANAGING OTHERS

'Management organises, ensures efficiency and maintains order'

From 'Leading for Quality', published by the Cabinet Office in 1994

7　Hoorah - Promotion to Principal

Each member of staff has an annual staff report, which contained one section which scored performance in the job and a second section which asked for Fitness for Promotion, and the four possibilities were Not Fitted, Fitted, Well Fitted, and Exceptionally Well Fitted. Few people are ever marked as Exceptionally Well Fitted because they should have been promoted before reaching this level. I had continued to keep a watch for suitable job vacancies, and this year for the first time I was considered Well Fitted for promotion, rather than merely Fitted.

I kept reading the Job Vacancy Notices which were sent out individually to everyone who might be eligible. In July 1984 I applied for a vacancy in the Mechanical and Electrical Engineering Division (MEE), in the Branch concentrating on support for the application of Advanced Manufacturing Technologies (AMT), which was defined as the application of computers to manufacturing operations. The work here was full of acronyms, most beginning with C for Computer, and only suited people with that special technical aptitude. It was not the sort of job which was going to appeal to a traditional administrator. The duties of the job covered responsibility for the software, control and manufacturing organisational aspects of the Department's AMT programme comprising CADCAM, Computer Aided Production Management (CAPM) and the software requirements for Computer Integrated Manufacturing (CIM). Alongside encouraging the application of the technology there was a complementary objective to develop a strong UK supply industry. The work involved close collaboration with the user and the supply industry, universities and research organisations. By now I could refer to my 135 Teaching Company Scheme programmes, most of which were centred on AMT topics, including CADCAM, CAPM and CIM. I could handle the alphabet soup although I only knew the technologies from a distance. For example, I had used a CAD system, but only in a University teaching laboratory. The vacancy was for someone who was a Chartered Engineer, and who would manage a small team, with two technical staff and a small shared administrative office. As a mathematician by training, who then became a computer specialist and was now considered to be a scientist, I had no problems becoming re-labelled again as an engineer. I also liked the idea of finally having my own staff.

My academic qualifications in computing from Oxford and subsequent research work were excellent and very similar in standard to that for a Chartered Engineer. I had also shown the ability to learn about new technologies, and manage projects. This was a good enough background because career civil servants did not usually have current engineering expertise; these could always be bought from consultants as necessary.

Engineering was not a very fashionable career option for bright young civil servants, and there was not a lot of credible competition for the post. When I applied for the job I was only thinking about the benefits of getting the next promotion, not how the job fitted into a career profile for subsequent promotions. In the DTI career development was a short-term game and in a rapidly changing world each move up the promotion ladder was worth grabbing. New challenges were always exciting and the extra money on promotion would be useful too.

My interview was on 31 October 1984, and I was interviewed by a small panel including Peter Adkin who as line manager and Grade 6 would be my new boss. I heard on 21 November that I had been successful. Who would take over my work in RTP when I moved? Of course there was a short delay while my own job was advertised, and my transfer took effect from 2 January 1985, with a starting salary of £12,737 plus London weighting of £1,300. So, at 32 years old I was now finally promoted to Grade 7, and would be leading my own small section. It had taken a long time. I was going to be managing engineers, with the special challenge that one of my staff had applied for the job in competition with me, been interviewed and failed. I discovered later that my new boss used to have my job and had been promoted, thus leaving a vacancy behind him. This also meant that my staff used to directly work for my boss, and now had to get used to working for me instead. It was not an easy situation for me and him, and it was a difficult learning curve for some of my staff.

It was an existing post, so I arrived at my new office on the fifth floor of Ashdown House to be greeted by a work programme and an in-tray as well as a diary of commitments. As a new Principal/Grade 7 I was also expected to find time to attend the Senior Management Course. Ideally I should have attended the course before landing in the job. But the first challenge was to work with and manage my two engineers, one who was an experienced Senior Scientific Officer (SSO) and the other a new Senior Professional and Technical Officer (SPTO), and my share of a small administrative office led by a Higher Executive Officer (HEO). The office staff explained carefully to me exactly what sort of work they were able to do, and how much time they would be prepared to spend on work from my area. I was surprised at the blunt way in which polite requests to do things for me could be robustly refused by junior staff if they thought I was asking too much. I knew in theory that being a senior manager involved getting out of one's office and actually managing. Nevertheless it took me the best part of a year before I really got to grips with the work and the subject area, and had begun to grow confident in my new shoes. It was known that it was my first post on promotion, and so I suffered from that too.

Although there was lots of work going on, it was time for a serious look at the problems of exploiting advanced manufacturing technology in industry, and one of the key enablers was standards. In September 1985 I worked with Peter Adkin to put together a paper titled: Standards: Problems, Activities and Actions. It was intended to become the foundation for the future work programme in my area. It was also the first time I had tried to put together my own policy ideas, albeit with lots of help. Five important problems were identified. Looking back it seems a brave list of work for such a small group, but much of the work was done by consultants, academics and industrialists. We in the DTI provided the vision, direction, catalyst and the means for them to work together. It cost money, but not a great deal, because we were limited to working within existing programme funding. And when I say 'we', I was still too inexperienced to be truly leading the work, but I had two good project managers in my group, and senior staff above me who could grasp the importance of what was being done, and supported it with Ministers. In a leading-edge technical area, the description of my work is inevitably technical, so please skip to the next chapter if and when your eyes start to glaze over.

The first problem was identifying the problems areas in AMT standards, and then specifying what work should be done, setting the priorities and deciding how the work should be carried out, and by whom. It sounds all very straightforward, in theory, but how was it all to be carried forward in practice? I tended to work by top-down rather than bottom-up principles. The first activity was that tenders were invited to prepare a survey of AMT standards, and within Europe there was a similar parallel activity, carried out by the European Commission. The work was led by the SOGAME, which we always called the Senior Officials Group on AMT, which was considering funding a multi-annual study on advanced manufacturing equipment. Mrs Pamela Denham, the Assistant Secretary for my area and Peter Adkin's boss, was the British delegate to SOGAME. When she attended meetings in Brussels either Peter or I went too so we were all three closely involved. The aim of the study was to provide up-to-date, comparable, accurate information on the markets, suppliers and users of AMT in industry across all twelve member states. It was to be a multi-annual study, so the information would be collected several times and trends could be identified. In addition it had been agreed that on 21 and 22 November 1985 the Commission would organise a meeting on standardisation for advanced manufacturing equipment in Brussels. This was an important event, with between 300 and 400 attendees expected from member states. It was intended to establish the priority of topics for discussion within the whole standardisation area, and a detailed work programme. Attendance was to be by invitation only, so each country was busily providing its lists of suppliers and users, valuable strategic information in its own right. We spent a lot of time getting our list right and speaking with the key players, as well as working with the officials from Brussels who were tasked with preparing papers for the meeting and who came to London to discuss ideas with us.

The second problem was to establish a set of standards so that equipment made by different manufacturers could be interconnected. This was a well known difficulty, and was a very important problem. Manufacturing companies said that their first step was to contact their existing equipment suppliers when they wanted to upgrade their equipment, and this meant that they were tied to the new products of their supplier. Equipment from other suppliers would not connect to an existing proprietary set-up. However, equipment from different suppliers might be more suitable. In the jargon, the aim was to ensure multi-vendor interconnection. Here there were already several activities.

Firstly there were the Esprit projects. There was the CIM Architecture proposal, CIM-OSA, led by the French company Cap Gemini Innovation, and among its many participants were British Aerospace plc and International Computers Ltd (ICL). The objectives of this project were to design an open systems architecture (OSA) for computer integrated manufacture (CIM), hence the acronym CIM-OSA, and to define a set of concepts and rules to facilitate the building of future CIM systems and to support migration of existing implementations. The work had begun in October 1984, and was due to be completed in 1989.

There was also the Esprit Communications Network for Manufacturing Applications (CNMA) project, led by British Aerospace plc and including GEC plc among the participants. The objective of the CNMA project was to select, implement and demonstrate profiles of existing and emerging communications standards in real production environments. This work only started in January 1986.

It was the first time I had been involved with the Esprit programme. Esprit stands for the European Strategic Programme for Research in Information Technologies, and was set up in 1984 to fund collaborative R&D, as a response to the Japanese 5th generation computer research. It was the most ambitious cooperative research programme ever embarked upon in Europe. Started in February 1984 Esprit was described as 'the key to reviving European technology.' The programme stimulated cooperation between several hundred large and small information technology companies and research institutions throughout the twelve countries of the EEC. The premise behind Esprit was matching funds. The Commission would put up half the money for a research project, and the participants would put up the other half. Rather than have researchers suggest some interesting research, the Commission would issue a call for proposals. To respond, a group had to have at least two industrial partners from at least two EC countries. Typically, a successful group would have up to a half-dozen members, including research institutions, consulting firms, telecommunications companies, and computer companies. The Esprit budget was significant. Esprit committed ECU 1.5 billion and involved 3,000 researchers in the first phase from 1984 to 1988. From 1988 to 1992, this rose to another ECU 3.2 billion, involving almost 6,000 researchers. Alongside Esprit there was also a similar UK collaborative programme in R&D, the Alvey Programme, which was set up for the same reasons in 1982.

The second activity to establish standards for interconnection was the new Manufacturing Automation Protocol (MAP). This would become a very important part of my future work programme. The purpose of MAP was to prepare a specification that would allow communication among these diverse intelligent devices, purchased from different vendors, in a cost-effective and consistent manner. It was founded by General Motors in the USA who had established the MAP Task Force in 1980. Their reason was strictly commercial. They expected to have some 200,000 intelligent devices in their manufacturing plants by 1990, purchased from different suppliers. The Task Force was set up to select protocols for the local area networks which would be used in all General Motors' plants.

The problem of communication between different devices from different vendors had already been addressed in the IT standards' world. The problem was complicated and the basic principle for dealing with complicated problems is to split them into simpler ones. Accordingly an international IT standardisation committee had divided the problem into 7 layers, making the Open Systems Interconnection (OSI) 7-layer model. This is how it all looked in 1985:

7	Application	User process and management
6	Presentation	Data format translation
5	Session	Control of sessions between end points
4	Transport	Reliable transfer of data
3	Network	Routing and switching of data
2	Data Link	Packaging of data
1	Physical	Cables, connectors, voltage levels

Imagine the difficulty of explaining all this to senior officials, many of whom thought IT was related to typing and was something for their secretary to do, or Ministers who did not have Mathematics at O-level and certainly had no IT background! It was exactly the same problem with many of the Chief Executives in industry. There was a need for a short MAP Guidebook, to help industry and others understand the bulky detailed MAP specification and to enable a UK input to future versions of MAP.

To explain the basic concepts, we found a helpful analogy, from Jim Heaton of General Motors, published in Modern Materials Handling magazine in June 1985.

'Suppose you are trying to hold a conversation with someone in another country, say Japan, by telephone. The first 3 layers enable you to dial the phone and start talking. If the other party speaks

English you are all set. But if he speaks Japanese and you don't then you'll need layers 4 through 7 to perform the translation. At that point, if you are discussing a subject you are both familiar with, you're home free. But if he's talking on a subject outside of your domain, you'll need more help. This corresponds to the fact that in factory communications you have to do more than just exchange data. You must use the data in a meaningful way.'

And, of course, it is always useful to see something which works, as well as read about it. General Motors was well aware of this too and had held a demonstration in Detroit, as part of the conference Autofact 6 in 1984. Progress had been made and Autofact 7 in Detroit, from 4 to 7 November 1985, would be building on Autofact 6. The theme was 'Manufacturing Integration becomes of Age'.

In the UK we had a policy of setting up mobile awareness vehicles in order to get out and explain to companies about new technology. This had begun in the Department of Industry in 1982 with the Minister of State Kenneth Baker MP as part of IT82, and had been shown to be a valuable means to get the message out to companies. One obvious idea was to do the same and set up a mobile demonstration unit for MAP, using a bus or a large trailer, which we did.

The DTI wanted to find an industry-led organisation to carry on the necessary work. After looking at what was there, and which organisations had expertise, the UK Centre for Communications Standards, ComCentre, was set up. It was sponsored by the DTI and industry, and operated by PERA in Melton Mowbray, in conjunction with the Institution of Mechanical Engineers (IMechE) and the Institution of Production Engineers (IProdE). Everyone recognised that communication standards were growing technologies, moving at a rapid pace. It was essential that data was collected and disseminated, thereby providing to British companies the most up-to-date information available from worldwide users. Companies needed to see at first hand how functional standards such as MAP, and the matching Technical Office Protocol TOP, worked, and discover how the technology could help their business. It was recognised that companies would also need guidance and training to implement MAP and TOP. ComCentre was set up to provide the following benefits:

databases of published material, Communication Standards, Conforming products – worldwide;

current information on this fast developing area of technology;

demonstration facilities;

international contact with other centres of communications expertise;

    awareness seminars, conferences and training;

    organised visits to demonstration companies;

    practical experience, and access to PERA's Networking Applications Centre.

Ministers were enthusiastic about these ideas and the Parliamentary Under Secretary of State, John Butcher MP, agreed to launch the first ComCentre seminar.

This is a long list of work already and so far I have only mentioned two of the five problems; the third problem was 'islands of automation'. One of my staff was responsible for promoting the use of Industrial Local Area Networks, under the new banner 'ILANs for Islands'. The idea was to link Computer Aided Design, Computer Aided Manufacturing, Computer Aided Production Management, Stores Inventory and other commercial operations so that data entered in one area may be made available to all others, avoiding manual transfer or duplication. We knew that early adoption of industrial networking would hopefully lead to competitiveness.

In 1985 the DTI had one large scheme to support R&D in industry, called Support for Innovation and usually shortened to SfI, and this was the only support scheme available. Current Ministers had decided that there were too many schemes, and wanted everything to be simplified and merged, with the same standard rules, and under the one banner. We wanted to promote the deployment of ILANs in UK manufacturing, so applications from industry and other interested parties were invited for projects to demonstrate networking in the context of Computer Integrated Manufacturing, and for the development of Industrial Local Area Networks. There was limited money available, up to 25% of development and implementation costs, as was standard under the SfI rules at that time. We insisted that any project should follow international standard recommendations, specifically mentioning MAP. In addition, any user company receiving assistance was forced to join the DTI Demonstration Firms Scheme, another useful awareness scheme managed by the Institution of Mechanical Engineers, whereby other people could visit the company, see what had been achieved and speak to those involved.

Of course, connecting equipment together doesn't necessarily mean that anything useful happens and there was also a need to establish standards for data exchange and transfer. As I quoted earlier, a simple analogy is if I am shouting down the telephone in English to someone else who only knows how to speak in Japanese. The connection is there, but no information transfers. This had been a technical area where my predecessor Peter Adkin had been very active, and I was to try and take on the same mantle.

In 1983 a working group from the Process Plant industry had examined the problems of exchanging data in a machine readable format between CADCAM systems from different suppliers, with the aim of facilitating the exchange of drawings and associated data. The pressure to do so was because there was the threat of mandatory computerisation, and even the simple solution of buying compatible or identical computer equipment will only work if a component manufacturer supplies only one customer. Firms cannot afford to purchase a range of different CADCAM systems because they have a range of different customers. The Initial Graphics Exchange Specification (IGES) was designed to deal with this problem, and was for the exchange of engineering drawings. The next stage was to develop a Product Data Exchange Specification (PDES), which included much more than just the drawing information. In 1985 we were also aware, through international standards meetings, that there was work going on in France and Germany. The master plan was that all this would come together as the international Standard for Exchange of Product Data (STEP), hopefully by the end of 1986.

At Leeds University 35 UK companies were, with the National Economic Development Office (NEDO) and the DTI, supporting the work of the new CADCAM Data Exchange Technical Centre (CADDETC) to try and take a leading role in all this international standardisation. I had more personal interest in the problems of data exchange than the problems of factory automation, probably because of my background working with software and drawings and CAD in the past. One of my tasks was to keep an eye on progress, attend the meeting of the CADDETC Executive Committee, and manage their DTI funding.

I was also responsible for the budget for the Geometric Modelling Project at Leeds University which was a R&D programme for developing new innovative software for modelling physical objects using solid components, rather than the traditional wire frame model which only defined the outline of the object. This involved another set of regular monitoring visits to the University of Leeds, and whenever possible the two different projects held their management meetings on the same day. There was some overlap with membership of the two groups at Leeds, and the two projects were led by the same Professor, Professor Alan de Pennington. If I was busy I found that I could drive up to Leeds early in the morning, spend the day at the meetings, and then drive back the same evening. It was typically just under four hours driving, each way. Usually common sense prevailed and I caught a train from London and stayed at the University Guest House for two nights, leaving a full day between for meetings. Because I had written off my car in the past I was being careful not to get too tired and do the same again.

Having supposedly practical experience of CADCAM I was able to offer myself in 1987 as tutor for the new Open University technology course on 'Computer Aided Design'. In those days the sites where OU teaching was carried out also had a special room where students could use a computer. People did not have computers of their own at home, and the 'open' aspect of the Open University meant that those who could not afford to have a computer were offered free access to one. These days it is obligatory to have a computer of your own in order to be a student. As a tutor, the Open University also provided me with a free Research Machines computer, which I found in a soggy box sitting around the back of the house one evening. It must have been there for several days and it was only at the weekend we spotted it. It was too dark when I got home at night to see anything. To my surprise the computer was still working, and there was special software provided so that simple CAD tasks could be carried out. It was the first year of the course, so I had to work hard to keep ahead of my students, and make sure that I had done all the project work well before they reached the tasks. There was a final project and I had great fun helping my third year undergraduate students use the simple solid modelling system to produce designs for a set of chess pieces. I continued teaching the course for six years.

Returning to my work programme in MEE Division, I have discussed three problems: identifying the problem areas in standardisation, establishing standards for interconnection, and dealing with 'islands of automation'. The fourth problem was the need for independent testing. We knew from talking with our colleagues who were responsible for IT standardisation and from discussions with General Motors that there were two distinct stages in testing, and it all needed to be truly independent. The first stage was conformance testing, which checked that the equipment does conform to the specification of the standard. Then it was necessary to join the equipment together for real and check on interoperability. As an example, this had been done in testing of MAP protocols for the Autofact 6 conference in 1984 and then for Autofact 7 in 1985. Both times, all of the vendors eventually were able to successfully pass the conformance test suite. When interoperability testing began most of the vendors then found problems affecting interoperability. It is possible for systems working on real networks to fail conformance tests and systems which passed the conformance tests to fail on the real network. Conformance testing centres for OSI were being set up in UK, including in Manchester at the National Centre for IT (NCC), at the NPL, and at a company named Eosys. Conformance testing for IGES was being carried out at Leeds University. There was certainly going to be a need for a UK conformance testing centre for MAP and the best practical idea in 1985 was to build on what was already happening. This is the usual approach taken. However initial contact with the NCC was not as positive as we would have liked, and a new organisation, The Networking Centre (TNC) was established at Hemel Hempstead. Later it was eventually agreed that NCC and TNC would to work together.

Finally, problem number five was described as the creation of a software engineering environment. This was one of several topics where manufacturing industry was using leading edge technologies from IT. Initial interest was on software engineering and project support environments. Later topics included artificial intelligence and intelligent knowledge based systems. It was all part of making sure that manufacturing industry was following in the footsteps of the enablers provided by the IT sector. In the UK, the IT Alvey programme had a number of projects in these areas, and the first topic I looked at was software engineering. The basic idea was to use the discipline of engineering to write better software. For too long the writing of software had been an art form, and that had to change. It was the time when there were problems with software maintenance and formal methods were being used to prove that software did really work. The idea in a manufacturing situation was to provide the enabling technology to ensure the integrity of systems design for total manufacturing operations. Of the trendy words, mention was made of new programming languages, project support environments, and expert systems. I was personally interested in expert systems, because it was interesting to be able to capture human expertise, as its name suggests. The technology was becoming used in industry, and PA produced a booklet 'Expert Systems: A Management Guide' during 1985. The ACARD working group on Software Engineering was due to report later in 1985, and I was watching their progress. It was really putting a stake in the ground that these, and other enabling technologies, would be useful to manufacturing industry in the future.

I seemed to spend a lot of 1985 writing my work programme, as did everyone in the DTI. So far it had been a bottom-up approach whereby the various things which were in progress had been assembled into a small number of related headings. Next that had to be incorporated into the Divisional Work Plan. So it was that my Section work programme was incorporated into the Branch work programme, and then into the Divisional work programme. Mine was just one small part of a much bigger portfolio of activities. By coincidence, I had identified five problem areas to deal with and the Divisional Work Plan had five approved headings:

Objective A was to encourage awareness, development and adoption of AMT.

Objective B was to work to improve the efficiency, competitiveness and trade balance of the AMT supply industry.

Objective C was to assist UK industry to increase its export share.

Objective D was in support of EC Programmes and standards.

Objective E was to improve the use of manpower and other resources available.

I sat with my boss and my actual work programme, and this list, and we tried to attach labels of A, B, C, D or E to each item. Some of the rough notes had an initial letter A, which was then replaced by the letter B. For example, making input to the Government response to the ACARD report on Software Engineering was a small part of my work, but should it be counted as part of Objective A? It didn't fit very well into any of the labels. By the end of October I had a neat work programme which had been pushed and shoved into the required shape. It was a good learning curve for me and it gave a firm foundation on which to build future work programmes. Each year a brand new statement of what we were going to do in the future 12 months needed to be prepared and approved by the Secretary of State and Ministers, and we had to report on our successes and failures.

International standards writing depends on using representatives from national standards bodies to contribute and only approved national representatives were permitted to take part. This meant that it was essential to set up a series of committees within the British Standards Institution, so that international standards for advanced manufacturing technology could be formally discussed there and drafted. There had been an old IT committee, named OIS/19, and I have no idea why it was called OIS or the number 19 was allocated. My best guess is O for 'open' and IS for 'information systems'. OIS/19 no longer met, and with the new emphasis on AMT standards it seemed best to start again with a new name and an expanded structure of sub-committees. We in the DTI suggested that there should be a new top-level committee which was called AMT/-. All top-level committees are /- and the top-level committee above OIS/19 would have been OIS/-. I attended the meetings of AMT/- as formal DTI representative and also attended a selection of its new sub-committees: AMT/4 on data exchange, AMT/6 on MAP-TOP and AMT/7 on real time communications. Many people think of standards making as dry and boring, but in this area it was exciting and had a real buzz. Everyone wanted to get involved and senior people from large companies turned up at the meetings and went away and worked on text.

One thing to be sure in the DTI in those days was that time passed and jobs changed. Also the Secretary of State kept changing, as did the Ministers. One year later and the name of the Division had changed from MEE to MMT. It was now Mechanical Engineering and Manufacturing Technology Division. This was good news for me because it reflected the new emphasis on manufacturing technology. Two years later and it was called Manufacturing Technology and Materials Division (MTM). Three years later and it was Manufacturing and Information Technologies Division (MIT).

After Lord Young of Graffham arrived as Secretary of State in 1987 there was a major new badging as we became the Department for Enterprise with its advertisements and Vroosh symbol. We went through an enormous amount of boxes of old headed paper, replaced by new, as well as, I am sure, confusing our customers in industry. The people around me changed too. Ray Mingay as Head of Division was replaced by John Cammell, and my Assistant Secretary Pamela Denham moved on promotion to the Quality, Design and Education Division to be replaced by Mark Lanyon who came to us from one of the DTI Regional Offices. Fortunately Peter Adkin stayed for 2 years, until he then moved and was replaced by Steve Owsianka who joined from IT Division. No-one who was ambitious and wanted to build a career in the Civil Service stayed for more than a few years in any job.

My staff stayed with me, although I worked with a number of different extra people who were bought in as experts from industry, research organisations and academia. There were usually three or four such consultants, at roughly my level or above, working part-time alongside for short term tasks. I recall Rod Duddin, Andrew de Vicq from the AMT Research Institute (AMTRI) which was previously the Machine Tool Industry Research Association (MTIRA), Colin Pye from the NCC, David Hughes from Kingston Polytechnic, and Andrew Harrison from Leicester Polytechnic. There were also dedicated staff from PERA and the National Engineering Laboratory (NEL), a research laboratory of the DTI located in East Kilbride near Glasgow. In addition, everyone belonging to the European Map Users Group (EMUG) worked very hard to maintain the bridge between the US and UK/European standardisation work. It was not only important to get the next version of MAP/TOP correct, it also had to be done to a firm deadline, unlike most standards work which drags on until each dot and comma is in the right place. EMUG members were senior technical people and also had responsibilities in their own organisations. For example, the first Chairman of EMUG was Colin Hoptroff, from Jaguar cars.

Everyone I met in MEE/MMT Division worked very hard. The size of my team gradually grew. My direct staff - Eric, Ron, and then Richard who joined later, and the administrators in the office, were augmented by one SSO-level secondee from industry, and junior scientific staff from the research establishments who joined for the experience of participating in policy work. I had been invited to be a member of the Interview Panel for Panel 2, which was the promotion board for DTI scientific staff deemed fit to be promoted from Higher Scientific Officer (HSO) to Senior

Scientific Officer (SSO). Remember these were often graduates aged in their late 20s who were doing research; I had been 28 when I was successful at Panel 2 and I had been younger than most. In the DTI the engineers at the equivalent grade of Higher Professional and Technical Officer (HPTO) were also seen by Panel 2. This gave me the chance to spot bright useful scientists and engineers who might be persuaded into a short secondment to work for me. This was formalised under a new scheme for Short Term Experience Postings, and although I found it took extra effort to help these young scientists and engineers contribute to my policy work, I made the effort because I felt it was part of my responsibility to widen their horizons. I made sure I defined a precise task for them to do, so we both could measure their success.

All my staff were special, and when they have latent abilities I try and encourage them. One special example is Ron. He joined my group in the DTI as an engineer just before my own arrival, and at his annual report review I suggested he might think about doing research, working towards a part-time PhD. It had the advantage that it would be useful in his work, if we found a project which was job-related, and would give him an added advantage over his colleagues when he came up for promotion interviews. At that time one of the consultants we were employing was Dr David Hughes, then an academic working at Kingston Polytechnic. David agreed to work with Ron towards the PhD, and took him with him as his student when he was promoted to Professor at Plymouth Polytechnic. Ron worked very hard, and although David left Plymouth, the research project was able to continue with a different supervisor. Eventually, in 2001 he was awarded his PhD from the Human-Centred Systems Design Group at what was now the University of Plymouth on the topic 'Improving design and administration of government support programmes for industry'. It is an interesting dissertation, with the benefit of being written with real examples with which Ron had been involved.

Towards the middle of 1987 I was asked if I would be prepared to write about my job, for inclusion in a glossy booklet titled 'A scientific or engineering career in the Department of Trade and Industry'. The booklet was targeted at new graduates and post-doctoral students who were suitable recruits for the Civil Service science and technology group, and highlighted career opportunities in the DTI. It was also useful to tempt scientists and engineers out of their research establishment and into scientific administration. My write up was first. I was taken into an empty Grade 5 office to be photographed, sitting at a desk smiling, with a neat pile of papers in front of me, pretending to talk on the telephone. To repeat my quote then:

> 'The job is what you make it. There is so much scope here (in Headquarters), more I think than in a research establishment. I get a lot of job satisfaction from what I am able to achieve. Of course, the

transition from technical expert to manager of a team needs effort. The most difficult challenge for me was certainly developing the best in my staff. But this skill is essential if I am going to make real achievements in future postings. And participation in the Department's Senior Management Development Programme helps me focus on acquiring the skills for good performance at Grade 6 and above.'

At this stage in my career it was expected that I would have to get promotion from Principal/PSO to Grade 6 and then to Grade 5, whereas fast-stream administrators who join the Civil Service, and were my colleagues doing very similar jobs, would go directly from Principal to Grade 5. In 1988 this problem had been identified, and the DTI did, for the first time, recruit a small number of graduates as Science Management Trainees. They were chosen for their exceptional potential and would undertake a challenging mix of research work and headquarters policy jobs, complemented by special training which was expected to earn them accelerated promotion. The aim was to develop scientists to fill senior posts in areas such as technology policy and R&D management. The scheme was too late for me, but useful for my junior colleagues. There were said to be 1,500 scientists and engineers working in the DTI, out of a total staff of 12,000. The majority of these worked in the four Research Establishments (LGC, NEL, NPL and the Warren Spring Laboratory) in applied R&D or providing scientific and technical services.

In 1988 I was asked to update my job description, and I include it here for comparison with where I started just three years earlier. The area was defined as Head of AMT Standards, and the duties now focussed on Systems Technology and Integration. There were two main objectives:

1. Support of the development of international standards acceptable to UK industry, to cover the information flow needs of all sizes of manufacturing enterprise but with a special emphasis on the needs of small and medium firms. The two main technical areas were networking (MAP/TOP/OSI) and data exchange for CAD systems.
2. Support of UK vendors and users in the application of these standards.

8   What are the competencies of a DTI Senior Manager?

Once I became promoted I had been invited to attend the Senior Management Course, and so I expected I should now describe myself as a Senior Manager, as did all my colleagues at the same grade. What did I learn when I attended the DTI Senior Management Course from 10 to 21 February 1986? Yes, this was really two whole weeks away from the office, just like the DTI Middle Management Course had been many years previously. Unfortunately the course was limited to DTI staff, and so I was not able to mingle with staff from other Departments. I should have realised that it was going to be of limited value.

Prior to attending I had filled out a Personal Development Plan. This was a new management tool and there were three stages in the development cycle: Assessment, Plan and Review. There are no new concepts here and it does sound very familiar compared with other management planning tools, although it was all brand new to the DTI. I was also provided with lists of competencies. These were groups of abilities, types of knowledge and skills which were said to be particularly important for staff at senior levels to develop. There were six Core Competencies and ten Important Competencies.

> Core Competence A: Management of resources/ organisations.
> It comprised Setting objectives, Deciding on priorities, Quantifying outputs and measuring performance, Financial management and Value-for-money principles and techniques.
>
> Core Competence B: Management of staff.
> It comprised Motivation, Communicating with staff and listening to their views, Assessing strengths and weaknesses of staff, Delegation/allocation of work and Development of staff.
>
> Core Competence C: Knowledge/Understanding of the context of your work.
> It comprised Your role in your own department, the Immediate context, Political context, and the Broader context, both the private sector and economic / social / technological trends.
>
> Core Competence D: Managing your own work.
> It comprised Allocating priorities to your work, Managing your own time and Coping with tight deadlines.
>
> Core Competence E: Information Technology
> .It comprised the Awareness of potential uses of IT and the Ability to make personal use of computerised equipment.

Core Competence F: More specialised knowledge/expertise.
It looked like a final heading put in to keep the lawyers, accountants, computer managers and other specialists and experts happy.

Without being informed, I assumed that Core A was more important than Core B, and so on down the list to Core F. I found aspects of both Core A and Core B which became my priority for my current job.

As well as the Core Competencies there was also a list of ten Important Competencies :

1.   Representational and presentational skills
2.   Written and administrative skills
3.   Policy management
4.   Economics
5.   Accounting and finance
6.   Quantitative skills and statistics
7.   Law
8.   Industrial relations
9.   Industrial and Technological Awareness
10. International

For each of these I had to think about what I had learned from experience or training, and then whether they were important for me to develop. The whole Personal Development Plan was nine pages long, and I still have my copy which I completed in January 1986.

After attending the course I wrote in my Personal Development Plan 'This course was very disappointing. Where are the bright people in the Department?' Of course, the answer is that the really bright staff, perhaps my colleagues at Oxford or graduates from elsewhere, had come in as graduate Administrative Trainees and moved quickly to Principal and then Assistant Secretary. They never attended a DTI Senior Management Course and their training was very structured and separate. They were part of a cohort of similar entrants across Whitehall with whom they were encouraged to network. Whereas I had arrived by a different route, almost through a side door, and others like me had come through the same slow route. The DTI Senior Management Course did reinforce some of the management lessons in the DTI Middle Management Course and gave me time to stand back and look at my job. The main benefit was that I could tick the box that I had attended.

Having identified my strengths I looked hard to try and identify weaknesses. I managed to identify one weakness which was participation in meetings. In some circumstances I got bored and found it was easier to sit and listen than to make the effort to take an active part in discussions. I was not the sort who needed to hear her own voice, but I knew that some of my colleagues were different. If I was going to make no contribution, then why bother attending the meeting myself? I should send one of my staff to observe instead. So I vowed to think beforehand about what I wanted to achieve at each meeting I was invited to attend, and do better preparation. Small meetings were not a problem, nor were large formal meetings where I had a specific role and had prepared a formal brief to follow. It was the informal meetings with 10 or 15 people present where I found it tempting to just sit back and listen, and even sometimes think about other things or write letters. A good Chairman would have made sure that I was not allowed to opt out, but such people were rare.

Of the long list of Core Competences those which I identified as a priority in my current job were Core A 'To set objectives and decide on priorities', and Core B 'The management of staff'. The latter was to be achieved by establishing their work programmes and ensuring they achieved their objectives. I started to hold monthly section meetings which I led. I felt it was important to start somewhere, although my recollection of the early section meetings was that I spoke and others listened. It was not an exchange of ideas, mainly because I was still not confident enough with the technical issues to allow an open and free-ranging discussion of the work programme, and my staff were not confident either. We all recognised that I had limited ability to change the work programme, given much of the work was part of a bigger picture already agreed between senior officials and Ministers.

Unfortunately much of my early experience of management was learnt by reading books and then trying an approach and seeing how well it worked. It was only much later that I could benefit from a better theoretical understanding of management, and also had the support of a mentor who was herself a good manager and useful role model. By then I had also become a tutor within the MBA programme of the Open University Business School.

Back in 1986 I had also noted in my Personal Development Plan that I wanted to do some private study on crisis management skills. Life in the DTI at that time seemed to always involve crisis management. It was also a fashionable subject to be interested in, and I decided to reflect on how to learn more about it. Being knowledgeable about fashionable subjects, whether of technology or management, has always been useful to me. One of my very senior colleagues, who also played rugby as a hobby, suggested that the best attitude when dealing with someone from the opposing team who had fallen on the ground was to give them a good kick to make sure they did not get up. This was not an approach which was overtly encouraged in policy making, but I am sure it worked well for some people in some circumstances. I will never be very good at rugby, but then it is useful to work with someone who is.

On 26 February 1985 the DTI Joint Permanent Secretaries, Sir Brian Hayes and Sir Anthony Rawlinson, had circulated to all staff a note about the general duties and responsibilities of civil servants. The information here was well known; indeed it had been reproduced as a Written Answer to a Parliamentary Question on that date. Then on 2 December 1987 that note was revised.

> 'The Civil Service is there to provide the Government of the day with advice on the formulation of the policies of the Government, to assist in carrying out the decisions of the Government, and to manage and deliver the services for which the Government is responsible.... The duty of the individual civil servant is first and foremost to the Minister of the Crown who is in charge of the Department in which he or she is serving.... It is the duty of civil servants to serve their Ministers with integrity and to the best of their ability....
>
> The determination of policy is the responsibility of the Minister. In the determination of policy the civil servant has no constitutional responsibility or role distinct from that of the Minister. Subject to the conventions limiting the access of Ministers to papers of previous Administrations, it is the duty of the civil servant to make available to the Minister all the information and experience at his or her disposal which may have a bearing on the policy decisions to which the Minister is committed or which he is preparing to make, and to give to the Minister honest and impartial advice, without fear or favour and whether the advice accords with the Minister's view or not. Civil servants are in breach of their duty, and damage their integrity as servants of the Crown, if they deliberately withhold relevant information from their Minister, or if they give their Minister other advice than the best they believe they can give, or if they seek to obstruct or delay a decision simply because they do not agree with it. When, having been given all the relevant information and advice, the Minister has taken a decision, it is the duty of civil servants loyally to carry out that decision with precisely the same energy and good will, whether they agree with it or not.'

That was all very clear, and I had no problems agreeing with the instructions. Indeed I wondered what disaster or clash between officials and Ministers had provoked such a stern repetition of the official rules. There were no problems in my corner of the DTI.

As an additional insight, recently I read the advice to new junior ministers from Michael Heseltine in his autobiography, from when he arrived as Parliamentary Under-Secretary to the Minister of Transport in 1970:

'Whatever you do on your first day, do something – preferably against the advice offered to you. Make yourself a nuisance. The message will soon get around that you're not there to be taken for granted. But remember, too, that the civil servants are usually right. Choose your decision with care. You are on your own. The instructions you give and your reasons for them – or the lack of them – will have been carefully recorded for any subsequent inquiry when things go wrong.'

9 Brussels: Meetings of the Senior Officials Group on Advanced Manufacturing Equipment

As my job developed there was an increasing amount of overseas travel on official business. I had not been asked to do overseas travel in my previous work, although I travelled abroad on holidays. The new Ad Hoc Senior Officials Group on Advanced Manufacturing Equipment (SOGAME) had been set up early in 1985, and I attended the meetings at the European Commission offices in Brussels with my Assistant Secretary, Mrs Pamela Denham. There were a number of Senior Officials Groups, and some are Ad Hoc whereas others are permanent and well-established. An example of the latter type was the Senior Officials Group for IT Standardisation (SOGITS). In contrast, SOGAME was an Ad Hoc Group, and set up with the deliberate intention of dealing with a particular topical issue and then be disbanded.

The meetings in Brussels were always supposed to be attended by an Assistant Secretary or above, a senior civil servant, because the emphasis is on the official national policy, more than the technology. Mrs Denham was therefore the named UK representative to SOGAME, and I had the task of doing the preparation of briefing material for the meetings, and preparing the notes of the discussions for circulation within the UK afterwards while we waited for the official minutes. Peter Adkin attended some of the meetings too, depending on the agenda. For the first meeting we took careful advice from our IT colleagues who attended SOGITS, particularly Harry Ivey and George Sidey. I learned a lot by watching how decisions were made at European level, and found Pamela Denham a good role model. I must have been doing a good job supporting her when we attended the meetings because on one occasion I was sent alone to represent the UK. Later, when I was teaching a course on Public Policy for the Open University, I wrote a fictitious role play exercise based around what actually happened at a Round Table meeting of this type in Brussels.

Travelling to Brussels became a normal and tedious part of the job. We flew out in the late afternoon, so that we were ready for an early start the following morning. Usually we managed to finish the meeting just in time to catch the last flight back home. Everyone at the meeting kept an eye on the clock, and the representatives from some countries had to leave earlier than we did.

In those days overseas travel came with a fixed 24-hour subsistence allowance and it was possible to stay somewhere cheap and eat well, or stay somewhere very posh and eat sandwiches. I always preferred the former. Colleagues often stayed in the Queen Anne Hotel, which was modern and clean with a good buffet breakfast, but on the edge of the town. It was not an area where I wanted to go out alone after dark, but interesting when passing through the area as part of a larger group. The hotel was within walking distance of the range of good restaurants in the Grand Place area in the centre of Brussels. In the narrow alleyways of the Rue Bouchers it was always possible to find a good selection of restaurants, and I was usually tempted by the fresh fish on open display, although on one occasion we found a Moroccan restaurant and ate couscous.

Staying at the Queen Anne Hotel had the disadvantage that it was a short journey by Underground to the Berlaymont Building for our meetings, and we had to take our breakfast early. Other colleagues who visited Brussels frequently chose to stay at the 5* Europa Hotel, which was very nice and very convenient for the Berlaymont Building. It was just a few minutes walk. At the Europa Hotel there was a special arrangement whereby the hotel cost was paid directly. The Civil Service got a special cheap room rate because of the vast number of people who stayed there. The Europa Hotel was said to be very comfortable and was a tempting option, although you only received a modest meal allowance. On one visit I stayed in a little 3* hotel actually in the Grand Place. My room had a spectacular view across the cobbles, and was not expensive. It was only with the regular chiming of the clock, all through the night, that I realised why no-one stayed there. I never went back. Too little sleep meant that I was not at my sharpest at the meeting.

The European Commission policy areas were divided into a number of Directorate Generales, or DGs. I recall that the work on CIM and AMT was part of DGIII, showing its background in engineering and manufacture, whereas the complementary work on IT and Information Systems was the responsibility of DGXIII. DGXIII took an active role in industrial policy, funding a great deal of research and development. The separation was not always convenient, although it was for good historical reasons. All the officials were based in the Rue de la Loi.

Meetings of SOGAME took place in one of many large conference rooms, with a horseshoe table. The delegates were seated in alphabetic order of their country, so the UK was always at one end. This was convenient because we were close to the Chairman and the Commission officials, who sat in a line completing the D shape. In 1986 there were twelve members of the European Economic Community (EEC) - the original six of France, Germany, Italy, Netherlands, Belgium and Luxembourg had been joined by Denmark, Ireland and the United Kingdom in 1973; Greece in 1981; and Portugal and Spain in 1986.

One of my travel souvenirs was a mug depicting the various member states characteristics - Cooking like a Brit; Available as a Belgian; Controlled as an Italian; Driving like the French; Organised as a Greek; Sober as the Irish; Humorous as a German; Generous as a Dutchman;

Discreet as a Dane; Famous as a Luxembourger; Technical as a Portuguese; and Humble as a Spaniard. I also had a bright blue golfing umbrella with twelve yellow stars which was left behind in my office in London and never claimed.

There were always interpreters, parked in boxes to one side, and one meeting had to be cancelled at short notice because interpreters were not available. It was very important that everyone could give their views in their own language, and for all the other countries to get a good real-time translation of what was being said. I was glad that my French was good, and that reduced the need to use the headphones to get a translated version of French contributions. It was also obvious to the French delegation that we could speak French. Mrs Denham could speak French too. The meeting operated as a Table Ronde, and because countries representatives were seated in alphabetic order, sometimes the UK was asked to give its view first, and sometimes we were able to listen to everyone else and give our views last. This gave a better chance to take account of other countries views, and to some extent summarise the different contributions before making our own known. Although we read the papers carefully beforehand, and had an agreed UK line, discussions at the table still involved a lot of quick thinking. Key words and phrases were scribbled onto pieces of paper and passed between us as we planned our formal, minuted, contributions.

We were always short of time, and notes of what had happened at the meeting were prepared while flying back home so that they could be issued quickly to our colleagues. It made it all a long and tiring day.

10 Funding and Setting up Demonstrations of Industrial Networking Technology

Having seen the success of Autofact 6 in 1984 and Autofact 7 in 1985 in the USA, in the UK we were jealous of the advantage which taking part and seeing such demonstrations gave to their companies. It was agreed between officials that it was time to explore what could be offered here. Setting up any new initiative can only be done by officials in partnership with the wishes of Ministers. The next step was to consult with key companies, who not only supported these views but were equally worried that there was an alarming lack of UK awareness of these initiatives in the USA - MAP and others. Consequently there was evidence of a need for a special initiative. An open meeting was held early in February 1986 at which the intention to promote a major MAP awareness campaign leading to a significant demonstration of MAP and relating enabling technologies was tabled. These intentions were enthusiastically accepted by the twenty or so key industrialists that were present. The plans were then further developed at a second meeting later in February, which was attended by 41 people representing 28 companies.

A paper was written, explaining to Ministers that the integration of islands of automation was recognised to be one of the most important problems facing British manufacturing industry, and that there were significant technical developments from the USA that could help overcome this problem. It was agreed that something should be done, and this became the DTI MAP Awareness Event. There were eight specific objectives:

1. To communicate effectively the basis upon which the MAP and TOP standards have been developed
2. To educate British industry in MAP and TOP technology, in terms of the principles on which it is based, the true status of the technology 'today', and the future developments that are planned
3. To position accurately MAP and TOP in relation to other communication technologies
4. To raise awareness of the status of existing MAP and TOP products and services by providing effective demonstration of their current capabilities
5. To demonstrate the wide range of manufacturing applications to which the technology applies
6. To demonstrate the effectiveness of the technology, particularly in the context of communicating between various applications and equipment across a wide range of vendors

7. To develop practical awareness of the technology by providing access to people who have practical experience in its use
8. To provide the participants in the demonstration with an opportunity to market their MAP and TOP products and services in the context of the Awareness Event

As an Awareness Event, the DTI MAP Event had three awareness levels - Publicity and Awareness, Application Demonstrations and Networking Demonstrations. There were orientation sessions to provide an overview of the MAP and TOP technologies and their significance, a technical workshop providing technical education, experience and demonstrations, and a full programme of business and technical seminars, as well as supporting documentation in the form of an Event guide and technical publications. Applications were grouped into industrial themes so that visitors could focus on applications of the technology as it applied to their own business environment. The primary objective of the network demonstrations was to show the true status of conformance and interoperability. A wide range of suppliers of MAP and TOP products and services participated. The DTI MAP Event included a demonstration of conformance testing, which showed the equipment used during testing and explained many of the procedures and the problems encountered. The network demonstration allowed visitors to gain 'hands on' experience in the use of the network, and the demonstration was attended by representatives of the participants to provide technical information and advice. By 15 May, 53 companies had agreed to be DTI MAP Event project participants.

The final name chosen for the event showed the links to CIM. We called it CIMAP, and it was advertised as the DTI MAP Event, showcasing Computer Communications into the 1990's. A central venue was needed, and so it was held at the National Exhibition Centre in Birmingham from 1 to 5 December 1986. Ministers were very enthusiastic about what was happening and it was opened by the Parliamentary Under Secretary of State for Industry and IT, John Butcher MP. Professionals were employed to bring together the project. It was managed by Coopers and Lybrand Associates, and used Electronic Data Systems (EDS) as network systems integrators.

In some ways I was pleased that I was not directly involved. I had a lot of other work, mainly about standardisation and pre-standardisation, and in the UK, Europe and internationally. My boss Peter Adkin kept a close watch on the CIMAP project, and worked closely with one of my engineers, as well as with colleagues with responsibility for the overall DTI OSI Awareness programme, of which the MAP Awareness Programme was part. It was an important demonstration of the potential of the technology and I went up to Birmingham to see it and share the success.

As well as the demonstrations, the lectures and the chance to meet with all the experts, one of the enduring and important outcomes from CIMAP was the publication of a glossy 24-page brochure 'Through MAP to CIM'. It explained, in terms which a managing director of a small or medium sized company could understand, the current issues in the computerisation of factory information, and where MAP and TOP fitted. Thousands of copies of this booklet were handed out, a second print run was made, and still there were demands for more copies. Other countries asked for the rights to translate it into their own language. It would have been one of the best-sellers for the DTI, except it was given away for free. This combination of free information alongside a real practical demonstration was a very powerful weapon in our aim to improve UK manufacturing competitiveness.

We know that CIMAP inspired many companies to consider integrating their own manufacturing organisations. Most small and medium size companies, however, found that the costs could not be justified at a time when MAP and TOP specifications were still being revised. In spite of the problems, it was accepted that, with time, the standards would stabilise and the costs would reduce. In the meantime, there was a need to demonstrate how Open Systems could be adopted by smaller manufacturing companies. The National Engineering Laboratory (NEL), took on this task and, using some existing and some additional equipment, designed CIMAC. CIMAC included all the elements of a typical manufacturing system: CAD, CAM, machining and assembly, cell control and an MRPII package. Customised products were designed and manufactured and all the information required to make each part was transmitted over the network. We learned that it was important that the hardware developed and the expertise gained during the major networking demonstrations did continue in some concrete way, and was not dispersed and lost after the event had finished.

11 Meeting Key Policy Makers in the USA

As I indicated earlier, the emerging networking standards for manufacturing equipment were based on IT standards, particularly the Open Systems Interconnection (OSI) 7 layer model. The DTI involvement with OSI was through officials in IT Division and they had a matching Brussels Group, the Senior Officials Group for IT Standardisation (SOGITS). This group had been established for some time when SOGAME was set up. Establishing good links with IT Division colleagues was essential and we often had to help each other prepare briefing.

The leaders in moving forward MAP and TOP were two large companies from the USA, General Motors and the Boeing Corporation respectively. IT Division had good links with leading OSI experts in the USA, which we did not have. However, they did not know the experts at General Motors and Boeing. So I was volunteered to take part in a business trip to the USA, from 26 to 30 October 1987, together with a senior colleague from IT Division, George Sidey, to meet with officials in our Embassy in Washington and visit the National Bureau of Standards (NBS), and then fly to Detroit to visit technical groups at General Motors and finally fly across to visit Silicon Valley in California and the Boeing Corporation in Seattle.

What do I remember of my first official trip to the USA? The answer is not very much now. The DTI organised a special official visa for my travel, and arranged that I have a new passport. The British Airways flight was comfortable enough. George and I arrived together in Washington DC and unanimously decided that I would navigate while he drove the hire car to our hotel. After dinner George said he liked jazz music, and so he went off in the evening while I had an early night and tried to get over the jet lag.

We had a very full schedule and met too many people in too short a time, and I collected a mound of visiting cards. Having made a success with the UK CIMAP Event, we were able to talk about the future on a 'level playing field' with our colleagues in the USA. For me, meeting people from the NBS and other standards groups, inside and outside Government, was new. They had generally come from an IT background, and were starting from established groupings who were working on OSI and the separate levels of the 7-layer model. Fortunately George knew everyone and took the lead in discussions, some of which were so technical that I was not sure that I had even spelled the acronyms correctly in my notes.

I remember the flight into Detroit because the weather was bad and the pilot didn't manage to land at his first attempt and we had to go around again. It was quite frightening as there was lots of thunder and lightning at the time. We made a quick visit to General Motors, hardly saw anything of Detroit, and were then on our way again. We had delightful weather in Silicon Valley, met more people and then continued north to Seattle. I didn't really look at the details of the geography of the trip until afterwards, but I wondered why there was snow on the mountains as we approached Seattle. Washington State is an awful long way from Washington DC.

At Seattle we met Laurie Bride, the senior enterprise architect for Boeing. It was memorable because there were few senior women in the engineering world, although there were more in the IT business. I caught up with her memories on the Internet through an interview for Network World's 15th Anniversary Issue in 2001, 'Locating Legends'. In 1985 she had her hands buried deep in the network protocol stack, forming methods for different computers to talk to each other. She had personally authored the TOP specification, worked on the OSI model, and was active in early interoperability demonstrations. 'We accomplished our goals, whether it was MAP/TOP or what has developed into the Internet,' she said at the 15th Anniversary celebrations in 2001. 'Our objective was to get users knowledgeable about the problem and to communicate to the vendors that we wanted a solution.' That was exactly the DTI position too.

There were many issues arising from our visit to the USA. Some involved the role of the NBS, where its workshops had been the focus for standards work and UK experts participated in these meetings. Misunderstandings can take place simply because people and organisations don't communicate, or they do not realise that there are reasons to share ideas. One key area involved test services, both the difficulty of estimating the market and the use of what is called independent third party testing. Large US vendors could afford to buy testing tools and then state that their products worked. Within the UK our vendors could not afford this and preferred to use independent testing. This is what is meant by third party testing - it is done by an independent third party. Here I am describing conformance testing, which is to check that the product satisfies, or conforms to, the MAP or TOP specification. Who in the UK would be permitted to do this conformance testing for MAP and TOP? The obvious existing organisations were The Networking Centre (TNC) and the National Centre for IT (NCC). The test tools were available from the USA, but at what price and to which organisations? We discovered that mutual recognition of testing or certification while well established as a principle in the UK was not well understood in the USA. There seemed to be a surprising total lack of awareness of UK mechanisms, including the role of accreditation. What sort of criteria would be applied to UK test houses which might license the test tools bought from the USA?

While all this sounds incredibly technical the basic idea was that only the right calibre of organisation did the testing, and that whatever was done in the UK should be recognised in the USA. And then, how should interoperability testing be organised? Factory implementations require that different equipment from different suppliers will actually work together. This is interoperability, and it is not easy. While we had no clear views on how to generate hardware/software 'fixes' to solve practical interoperability problems, we were convinced that national arrangements were needed. This was all in the context of getting ready for UK participation in the next major demonstration of the technology, the international Enterprise Networking Event (ENE '88i) in Baltimore in 1988. We had behind us the experience of what had happened at CIMAP in December 1986. For ENE '88i, we hoped that the staging areas in the USA and the UK would form the basis for subsequent interoperability testing, and not be dismantled and discarded after the event.

12 Lord Young makes the DTI the Department for Enterprise

While we had been deep in the technology, our Secretary of State had changed. Lord Young had some good management ideas when he joined the DTI in June 1987 with the aim of changing it from what he called in his autobiography 'The Department of Disaster'. I never felt it was the Department of Disaster, but then I did not see the DTI from the viewpoint of an industrialist who had newly arrived as Secretary of State. And it must be remembered that he had also worked in the DTI some 5 years earlier as a Special Advisor.

We suddenly found that all our programmes were to be reviewed by Ministers and there was an attempt at zero budgeting. The old Policy Planning Unit disappeared, to be replaced by a new Central Unit. The idea was to initiate suggestions for re-organisation.

Lord Young also thought that staff generally did not know what the objectives of the DTI actually were. This was in spite of Norman Tebbit having published his Central Aim with its emphasis on Climate, International Competitiveness and Innovation just three years earlier. According to his autobiography, Lord Young wrote the new objectives for the DTI himself, having been unable to get the right flavour from senior officials. He actually said that the first version offered by the DTI Permanent Secretary, Sir Brian Hayes, was too long and unsuitable. Perhaps it was derived from Norman Tebbit's Central Aim. I must admit that there is an advantage in having clear objectives, written in plain language, and on just the one sheet of paper.

Soon after the Conservative Party conference in Blackpool, in October 1987, a copy of the new objectives was issued to each and every member of the DTI, and they were displayed in the entrance hall of every DTI building. At the same time, Lord Young spoke to all staff at Assistant Secretary and above to allay fears about the extent of the review and the re-organisations. Staff were all told that they were now the Department of Wealth Creation.

The Objectives of the Department of Trade and Industry

The needs and demands of society can only be met by increasing prosperity. The prime objective of the Department is to assist this process throughout the economy and to champion all the people who make it happen, rather than just individual sectors, industries or companies.

We work with business to promote best practice and within Government to create a climate that stimulates enterprise and reduces red tape.

Business flourishes in a competitive and open economy and we aim to secure this both at home and abroad. We will continue to promote the growth of international trade and work towards a single market within the European Community.

We seek to:

produce a more competitive market by encouraging competition and tackling restrictive practices, cartels and monopolies;

secure a more efficient market by improving the provision of information to business about new methods and opportunities;

create a larger market by privatisation and deregulation;

increase confidence in the working of markets by achieving a fair level of protection for their individual consumer and investor.

We will encourage the transfer of technologies and co-operative research, the spread of management education and the growth of links between schools and the world of work.

Our objective will be to produce a climate which promotes enterprise and prosperity. In all our work we will take account of differing circumstances of the regions and of the Inner Cities to enable those who live there to help themselves.

These objectives were amplified in the White Paper, 'DTI - the Department for Enterprise', which was launched in January 1988. Everyone, and I mean everyone, was simultaneously briefed on the launch of the new Department, and we all sat and watched the short video which explained the Enterprise Initiative and then covered the changes to policies, to services and the new approach of the Department.

A comparison between these Objectives and the Central Aim of Norman Tebbit previously shows that many of the same themes are still running through Conservative policy. The Central Aim had three main headings - Climate, International Competitiveness and Innovation. The central theme of the Objectives still remained the belief that sensible economic decisions were best taken by those competing in the market place. The responsibility of Government was to create the right climate so that markets work better and to encourage enterprise. The aim of the policy was thus to encourage the process of wealth creation by stimulating individual initiative and enterprise and by promoting an understanding of market opportunities combined with the ability to exploit them. The DTI would be playing the key role within Government in encouraging enterprise.

Those of us who were using the Support for Innovation (SfI) programme for funding R&D turned quickly to the part of the White Paper which dealt with innovation. Here it announced that greater emphasis would be made on technology transfer - especially linking educational institutions with industry - for small firms, for the regions and for new technologies. Greater emphasis would also be placed in collaborative programmes of longer term research between companies and to encourage collaboration between Higher Education Institutions (HEIs) and companies. Finally, initial assistance would be given to technologically-advanced projects in small companies, and to a very restricted number of projects offering exceptional national benefit. The general scheme for providing innovation grant assistance to individual companies would end.

It meant some quick thinking to make sure that the existing projects on MAP/TOP and conformance testing which were in the pipeline were still able to be supported. We had not expected that the rules for funding R&D would change so quickly. Fortunately much of what we were doing was collaborative, was with small firms, and included academics.

More money was going to be needed to support ENE '88i, and for the support of standards and the collaborative application of standards for manufacturing industry by small and medium companies. It was with some nervousness that the proposal for funding was put forward. The programme, named the Systems Technology and Integration Programme (STIP), went through the usual approval process. First it was agreed by the people around me who were doing the work, then it was signed off by more senior officials within MMT Division before going to the Innovation Policy Committee (IPC), a group of senior officials chaired by the Head of RTP Division, who had formal policy responsibility for allocating the Innovation budget. However, since the amounts involved were significant, the programme could not be finally approved by officials; it had to be approved by the Secretary of State. His approval could not be sought directly; the appropriate Junior Minister had to agree first and in this case the proposal was sent to John Butcher MP. He liked the programme and I was relieved when the approval by Lord Young was finally given.

While details of the programme are not in the public domain, the structure of such submissions is generally known. The headings for the submission were standardised: Issue, Recommendation, Timing, Background, Argument and Funding Requested. There had also been a ROAME statement prepared as part of the submission to the IPC, which contained the Rationale, Objectives, Appraisal, Monitoring and Evaluation, hence the acronym ROAME. Total funding for this activity, including existing commitments, was just over £21 million, from 1988/89 to 1991/92. The proposal went forward for approval on 7 April 1988.

The real change in policy in 1988 was the launching of the Enterprise Initiative. It was the first time there had been serious professional advertising of the DTI, including spectacular and expensive TV advertising. The Enterprise Initiative was advertised as providing the most comprehensive self-help package offered to business by Government. Lord Young admits that his original idea came from discussions about the way that advisory services were available in the agriculture sector. I smiled because it reminded me of the time some seven years earlier when I had looked at ADAS as a model for the SFTES. The emphasis of the Enterprise Initiative was on transferring best practice and providing information.

The most popular initiatives were the business development initiatives. To be eligible, companies had to have fewer than 500 employees. Subsidised consultancy help was available to them under six headings: Design; Marketing; Quality Management; Manufacturing Systems; Business Planning; and Financial and Information Systems. Hundreds of Enterprise Counsellors were recruited, each with a wide range of private sector experience in the management problems encountered by small and medium sized businesses, to work directly with companies. Project managers were engaged to make sure that companies were advised by the most suitable consultant. There were also research initiatives so that businesses could innovate and develop collaborative R&D, and there was a regional initiative so that businesses had greater help to develop their potential. Everywhere there was an initiative. Everywhere there was the Vroosh symbol. These services were provided in partnership with business, often delivered by the private sector, and offering limited grants of rarely above 50%. Lots of consultants did well out of the new initiatives, and lots of companies benefited.

13 Enterprise Networking Event, Baltimore USA

When Laurie Bride of the Boeing Corporation participated in the international Enterprise Networking Event (ENE '88i) from 5 to 9 June she rated it as the most important network event of the past 15 years. 'The Enterprise Networking Event established that there were solutions to the information-sharing and communications problems among different vendors.' Bride said.

It was reported that 131 different computing systems were linked and simulated an enterprise network. I am not sure about the accuracy of the number 131, but there certainly were a very large number of different computing systems.

When my part of the DTI first got involved with ENE '88i a lot of the elements of the network were already agreed. There were seven cells from US suppliers and we were allocated the last cell, cell number 8. From the UK perspective, and our emphasis on smaller firms acting as subcontractors, it was appropriate that the application theme which we chose was The Jobbing Shop. The cell acted out the role of a subcontracting company, which manufactured a range of components and sub-assemblies for a number of prime contractors. The cell assembled several different types of water pump, machined a turned component, inspected several items, carried out some structural steel design and manufactured steel puzzle pieces on a laser cutting machine. It was the principle of transferring the manufacturing data around the network between the cells which was most important.

Companies involved on the TOP side included CSD/CIMTEL with estimating, tendering, process planning and drawing office management, Ferranti CAM-X with computer aided design, numerically controlled part programming and nesting, Kewill with production management including scheduling, bill of materials, work-in-progress, invoicing and sales and order processing and CSC with structural steel design, bill of material output and computer aided drafting for construction.

Companies involved on the MAP side were Reflex with area/cell controllers including work to list handling, instruction and data distribution, assembly control and manufacturing control, BIT with a fibre optic token ring network, Ferranti with a laser cutting machine and a co-ordinate measuring machine, Prodel with an assembly system including vision part recognition and water pump assembly, and a numerically controlled turning centre.

The DTI involvement had four aims :

1. To demonstrate the interworking of enterprise MAP, TOP and X.25 wide area networks, in the spirit of ENE '88i.
2. To demonstrate clearly how MAP and TOP network systems may be employed to form the communications infrastructure in a contracting organization.
3. To show how MAP and TOP version 3 protocols may be employed to integrate industrial computer-based applications to form a single cohesive system. CIMAP had only been using MAP version 2.1.
4. To demonstrate the use of electronic mail to support the day-to-day dialogue, endemic to the commercial operation of a subcontracting company.

The scenario to be acted out was:

1. Cell will receive orders via the electronic mail system. It will be possible to enter orders and any other documentation into the mail system both from other booths and from within the DTI cells.
2. Customer orders will be processed and manufacturing documentation raised (e.g work orders, routing cards etc)
3. Mechanical design of components and assemblies to customer specifications.
4. Manufacture or simulated manufacture of assemblies and components.
5. Mechanical and electrical inspection.
6. Raise inspection reports and shipments advice notes, forwarding to customer.
7. Raise invoices, receiving dummy payments from customers.
8. At regular intervals, update dummy bank account.

In addition, every cell taking part in ENE '88i had to take part in the Enterprise Product Global Application. An order for metal puzzle pieces would be received from the John Deere booth. The order was acknowledged. Then a job complete note was sent back to the Deere booth after some pre-defined time interval. In detail, the activities of the booth would be interrupted by the arrival of an urgent 'Request to Tender' from the Deere booth. The items required were metal puzzle pieces that had been made before but which now require a design modification. The request to tender was handled by the CSD/Cimtel node which would return a tender document and accept an order. The design modification required would be described in text form only. No drawings would be involved. CSD/Cimtel would send a work ticket to the Ferranti CAM-X CAD system to initiate the design change. CSD/Cimtel would send a copy of the order to the Kewill node. CDS/Cimtel would update the process plan for the parts and transfer to Kewill. Ferranti CAM-X would make the design changes, would re-nest the components on a sheet, produce new numerical control programmes for the laser machine and for the co-ordinate measuring machine, and create a new bill of materials and transfer this to Kewill. Kewill would schedule the work for each operation required and produce work tickets for the laser machine and co-ordinate measuring machine. The Reflex area/cell controller would collect work tickets from Kewill, collect numerical control programmes from Ferranti CAM-X and transfer the relevant data to the cell controllers. The Reflex cell controllers would control the operation of the machine tools and co-ordinate measuring machine. The Reflex cell controllers would notify the Kewill shop floor data collection system (SFDC) on completion of each job. The SFDC system would inform Kewill production management when the work was complete. Kewill would prepare and transmit the invoice to the Deere booth. The computers used were VAX, PC and Sun workstations. Staff from PERA, who were responsible for managing the project, went to Washington on 18 and 19 November 1987 to describe this scenario. The scenario was accepted, and serious work to deadlines began.

This was all leading edge technical work. There were no factories in the UK using this technology, but we knew that commercial products would be available in the near future. The UK participants at ENE '88i were carrying out product development, and were able to benefit from the standard DTI Support for Innovation (SfI) funding. At the time we started organising the cell we didn't know that Lord Young would end the SfI funding for product development in 1988, to be replaced by his new Enterprise Initiative. There were some eight collaborative projects, each with a milestone at ENE '88i where new products or prototypes would be demonstrated.

A pre-staging location was organised so that all the equipment and products could be brought together for testing. The aim was to use the conformance testing capability in the UK to show that products conformed to the MAP/TOP specification and then to use the pre-staging area to do the practical interoperability testing. One important lesson which had been learned in CIMAP was that provision needed to be made for after-CIMAP work. There the companies, systems integrators and test centres had each gone their separate ways with a dilution of the knowledge gained jointly while putting the event together. There was some continuation demonstration in CIMAC at the NEL, but opportunities were lost.

At ENE '88i there was also an extra external link to cell number 9 which was sited in Europe, based around the Esprit Communications

Network for Manufacturing Applications (CNMA) project. CNMA was led by British Aerospace, with other participants including BMW, Aeritalia, Peugeot, ICL, Siemens and Olivetti. Three major pilot production sites were operational at Preston (BAe), Regensberg (BMW) and Turin (Aeritalia) using Open System approaches. The achievements of the first phase of the CNMA project were demonstrated at the Hanover Fair in April 1987. A typical manufacturing cell was controlled by computing hardware from 5 vendors, interworking by using CNMA communications software. The success of this demonstration was intended to draw attention to the feasibility of multi-vendor systems and influence the development of the relevant international standards. With this experience, CNMA was well placed to be an external cell for ENE '88i, and their participation was intended to underline the compatibility of the CNMA and MAP profiles of communications standards.

There was a lot of work to do, only a short time to get ready, and the challenge was to obtain more staff and of the right calibre. So alongside the DTI permanent staff there arrived more consultants and secondees to cover specialist areas. I was also keen to accept good scientific staff from the DTI's research laboratories, particularly engineers from the National Engineering Laboratory at East Kilbride. All the serious work, burning the midnight oil, took place at the pre-staging site.

Finally everything came together at pre-staging, was then packed into crates and shipped to the USA, where it was all re-assembled in our corner of the Baltimore Convention Centre.

The event was scheduled to be in early June and I knew that it was going to be warm. I remember wondering what sort of formal office wear I would need. Even on the coast at Baltimore it was going to be very hot. I bought my first set of pretty cotton skirts and blouses from Liberty plc in Piccadilly, so that I would survive the heat, and worn with a formal jacket I was set for anything. It was the start of my many purchases of clothes from Liberty plc. I recalled that my mother used to buy Liberty cotton to make me clothes when I was an infant.

I did not feel that I fully deserved my flight ticket to attend, after all it was other people in my team who had done all the hard work. I felt even more guilty when I was shown my beautiful room in the Harborplace Hotel. The room was enormous, and included a big Board Room with a large table and lots of chairs and an amazing view down on to the waterfront at Baltimore. The catch was that we all used my room for meetings during the day. I wondered where the bed was hidden, and then was shown that the bed was flipped up vertically and hidden into the wall when it was not in use. Conveniently it was only a short stroll from the hotel to the main Convention Centre. We took turns to attend the event and in my spare time I was able to walk along the waterfront, buy a few souvenirs in the shops and admire the posh boats. We all met together in the evenings to discuss problems and compare notes on what had happened and how successful it was. Close to 10,000 people were supposed to have attended the event.

I thought I remembered a special treat when Concorde flew over the Convention Centre at Baltimore, but I can find no record now that it actually happened. It must have been a bright idea which never took place, and shows how memory should not be trusted. In spite of the major contribution of ENE '88i to multi-vendor industrial networking there is no evidence that the event ever happened, except for one or two specialist technical articles and conference publications published in the USA at the time. If I had not been involved with the UK contribution then I would not have any details of what took place.

I still have the Liberty skirt and blouse, and my sweat shirt of Baltimore Harborplace, and my grey ENE '88i souvenir coffee mug. It was from that coffee mug that I finally found the exact dates of the event, 5 to 9 June, such are the gaps in the Internet!

After the last day and the event closed I said 'Goodbye' to everyone, flew home, and moved out of the DTI.

14 Relaxing on the River Thames

Looking back in 1988, the three years had involved a steep learning curve, gaining a lot of experience, and working hard. But it is dangerous to be dedicated to work for 7 days a week, every week of the year. I did bring work home, and often worked on the train travelling to London, but we had both decided to keep evenings and weekends clear. In the beginning, when Pete worked in the Ministry of Defence, he was strictly unable to bring any work home, and so we kept that rule later when we had different jobs.

Once we had done most of the renovation work on the house, and were back to normal maintenance, we discovered the River Thames at the bottom of the garden. It had always been there but we had been too busy to exploit it. Our riverbank was quite rough with a lot of bushes and blackberries which had been left to go wild by the previous owners. The garden by the riverbank was basically only rough chalk with a thin layer of soil. It had been made when the foundations for the houses were cut into the hillside, and the spare chalk was used to build up the road, the footpath and the gardens. We did find a little modern concrete landing stage, in good condition, and after some exploration we found a line of waterlogged old posts, which would have supported the original wooden edging along the riverbank seen in the old photographs of the 1890s. We decided that we could afford to have some work done. We had several tenders and chose Ian Cook, who was just starting out in his business of riverbank repair. We heard that his father had worked on the river all his life, and that Ian was just getting started, hence the cheaper price. He did not have a barge so all the hard work was done from the bank. The old plants and weeds were removed, a line for new steel piling was agreed with the officials responsible, and the work was done. The price had been agreed but not the timing. Some days Ian decided that he wanted to stay home and play cricket, and we did not mind. We had a plan of what we wanted to put back in the garden, including apple trees, a cherry tree, a plum and a greengage. Ian made sure we had nice flower beds dug into the chalk so that the new trees would thrive. Then we ordered lorry loads of soil and top soil and turf to make it all look pretty. At the Chelsea Flower Show we admired and then ordered a large hardwood picnic table, with folding bench seats. We were all ready to sit down by the river, with a nice glass of cold Champagne, and enjoy our new garden.

We had not thought about getting a boat. But one weekend the next door children pulled on a rope which was hanging from the edge of their garden and brought up an old dinghy from their moorings where it had been sunk. The following week we saw a second hand outboard for sale in the Harwell magazine, bought it and went round to discuss how we could put the two together. We all enjoyed a summer with the little boat which we named Amazon, after the classic book Swallows and Amazons. Our first surprise was when we set off down stream and found Whitchurch Lock. We had set off without any charts of the River Thames, and although we knew that there were locks in Oxford, we had not noticed that there was one just a short distance downstream. There followed another much larger lock at Mapledurham, and then we had a long straight stretch to Reading.

There was a posh chandlery and shop which sold expensive Fairline cruisers near Tilehurst, and we stopped to buy a Guide to the River Thames, and get a new buoyancy jacket. I was not very good at swimming, and the old kapock life jacket needed to be replaced. They also sold petrol, which was useful. Other items were obtained from Force4 Chandlery at their shop in Bressenden Place, just opposite one of the DTI offices. Amazon did not have a cabin and when it rained we just got wet, unless we were able to shelter under a tree or a bridge. There was a little footbridge at Mapledurham lock and the lock keeper suggested we sheltered there one day while it was raining.

I commuted by train to London and often caught the early train with one of our neighbours, David, who worked in a bank in the City. In 1985 he was asked to move to the Channel Islands, and this meant he had to sell their house. Long after he had moved out, and the house was still empty, we noticed that his boat was still moored in his garden. We contacted him and he was surprised; it was not his boat but belonged to a friend who had promised he would move it. We knew that the boat had never been out while we had lived in our house, and guessed that the owner was going to have problems finding somewhere new to keep it. David gave us his telephone number and as a result we were able to contact the owner and ask whether he was interested in selling it. It had been arranged that the owners would let us look at it on the Sunday, but we guessed that they would come along on the day before and make sure it was clean and tidy, and that the engine started. And so we kept a watch down the road and when we saw a strange car we set off to meet them. The engine behaved very well, and in spite of having been unused for a long time, and still having the same fuel in from when they had purchased it originally, it started. We had to go and get a different battery, but that was no surprise. They were really caravan people, had bought the boat at a good price knowing that it needed some minor repair work, and then not done the work and not used it.

It was a little Shetland 535 fibreglass cabin cruiser, it was just 18 foot long, and had a lovely old Mercury 20hp outboard engine with an electric start. We were pleased that the engine had an electric start because we knew from having petrol lawn mowers that pulling the starter cord can be difficult. Something disastrous had happened to it, we guessed a weight had fallen onto the back corner, and it had a hole which had to be repaired, but it was not structural and the main aim of filling the hole was to stop the rain coming in. It was a simple fibreglass repair, compared with some of the repairs which Pete had worked on with gliders, and the only pity was that we couldn't match the faded brown colour of the original gelcoat.

The cabin had sleeping accommodation for two people and there was just space for a double burner camping stove, a chilly bin, saucepan and utensils, and a Portapotti. We did not know what a Shetland cruiser was, so we asked a friend from the NPL who had a larger boat, told him the price and asked for advice. He said it was a well known boat, and we decided to buy it.

We only had to pay for a license and for insurance and we were ready for the summer. The boat had been named Danabo, but we didn't like the name and decided to call her Corinna, after the boat which was used for the kidnapping in the John Buchan book 'The Courts of the Morning'. Fortunately the name was available, else we might have had to choose another name. Boat names on the River Thames are unique.

After a busy day working in London it was relaxing to get on the boat and spend an hour pottering up to our favourite pub in Goring-on-Thames, have a pint of Brakspears bitter with dinner and then potter slowly back, usually with the navigation lights. At first we did not appreciate that not only was the Shetland a perfect size for two people on the River Thames, it was also narrow enough to fit into the locks on the canals. As well as not knowing about locks on the River Thames, we had no idea there was an extensive canal system which joined at Oxford, Reading, Weybridge and London. In 1985 the Kennet and Avon canal which joins the River Thames at Reading was still under restoration, but the Oxford canal was ready and waiting for us to explore. In the first year we spent two weeks in August exploring the Oxford canal and also part of the Grand Union canal, and on that trip we did 139 locks and 261 miles. The first year we did a total of 1117 miles and managed to get out on the boat every week until Christmas, when the weather became too bad.

The most exciting parts of boating on the canals were when we shared locks. On the River Thames locks are not an excitement. During normal hours they are worked by lock-keepers and we simply waited on the lay-by until the lock was ready and then entered it. Most boats on the River Thames were also made of fibreglass and everyone had a good selection of plump plastic fenders so it was never a contact sport. Our scruffy little cruiser was treated exactly the same as bigger, posher boats, and many people said that they had started boating with a Shetland cruiser before buying something larger. We soon found it had been a classic design in its time, and ours was the De Luxe model. We never discovered exactly how old it was, although the previous owners thought it was built in 1974 and that was what we said when we organised insurance. Now we believe it was probably older.

On the Oxford canal the locks are DIY. It was OK to share if there was another fibreglass boat but sometimes we met with a small narrowboat and the mix of fibreglass and steel could be a problem. In our area the canal locks were all a standard 70-ish feet long and precisely the width of our boat, and in theory we would fit with anything which was less than 40 foot long. There was always a water shortage on the Oxford canal in the summer and hence a pressure that locks should be shared whenever possible.

Going through tunnels was fun too. We had an expensive large rechargeable torch which was positioned with Velcro on the front of the boat, and it worked well when we were on our own in tunnels. Being based on the River Thames we also had navigation lights, red on the port side and green on the starboard side. When they were all lit we used to say we looked like a Christmas tree. Few boats on the canals carried navigation lights. Some tunnels are single width but there are other tunnels, at Braunston near Rugby on the Grand Union canal for example, which are double width and so boats can travel both ways and just pass each other with care when travelling in opposite directions. The locks on the Grand Union canal are double width too. For a little 18 foot fibreglass cruiser the most frightening noise is the thump of a narrowboat engine coming closer, mixed with the shouts and screams of children and their parents travelling on their hire boat for the first time, bouncing off the tunnel walls. Fibreglass squashes very easily. Fortunately we had no problems.

1986 was the year when the National Garden Festival was held in Stoke-on-Trent and we took the Shetland up to Oxford and then continued north on the canals. We had decided from the holiday in 1985 that we enjoyed travelling on the canals and we really wanted a larger boat with a shower and a fridge. After trying to wash feet in muddy canal water, and using a series of frozen chickens to keep the chilly bin cold it was time for a change. As we headed north in June we stopped to look at a few narrowboat builders, particularly Peter Nicholls at Napton, Colecraft at Braunston, Mike Heywood at Great Haywood and Stoke-on-Trent boatbuilders at Longport. We moored at Stoke-on-Trent and spent a day exploring the site of the National Garden Festival.

During our trip we had been taking a lot of photographs of nice boats and when we sat down with the pictures we found that they were mostly made by David Piper. His boat building business was at Red Bull Basin. This was not far north of Stoke-on-Trent, we had a spare day in our schedule, and we were soon waiting at the southern entrance to the Harecastle tunnel. Red Bull Basin is on the Macclesfield canal where it crosses the Trent and Mersey canal, just a mile beyond the northern end of the tunnel. We had discovered tunnels already at Braunston and Newbold, but the Harecastle tunnel is a serious challenge. It is very long, just under 3000 yards and wiggles. It is only single width and so boats are sent through in batches, under the control of a tunnel keeper. We survived without hitting the sides too often in spite of travelling mostly in neutral because we were much faster on tick over than the narrowboats ahead of us in our batch.

So, on 12 July, we arrived at Red Bull Basin and met David Piper and his wife Dot. We looked at boats under construction, and were shown into some boats which had been recently completed. We liked what we saw, but were disappointed that the waiting list for a complete boat stretched over a year ahead. They were also quite expensive; David was one of the best boat builders in the country. However, David also built hulls which people fitted out themselves, and he provided all the materials for purchase. This option meant that we could get our hull much sooner, and the costs of fitting out would be spread over the months as we purchased the materials. The only disadvantage was that we had to do all the work ourselves. We needed to think about it.

We turned around, went back through the Harecastle tunnel and worked our way slowly back home. The whole trip was 267 locks and 534 miles, achieved over 4 weekends and with 2 weeks continuous cruising in the middle.

Back at home we thought about it, drew pictures of internal layouts so we knew what we wanted, and decided to order a 46 foot shell from David Piper for delivery in May 1987. With a long outdoor front sitting area, which would enable her to swim well on the River Thames, the design had a cabin which was 31 foot long. We started to count the inches in order to decide where the walls and windows would go, and it did not take much persuasion from David to add an extra foot to the overall length. It seems that steel came in standard sizes, and a 32 foot cabin used the same number of pieces of steel as a 31 foot cabin, and so would have no extra welding marks. Of course, it also meant that we paid full price for the extra foot but it cost David no extra materials. So 47 foot was the final agreed length, just two thirds of the size of a full size narrowboat. It also meant we would just fit in a lock with our little Shetland, although we had no plans to take the two boats together down the canals. We decided to call the narrowboat Corinna, taking over the name presently used by the Shetland which would then become Corinna Too. Although no joinery work was going to be done, David Piper did agree to install our engine and to fit the windows, which in his view still counted as steel work. So we were pleased that the hull was going to be reasonably watertight from the beginning.

15 Fitting out our new narrowboat

Early in 1987 we realised that the time was approaching for us to think about starting work on our nice brand new narrowboat. We had never handled anything with a tiller before because our little cruiser was steered by a wheel just like steering a car, so we wanted to get some practise with a tiller. At short notice we rang up a hire boat company in the middle of Birmingham and arranged to rent one of their 42 foot narrowboats, named Blyth, for the Easter weekend. Although shorter than our new boat it still contained the same main essentials: saloon, kitchen, bathroom and bedroom (with bunks!). The dining room table converted to a comfortable double bed at night.

We knew that there were only a few locks if we stayed within the Birmingham and Wolverhampton area, and our main aim was to get used to handling a narrowboat. We thought it would also be the only chance we would have to travel through Birmingham. We had heard such stories about the problems, from hitting shopping trolleys and other rubbish, from being left high and dry by empty pounds or being shot at or hit by other missiles. The only incident was when we approached a junction, where we had the choice of turning either left or right, and there was a mound of rubbish around the propeller and the boat continued in a straight line towards the opposite bank. We just manage to stop without damaging anything, but we were stuck across the whole width of the canal while Pete went down the weed hatch to cut away all the rubbish. Fortunately there were no other boats moving. We found the holiday to be a series of contrasts, but not as bad as we expected. There were some areas of derelict buildings and flat wasteland. Local people either ignored us and the canal, or smiled a cheerful greeting. Only once were we concerned about local groups of teenagers in the distance, and even then most young people didn't go out of their way to cause trouble if it involved them in a long walk. Those with motorbikes were more of a problem as they rushed at high speed past us along the towpath. Blyth survived all that without any damage, and only needed washing to remove the splashes of mud.

Meanwhile I had been accumulating my Annual Leave so that I could find time to work with Pete, fitting out the boat. We knew that the fitting out could be done at David Piper's moorings at Red Bull Basin. We wanted to work there because we could watch how his professionals fitted out their boats, and this would also give us access to the right materials. We wanted our boat to look exactly like the best of the fitted-out boats. It was a long drive up to Kidsgrove so I had the idea that we should spend some long weekends, say every other week, during the summer. That way I would nibble away at my Annual Leave, without taking a proper long summer holiday. This caused real distress back at the office when I made the suggestion, and it was flatly refused. So it meant that we were limited to planning what we would do during the week, driving up late on Friday or very early on Saturday and then working hard all day Saturday and Sunday, finally driving back home on Sunday evening.

We stayed at Cuttleford Farm, just opposite the National Trust's Little Moreton Hall, and had a large self-contained en-suite room, although without cooking facilities. We were still able to cater for ourselves in the evening, and we often went back late on Saturday night with cold meat and salad and a treat of a Viennetta ice cream to divide between us. Fitting out the boat was supposed to take 1,000 hours by a professional, and we measured over 1,400 hours. We had a plan, and worked to a timetable, just like for any project at work.

The first job when we entered the boat was to put lots of Bitumen onto the inside walls. Then David Piper told us that we must paint the engine room with white paint quickly. He wanted to put the engine in, but first we had to have a nice bright white engine room. His son Simon Piper, now with a boatbuilding business of his own, soon fitted the windows. We found that having a boat which had been built in the summer was much better than a winter boat. The steelwork did not rust as easily, and we were very careful to touch up the grey primer on the outside whenever we saw a scratch.

Several other boats were in varying stages of completion and we arranged to purchase duplicate sets of woodwork. For example, the frames for the panelled doors, the edging for the shelves, and the turned posts were all purchased as a second set when one set were being made for one of their fitted-out boats. On weekends we were able to borrow the spider, a frame which made it easier to mark out the exact shape for the bulkhead walls between rooms. The boat was literally a big long steel box when we got it, with no internal walls and no bulkheads. It was also light and heavy slabs of concrete, each sitting on little hardwood blocks, were used as ballast. David had designed the floor so that the standard slabs which he sold were an exact fit. They were still very heavy to carry around.

On Saturday evenings we used to choose our pieces of wood from their stock. The long pieces of pine tongue-and-grooving could be bought either plain or varnished, and we took the easy option and paid the extra so that someone else did the varnishing. The expensive veneered plywood came in a variety of patterns. Generally it did not matter, and David's carpenters took whatever was on the top of the pile. We were more discerning and tried to choose pieces with pretty patterns for the bulkheads. When we started to do the walls of the front saloon then we wanted the veneers to match on both sides of the room. This meant that we looked through the complete stack of wood until we found the pieces which matched. Payment was on an honesty basis. Everything which we took from their stock was signed for in a book, and then the amount was totalled at the end of each weekend.

Our first trip was logged as 25 July 1987, and was just two miles and one lock along the Macclesfield canal and then return. There is always a short trip to commission the engine, and check any problems. We finally left on 13 August with the boat full of the extra materials we were going to need to complete the work. Pieces of 8-by-4 veneered plywood were stacked on both sides, and we had a narrow gap through the middle where we could walk, and sleep in a line. Many standard items could be collected by car later, but all the large heavy pieces of plywood had to be taken by boat.

We took the pretty route home, starting by travelling north up 'Heartbreak Hill' along the Trent and Mersey canal, then across at Middlewich to the Shropshire Union canal and turning west at Hurleston Junction up the Llangollen canal. This canal has some spectacular and unusual features. Firstly there are three lift bridges at Wrenbury, of which two are the classic scissors shape and are raised by hand using a windlass. Then there is a staircase lock at Grindley Brook, which is managed by a lock keeper. And thirdly there are the glorious aqueducts at Pontcysyllte and Chirk. It is just over 40 miles and 21 locks to the basin at Trevor, and then a further 4.25 miles along the narrow channel to the terminus at Llangollen. In two places the channel is only single width. We managed to find a mooring at Llangollen, within walking distance of the town, but the canal was very narrow. That part of the canal is really just a feeder channel, and was never designed as a waterway. We were trying to paint our walkways, and were bothered by people on passing boats coming alongside and holding our handrails, in spite of signs saying that the paint was wet. We didn't stay long.

It was also our first experience of the problems of speeding. The Llangollen canal is very beautiful, and many boats want to explore it. Unfortunately it is often attempted without allowing enough time, with the consequence that people try and travel at the official speed limit, 4 mph, rather than at the lower speed which is acceptable. Too much speed causes wash, and for much of the canal it is only possible to travel at 3 mph or less. More importantly, when a boat goes past a moored boat the motion of the water pulls moored boats forward and back, and can pull out mooring pins. Moored along one of many beautiful Meres we had our ropes cut because we had tied directly on to the steel piling, then got our mooring pins pulled out when we used them instead, and only got abuse from passing boaters when we complained. We looked at what other boats had done. The solution was to go into Ellesmere town and buy two lengths of chain, which we looped around the piling, and then our rope was linked through the chain. It doesn't do a lot of good for the steel piling, but at least it stopped the boat escaping when the ropes were torn.

We left the Llangollen canal, and went through the middle of Birmingham, having been encouraged by experiences on our hire boat the previous Easter. Then it was directly home, through Warwick, Banbury and Oxford. The canal and the railway follow the same basic routing.

Whenever we stopped we did more external painting, managing to paint whatever we could on the towpath side, and then doing the other side having turned around. The steady noise of our power tools cutting wood could be heard for some distance. We had an inverter, which converted 24 volts (from two standard 12 volt batteries) to 240 volts, enabling us to use standard household DIY tools while we were on the move. It was not a perfect sine wave, but was OK for the sort of work we wanted to do. Usually the engine had to be run at the same time, to keep the batteries up.

We already had a licence to travel on the canals and when we got to the junction of the Oxford Canal and the River Thames at Duke's Cut we had to buy a transit licence for the River Thames, and it was supposed to be just for the one day. However we were delayed for several hours due to a broken lock at Clifton. When the lock was repaired we were beckoned in as the last boat into the first locking and then the lock-keeper found we were just too long to fit. We had to reverse back out and wait for another twenty minutes until we could go in to the next locking. It is very unusual for lock-keepers to get packing wrong, and it can only have been because they knew us and our little Shetland and wanted to help us get home, and they did not know that the new boat was 47 feet long. We continued downstream with no problems but had to moor up when it got dark because we had no navigation lights. We eventually got home early the following morning, having wound two locks at dawn. We then had to order a full licence, and because it was now September the licence would be at a reduced price. Normal licences are for one year and start on 1 January. The boat had to stay on its mooring until our proper River Thames licence arrived on 27 September. In 1987, the first year with Corinna we travelled over 500 miles, as well as using Corinna Too for a lot of short trips.

16 Secondment to Kewill Systems plc

Each year in the Civil Service there is an individual staff performance review. During my review in 1987 it had been suggested that I think about a secondment to industry. I welcomed the idea. Indeed I had kept a copy of an article in the Financial Times of 19 August 1983 on The Private Civil Servant, which reviewed the experiences of Whitehall's men in industry. And they were all men, generally in their early 40s and high flyers at Under Secretary level. This breed of seconded Civil Servant sits in on Board meetings every month or so, and the arrangements are usually for two or three years. Their main contribution is asking questions as well as explaining about Whitehall, and talking about economic issues. The chosen few must have good potential for promotion within the Civil Service and with the capability to make a contribution at Board level. Recall that promotion onwards from Under Secretary is to Deputy Secretary and then to Permanent Secretary. As an example, Alistair Macdonald, then an Under Secretary aged 42, was on the board at Rank Leisure. He eventually became Deputy Secretary, but not Permanent Secretary. The scheme had been started in 1978 by Sir Peter Carey when he was Permanent Secretary at the Department of Industry. Sir Peter was concerned about a lack of understanding between industry and the civil service. When he retired in April 1983 he admitted that 'Whitehall suffers from the cult of the gifted amateur'.

In my Senior Management Development Plan for December 1986 I had made sure it was made explicit that I wanted to get direct experience in industry or commerce, either as a non-Executive Director or as a manager in a manufacturing company. I wanted to spend my career in the DTI but I needed to know more about the problems which our 'customers' were dealing with. In December 1987 it was agreed in principle that I should have a six month posting into a company, starting soon after ENE '88i in June 1988. In the DTI we knew a lot about companies of all sizes, and there were some impressive smaller companies. The challenge was for me to get the right opportunity so that the experience was valuable for the company as well as useful for my own career. Here I was able to rely on contacts we already had, and it was through those networks that my boss Peter Adkin had a discussion with Derek McAraBrown and John Faulkner of Kewill Systems plc and agreed I should move there. Although Peter then moved elsewhere within the DTI, my new boss Steve Owsianka still encouraged my move to Kewill Systems plc. I was to work as an Assistant to the Chief Executive, Kevin Overstall.

Kewill Systems plc was founded in 1972 by two management consultants, Kevin Overstall and William Loeffen, hence the name Kewill. They moved from management consultancy into application software at the end of the 1970s. I didn't know at the time but Kevin had gained a Mathematics degree at Pembroke College, Cambridge, so his academic background was similar to mine. Following a career as a scientist and then as a management consultant, he formed Kewill Systems and built it up to be a leading international software company. Kevin retired from Kewill Systems plc in 1998.

But this is all in the future. When I visited Kewill Systems plc on 26 November 1987 all I knew was that the company was said to employ 95 people on five sites, with the main site at Walton-on-Thames employing 44 staff. I knew from ENE '88i that their business was the development of the MICROSS manufacturing management software package, which the founding members of the company had developed and enhanced over several years. It was the market leader in manufacturing management systems in its price range. I convinced myself that a secondment there would be an exceptional opportunity. Kewill Systems plc was an ambitious, growing company in a growing industry. It was quoted on the Unlisted Securities Market with the latest published turnover for 1987 just £5 million. In March 1988 the published turnover was over £6.5 million and there were 148 employees spread over six sites. In January 1989 I reported that the Group was now estimated at over £13 million turnover, with 200 specialist staff, over 1700 customer sites and £2 million invested in research and development. Things had certainly changed very quickly. There had been a recent acquisition of Trifid Software Ltd of Congleton in November 1987 which increased the number of employees and broadened the product range to include planning and control software on minicomputers. Until then Kewill's products were all microcomputer-based. There was also the acquisition of Xetal Systems Ltd of Salford, which would happen later in November 1988.

On 1 December 1987 I sent in the proposal that I should go on Industrial Secondment. I wrote in my application that the company was well considered by the DTI. This was important because there was theoretically a slight risk of civil servants landing in companies who proceeded to go bankrupt. But Kewill Systems plc had been awarded a 40% grant under the DTI's Support for Innovation programme of £1.5 million, and two further collaborative projects were under consideration. They were going to be taking part in ENE '88i at Baltimore as part of the jobbing shop cell. The DTI accountants had put their magnifying glasses over the company accounts. Compared with the average small firm, Kewill Systems plc was a good place to go on secondment.

The company had two ideas for projects for me. The first was that I should prepare a proposal for funding from BRITE 2. This was a European funding programme for Basic Research in Industrial Technologies, hence the acronym. The original BRITE programme was launched in 1985, and BRITE 2 was its successor. I was reluctant to do this task because of the ethics of being poacher and gamekeeper simultaneously. The second project was to work on the financial strategy for the business. This sounded more fun because I did not know very much about finance, accounting and economics, but was eager to learn.

Time passed and eventually in April 1988 the following job description was agreed with John Faulkner, the Director who ran the Kewill Systems plc office in Sale near Manchester, and was now supposed to become my manager. Note that it had no mention of BRITE 2 nor anything about finance. Nevertheless it was an achievement. I should have realised that the problems about agreeing the task were an indication of what was to follow. However I was young and hopeful, and I recall that I wrote Hooray ! in my day book.

DEVELOPMENT OF KEWILL GROUP MARKET ANALYSIS FUNCTION – PROPOSED PROJECT FOR PAULINE CURTIS IN APRIL 1988

Objective :
　　To prepare a dynamic model of the European Market for IT in Manufacturing Enterprises.

Tasks
　　Define the critical characteristics which differentiate classes of users of IT in manufacturing, identifying actual and potential buying behaviours

　　Obtain, from secondary sources, data on market size for served and potential markets over time

　　Design and populate a data-base which will be the market model and set up procedures to maintain this database and to identify trend information

　　Make a series of policy recommendations based on the above data for product and service development and for distribution

I hated the idea of the drive to Walton-on-Thames from home, 90 miles round trip each day, but was prepared to go for just the six months from June to December, hoping to miss the worst of the bad winter weather. I would have preferred to go somewhere which was more local, but it was too late to set up an alternative option. The deal had been made for me and there was no real choice but to go. I now wish I had been more pro-active in my search. High tech IT companies in Oxford, or even Bath where I could stay with family during the week, would have been much better. Then I might have developed my move into a longer term relationship.

Looking back, it is clear from the notes made during my secondment that I was totally unprepared for village life in a small firm. If I had been returning to my old responsibilities in MTM Division at the end of the secondment then I would have been able to ask for a car from out of MTM Division's budget. There was an existing precedent. Unfortunately I truthfully admitted that I was expecting to return to a different area, and so this was not an option. I then asked at Kewill Systems plc because they did have leased cars for their sales staff, and they agreed that I should have one. I contacted a number of car leasing companies but even a little Austin Maestro 1.3 was going to be over £2,000 plus insurance for the six months, and a Ford Escort 1.3 was going to be over £3,000. When we got down to the detail, and the costs and the income tax situation, the idea had to be abandoned.

It was impossible to get to Walton-on-Thames by public transport, so we replaced our car with a brand new Maestro, which we hoped would be reliable, and I started the tedious commute along the M4 and M25 in the rush hour. Pete was still at the Rutherford Appleton Laboratory at Harwell, so he was able to go to work by company bus. I did get a mileage allowance, as if I was on a detached duty allowance, but that was only between my old office in the DTI in Central London and Walton-on-Thames. Those were, and still are, the rules. Although Kewill Systems plc was located in the middle of Walton-on-Thames the offices had a large car park, and I always arrived at about 7.30 to avoid the worst of the traffic, and make sure I could get a space. The hardest part of commuting was driving home, especially towards the end of the year when I was driving in the dark. My night vision has never been very good, and the M4 was not a kindly motorway at rush hour.

I started on the agreed date, 4 July 1988, at their offices in Ashley House, Church Street, Walton-on-Thames. I left home just before 7.00, driving through horrendous rain and arrived at Kewill Systems plc at 8.10. Fortunately I bumped into a member of staff at the door who had a key; no-one had told me that the normal starting time was 9.00. I found that the staff divided into the techies who lived downstairs, and the consultants/sales/accounts people who lived upstairs. I was given a desk upstairs in a cramped smoke-filled office sharing with the three sales reps. I was horrified after my individual office in the DTI and the compulsory no smoking policy. I nearly turned tail and ran. I have a long-standing allergy to cigarette smoke, which leads to hay fever symptoms. Fortunately the sales people spent a lot of time on the road, so it was only on Monday mornings that they were all at their desks. I never really got to know them very well. They were all younger than I was and we did not have a lot of common ground, except of course for all working at Kewill Systems plc. As a welcoming gesture, John Faulkner came down from Manchester and took me out for a beer and lunch. It was still raining. Only Directors of the company had rooms to themselves, otherwise it was all open plan offices. I started to spend time out of the office too, although it was mainly spent sitting in the Reading Public Library trying to get my mind around European statistics and the Kompass book of industrial companies.

I knew there were other DTI staff out on secondment and I suggested to my Personnel Manager that it would be useful for us all to meet on a regular basis, so that we could exchange experiences and keep in touch with what was going on in the DTI. It was lonely being a DTI official out on secondment. I proposed that I should organise a regular meeting in the Squash Bar of the United Oxford and Cambridge University Club, of which I was still a Lady Associate member. This was agreed, and I sent a letter to the other secondees, suggesting a time and place for the first meeting. We had a number of meetings, but gradually the novelty reduced and it became just three or four of us. By then my six months was completed and I was due to go back to the DTI.

I made some progress on the task of the job, read a lot of books about marketing and export marketing, and poured over out-of-date statistics about company profiles and industrial sectors in each of the European countries. The problem with statistics is that it takes so long to assemble them, and in 1988 the best official information I could find was for 1982. It was my only job when I kept a very detailed daily diary of the contacts I made, the information I collected, and the analysis of that information. During July I collected information about each European country. It was an academic and theoretical study. My suggestions of Spain, Italy, Denmark and the Netherlands for expansion opportunities were soon criticised, but at least it got some extra information and prejudices out onto the table. Kevin Overstall wanted to export to Australia, and definitely not to Spain, whereas John Faulkner was more interested in Spain. There was already a French distributor, much to my surprise, which took UK source code and translated it into French. There was also a Greek distributor who had just popped up but had not yet sold anything. I asked why there was a Greek distributor because it was an unusual strategic choice. I found there seemed to be no strategy in choosing distributors and if an organisation asked to be the distributor in a country where there was no existing presence, then the usual philosophy was to agree. I was reminded that Bill Loeffen, who was one of the original founders, was Dutch born. It was decided that I should do more work on the markets in Australia and the Netherlands.

With hindsight, I think it may have been more difficult than I realised for the Directors at Kewill Systems plc to decide what to do with a civil servant on secondment. By 14 August 1988 I had a new list of six tasks, proposed by Kevin Overstall. My final report to my DTI manager in December 1988 gave progress against each of these tasks.

KEWILL SYSTEMS PLC MARKETING STRATEGY - PROPOSED PROJECTS FOR PAULINE CURTIS IN AUGUST 1988, AND ACHIEVEMENTS

1 Publish Kewill Newsletter for Autumn 88 and develop Internal News Sheet

> The Autumn 1988 Newsletter was edited and published in October 1988, and a draft copy for the next Newsletter for February 1989 was prepared

2 Plan and control Kewill's Advertising Campaign (September 88 to March 89)

> Design of new adverts based on (a) Unix product and (b) Moog story
>
> Analyse past leads data to select best magazine schedules
>
> I found that I was not good at writing and designing adverts, but nor were Kewill's professional agency. Nevertheless I did participate in the writing of the text, and the two adverts were produced. Past leads data was analysed and I made a list of best magazines, with recommendations for changes in advertising for 1989.

3 Design and implement an Analysis of Competitors Details on top 20 main competitors, to be obtained from Kewill/Trifid salesmen, consultants and journalists.

> I identified the Top 21 competitors. Sales people provided information on three of these, but no more. I wrote that this was a disappointing response from them to something of long term benefit to all.

4 UK market research

> (i)Analysis of trends in Benchmark survey
>
> The Benchmark survey on Engineering Software was published in 1986 and 1988 in the magazine Engineering Computers. It was impossible to use their results to make any meaningful statement about trends.
>
> (ii) Kewill market penetration (based on Kompass etc)
>
> Kewill customers were identified by size and Standard Industrial Classification in Kompass and a general statement on Kewill's customer base was extrapolated. Recommendations for improving the company's knowledge of its customers was made.

5 Investigate two overseas markets in detail. These are to be Holland and Australia

The two overseas markets were investigated in detail. Also the market for software for the clothing sector was investigated prior to the acquisition of Xetal Systems Ltd.

6 Create model/analysis of other European markets

A detailed analysis of the European market was made, including for each EC country: a country profile, published statistics of its manufacturing industry (for the market) statistics of its CAPM industry (for competitors) and recommendations. For example, I noted that the Netherlands had a marginal market size, its manufacturing industry being 17% of UK, and with already a strong local CAPM industry. This did not seem to me to be a good opportunity for Kewill. Whereas Spain was a growing market with better opportunities, and had a very weak local CAPM industry. Unfortunately my analysis was too logical, and admittedly was based on old statistics.

On Wednesday 14 September I was surprised to arrive in work and find the office was all set up for a large meeting. It was the day of the Annual General Meeting of Kewill Systems plc and an unknown number of shareholders were expected to be arriving at 10.00. There were tea and biscuits laid out ready for them. I wondered whether to buy some shares myself, but being a shareholder and having staff who were managing a DTI grant with the company at the same time was not a good ethical combination.

Working on the Kewill Systems plc Marketing Strategy was all made more difficult by having another operation on my right hand to get more windscreen glass out, following my car accident in 1982. Much of my notes at Kewill Systems plc for that time were written left-handed. I was becoming quite proficient, which was useful because I was also teaching three different courses for the Open University and all the student work was paper-based and needed to be marked and annotated in the traditional way with a red pen.

As well as the Marketing Strategy, a marketing manual was prepared which detailed Kewill's marketing activity under the headings: Advertising; Press Releases; Mailing Lists; Newsletter; System Summaries and Leaflets; Technical Articles; Exhibitions; Surveys and Competitors; Kewill Customer Profile and International Marketing. Finally, I was asked to produce a draft job description for the marketing role as I perceived it for 1989 onwards.

As an additional task, perhaps best thought of as a fill-in, there was concern about the impact on the business of the Single European Market in 1992. I had by now learned that it was a bad idea to try and answer the question, but I thought I could make a useful contribution by setting out 8 key questions for discussion. Some issues were about the changing market, others concentrated on the competitors, and how to strengthen market presence, broaden the product range and spread financial risk. There were extra concerns about changes to the management structure, the need for extra skills, and who was going to take on the lead responsibility for all this.

I had not been forgotten in the DTI and was asked to write an article about my secondment for DTI News, the staff newspaper. A photographer came up from London and I was seated at Kevin's desk and made to look as if I was busy on the telephone with lots of papers spread around, and a PC to hand. I wrote about the differences between the DTI and Kewill Systems plc, the benefits to the company and to the secondee, and something about my task which was to establish their Marketing Strategy. It was all taken through a nice rosy window, aiming to get other DTI people interested in going out on secondment, but also recognising that writing an article might help me find the right job when I went back to the DTI.

Civil servants on secondment were also of wider interest and the Daily Telegraph asked for me to be one of their examples for an article which was going to be published at some indeterminate time in the future. There are always articles sitting ready for publication, for when a suitable slot arrives. So on 30 December they sent a photographer across to Kewill Systems plc, and took a series of photographs of me. There was one taken with Kevin Overstall which was eventually used on 16 February 1989. It was a short article, on the front page of the Appointments Supplement. Some extracts from the DTI News article were included, as well as the quote 'It was interesting to see Government from the outside. My biggest task, a research study into future European marketing opportunities, provided an insight into sales and marketing operations, areas which civil servants don't normally experience.' Thankfully there were no questions about whether it was really worthwhile to either Kewill Systems plc or to the DTI, and how that was measured, as the measures for assessing success would have been less than robust.

I was due to leave at the end of December 1988, and I was kindly invited to the Kewill Systems plc Christmas party, which was held at the Runnymede Hotel near Walton-on-Thames. It was an excellent venue, on the banks of the River Thames and looking directly over Bell Weir Lock. Everyone was able to bring their spouse or partner and it was a very pleasant social occasion. I was actually sad to be leaving, now the time had come to go, but I did not hide the fact that I was pleased to be going back to the DTI. I had made it clear that I could not face driving from home to Walton-on-Thames in the winter and along the M25. And I wanted to be back in Whitehall, where I could continue my career. The saying 'Out of sight is out of mind' is a very true threat for a secondee.

I had taken advice on what to look for in my next posting from friends and colleagues. One particular note I have is of a discussion with Mark Lanyon, who had been my Assistant Secretary in MTM Division, and who suggested that I avoid IT and the Information Engineering Directorate (IED) because they were too close to my previous posting. He suggested that I instead consider the Regional Offices, and said that some of the Grade 6 posts there were OK. This was flattering because it implied that I should be looking to return on promotion, but based on my DTI career I was not yet deemed ready for promotion to Grade 6, and I was sure that Kevin Overstall was not sufficiently impressed with my work at Kewill Systems plc. Peter Adkin had moved to the Regional Office in the South West, located at Bristol, and from what I heard I was not convinced that going into a Grade 6 job at a Regional Office was a good idea. It was only possible to move into jobs which are vacant and so my choice was limited anyway, given that I had a fixed date for my return of 3 January 1989.

During the Autumn I had been looking at vacancy notices, and had been successful in applying for a post at Principal in IED with responsibility for software quality. The job had previously been held by Dr Monica Darnbrough, whom I knew, and the Grade 6 there was Dr Peter Wilkinson formerly from the Division of Numerical Analysis and Computer Science at the National Physical Laboratory. I was content. I knew exactly what I would be doing when I left Kewill Systems plc, and I did not have a spell on 'gardening leave'.

17 The Death of a Senior Colleague

On 8 January 1989, a British Midland Airways Boeing 737 Series 400 took off from London Heathrow in the evening, bound for Belfast. At 20.05 the aircraft was climbing through FL283 some twenty nautical miles south-south-east of East Midlands Airport when the aircraft began to shake and smoke fumes filled the flight deck. The captain took control of the aircraft and shut down the right engine which was not the damaged one. The three flight attendants and some passengers had seen signs of fire from the left engine. It became clear that there was a catastrophic mistake when there was a sharp decrease of power from the only engine, on the left. Attempting to reach East Midlands Airport for an emergency landing, the impact was on high ground just to the east of the M1 motorway at Kegworth. Thirty nine passengers died in the accident.

The images on the TV news were horrific, but I had no personal reason to be concerned. Then a photograph of Dr Barry Copestake recovering in Leicester Royal Infirmary from a fractured leg was published in the newspapers. It was to the Leicester Royal Infirmary where I had been taken when I had my car accident, and I had not been very impressed compared with my local hospitals in Reading and Oxford.

I had worked for Barry in my first job in the Department of Industry in 1981, and he had been very kind when I had my accident in 1982. Then in 1984 I had moved, and later he had been promoted from Grade 5 to Grade 3, and moved to Northern Ireland. In the newspaper, he was described as an engineer working in Belfast. In fact he was then the Chief Scientist in Northern Ireland, which was a very senior post although less influential than being Chief Engineer and Scientist in London. He had not moved house and was still living at Caversham near Reading and commuting weekly by British Midland to Belfast. He had his favourite seat near the front of the aircraft on the flights, the same seat as I chose when I was flying.

Shortly after his picture was in the newspapers, he died from his injuries. Being forced to lie stationary in a hospital bed can have serious side effects, and that was the problem. I regretted that I never had the chance to go up to Leicester to visit him. For all of us who had worked with him, it was a tragedy. He was too young to be taken away, and still had so much to offer as Chief Scientist. A handful of us took time away from work and made the effort to come up from London and attend his funeral in Caversham. It was an occasion to reflect on a special career, and for me it was the second time when I thought about my own career and the fragile line between life and death.

18 Software Quality and Safety Critical Systems

Immediately after celebrating the New Year of 1989, and in spite of advice to the contrary, I joined the Information Engineering Directorate, responsible for software quality and safety critical systems. My annual salary was £20,798 including the London weighting of £1,707. I was delighted to give up driving and bought an annual season ticket for the train and London buses and tube, which cost £1,508, and the DTI offered me a tax-free season ticket advance which was repaid monthly. In spite of all the problems of commuting by train I was really pleased to get away from the driving. My new office was in Kingsgate House, just opposite to Ashdown house where I had been working previously. Both were in Victoria Street and I could settle into my routine of buses and tubes across London from Paddington Station, and the weekly escape across St James's Park for lunch at the United Oxford and Cambridge University Club.

I don't want to give a boring history lesson on the setting up of DTI's Information Engineering Directorate (IED), but a short introduction to the policy changes at that time is useful background. The IED was created as a consequence of the Alvey programme which had started in May 1983, following the deliberations of a committee set up in March 1982 by the Minister of State Kenneth Baker MP, under John Alvey of British Telecom, to advise on a strategy for a research programme in advanced IT. At that time it was partly a response to the Fifth Generation computer initiative of the Japanese, which had been unveiled in October 1981. Seeing the Japanese initiative made UK Government and industry and the academic community realise that the UK had to get its act together. The first phase of the Alvey programme had a total budget of £350 million, of which £200 million was from Government and £150 million was from industry. The Government portion was from the DTI, the Ministry of Defence (MOD) and the Science and Engineering Research Council (SERC). Projects were generally funded 50% for the industry collaborators, and 100% for the academics.

The Alvey programme was set up to last 5 years, and was to fund collaborative R&D. It aimed to strengthen the academic and industrial science and technology base, transfer academic know-how into industry, and enhance the competitive potential of the IT sector. There were four main technology themes: VLSI (very large scale integration or 'chip' technology), Software Engineering, IKBS (intelligent knowledge-based systems) and MMI (man-machine interface, now commonly called human computer interface). There were also five Large Demonstrator projects, intended to demonstrate emerging enabling technologies. One of these, the Design to Product Demonstrator, was in my old area of AMT. It had academics from the Universities of Edinburgh, Loughborough and Leeds working with the National Engineering Laboratory and with industrial collaboration from three companies of the GEC Group.

In 1986 there was a review of the Alvey programme by the IT86 Committee led by Sir Austin Bide, which recommended further funding should be made available. Three things were essentially recommended: a continuation of the Alvey process in R&D; the participation of the UK fully in the European programme ESPRIT; and what might be called an experimental programme to try to apply the Alvey process in the application area. This is not my summary, but came from Sir Brian Oakley, who led the Alvey Directorate until his retirement in October 1987. There was no detailed DTI response to the Bide report. This was later justified on the basis that the amount of public money available for collaborative R&D was broadly as recommended by that report, although with a greater emphasis on European programmes such as ESPRIT. So Ministers said there was no need for a formal response.

I had previously been interested in the ACARD report 'Software - a vital key to UK competitiveness', which was published in June 1986. Now I had my first real involvement with the same ACARD report. When I had been in my previous post in MMT I had read the ACARD report, and others, as one would read a daily newspaper. It was interesting but I recognised that I could only have a role as an observer whereas other DTI people had responsibility for carrying forward the ideas and getting involved. In 1986 the Chairman of ACARD was Sir Francis Tombs FEng, Chairman of Rolls Royce, and there were 14 members of Council over half being industrialists. The first ACARD report, on the Applications of Semiconductor Technology, had been published in 1978, and this ACARD report was number 14.

The format of an ACARD report is that there is always a short introduction to the problem, followed by a list of detailed recommendation, in this case targeted at industry, Government and the Professional Institutions. Of course, ACARD members, although eminent, cannot be expected to cover all important subject areas themselves, and an ACARD report is prepared by a Working Group, which is chaired by a member of Council, but includes a good mix of experts who understand the problem. Once the Working Party had prepared their report it was offered to Council, who are able to discuss the recommendations before approving publication. John Coplin, Director of Design at Rolls Royce Ltd was the Chairman of the Working Group. Government officials were also invited to meetings. This ACARD Working Group included two people from the Ministry of Defence and someone from the Software Engineering part of the Alvey Programme.

The terms of reference of the Working Group were:

to identify measures to assist in the understanding and use of software engineering by industry and business through education and training;

to report on the nature of existing and prospective management and organisation practices in software development, in the light of changes being and likely to be brought about by software engineering;

to report on current and prospective techniques and aids in the specification, design, integration and testing of software in the assessment of quality and correctness of product;

to report on the international competitive position of the UK with respect to the above, including restrictions on international trade in software and its implications for UK industry and business;

to make recommendations.

In the event a broader interpretation was adopted. The approach taken was to seek to identify the macro-economic significance of software to the UK; then to develop an understanding of the actions required to produce a better market performance; and how to develop the methods, skills and tools to achieve better software technology. Particular emphasis was placed on the users of software and on the collective behaviour of users, appliers and suppliers of software. In the usual way, many individuals and companies gave evidence to the Working Group.

Full details of the recommendations can be read from the ACARD report. However, I want to concentrate on the areas where they were relevant to the work of my team and my consultants.

The recommendations began with the recognition that the widespread application of soundly engineered software can enhance the overall financial performance of the UK. To maximise this potential, companies, government departments and educational establishments needed clear visibility of the broad picture. Thus informed about national targets, and the general direction to be taken, they can then strive to achieve the overall targets by mutually coordinated actions. The first recommendation was therefore the formation of an expert body to monitor the implementations of the recommendations and their effectiveness in use against the targets set. The first step in getting anything started is often to set up a committee. But this expert body had real targets to measure progress against and tasks to achieve. One task was to hold an annual, large scale, formal review meeting, to consider a performance report of software users, appliers and suppliers. ACARD required an annual summary report from the expert group in order to monitor the effectiveness of the mechanism and the progress towards its targets.

Initial targets to report progress against were:

> that the UK should have a software balance of payments surplus by 1995;
>
> that UK-owned companies should by 1995, supply:
>
> 80% of bespoke/custom software produced in the UK;
>
> 50% of the new packages purchased in the UK;
>
> 30% of the systems software employed in the UK;
>
> 10% of the total world market for software.
>
> that companies operating in the UK should, by 1990, increase their formal, in-service, training for Board and senior managers, Middle Managers, Technical IT staff, non-technical IT staff, other professional staff to specified levels.

Written in 1986 these were the elements of a long-term ten year plan. At that time there was the view that there was a real possibility that these targets might be achieved, if work was set in progress quickly. There were specific recommendations to industry, to Government and to the relevant Professional Institutions.

The main recommendations for industry were

> in-service training initiative for all users, appliers and suppliers;
>
> increased application of software to improve the competitiveness of the manufacturing and service industries;
>
> marketing initiative for UK software products and services.

The main recommendation for Government was the formulation and implementation of a long-term (10 year) plan for interdepartmental co-operation on:

> public purchasing to exercise demand-led leadership;
>
> a new technology transfer initiative, similar to the Software Engineering Institute in USA;
>
> better public sector R&D planning, including the follow-up to the Alvey programme;
>
> in-service training initiative, similar to industry and with similar targets.

The leadership role of the professional bodies, in particular the Institution of Electrical Engineers (IEE), was recognised, and it was recommended that the IEE should lead a study into the issue of professional certification of software engineers, safety critical software and quality certification. The IEE was told to involve the Engineering Council, the British Computer Society (BCS), industry, academia and the government in these studies.

There were also three important Appendices. The first was on Education and Professional Qualifications, the second was on Safety Critical Software, and the third was on Product Standards and Certification. The last two of these were followed up in my area.

On safety aspects of software system construction and operation there were needs for safety certification. These included:

> certification of the mathematical soundness of the methods of construction;
>
> certification that certified methods are properly applied during construction and subsequent maintenance (rectification and development);
>
> certification of the tools used during construction and maintenance;
>
> certification of the software engineers who build and maintain the systems;
>
> certification of the end product, that is, the software itself.

There was awareness in practitioners that safety and reliability required more rigorous theoretical bases than existing 'good practice', so that system behaviour could be accurately and consistently predicted. Hence there was a need for mathematical soundness to enable prediction to be based on mathematical proof. And, as in other branches of engineering, the rigour of the inspection procedures should be adjusted to the degree of risk, the severity of the danger and the cost.

On Product Standards and Certification, the appendix discussed the opportunities and benefits of standardisation of the designs and interfaces of software products, with particular mention of programming language compliers, applications-oriented packages, operating systems, word processors, spreadsheets etc. The recommendation was of a policy of long-term, goal-directed research into software standards, which should be coordinated internationally, with the expectation of a variety of spin-offs to our local suppliers who would secure a competitive edge.

In 1986 the House of Lords Select Committee on Science and Technology made an important review of the policy and practice of public support for civil science and technology in the UK. It had the boring title of 'Civil research and development: First Report of the House of Lords Select Committee on Science and Technology'. There were many eminent scientists in the House of Lords, and their report was awaited with interest from those who would be tasked with writing the Government response, which was published in July 1987. Recommendations were considered; some were accepted and others were not, and it is all clearly explained in the Government response. One relevant action here was that ACARD was absorbed into a new body, the Advisory Council on Science and Technology (ACOST) with a wider membership and terms of reference to embrace all science and technology. The idea was that the central structure should be strengthened. None of these administrative changes had an obvious effect on the content of the ACARD report, and the imperative to follow through their recommendations.

As well as the formal Members, like its predecessor ACOST had a number of Assessors. Some were from Government Departments and Dr Bob Whelan of the Centre for Exploitation of Science and Technology (CEST) was invited to become an Assessor. CEST had been launched in 1987, and represented a partnership between leading industrial companies and the Government. Its major aim was to stimulate more effective exploitation by industry of the findings of scientific and technological research. It was supposed to be a market-driven organisation which sought to take a pro-active role in enabling research and stimulating the involvement of industry in particular areas of science and technology. CEST worked on well-defined project areas, each having a clear agenda and a finite lifespan - normally around two years. Projects were grouped around certain key factors which CEST considered were facing change in world markets. These factors included four areas of project work: demography and social change, environmental pressures on industry, materials and advanced manufacturing and food and agriculture. There was a fifth area of project work related to the process of managing exploitation. I have no results for the early years, but in 1993 it was reported that the Centre had a budget of around £1.5 million.

The White Paper 'DTI - the department for Enterprise' was then published in January 1988, so everyone in the DTI was very aware of the new policies which Lord Young defined for the Department. I am sure that in IT Division the changes to innovation policy had exactly the same impact as I had felt in MTM Division. The general Support for Innovation (SfI) scheme for providing innovation grant assistance to individual companies would end. In its place there was the Enterprise Initiative. There would be greater emphasis made on technology transfer - especially linking educational institutions with industry, for small firms, for the regions and for new technologies. Greater emphasis would also be placed in collaborative programmes of longer term research between companies and to encourage collaboration between higher education institutions (HEIs) and companies. Finally, initial assistance would be given to technologically-advanced projects in small companies, and to a very restricted number of projects offering exceptional national benefit.

The new Alvey Directorate lived alongside DTI's Information Technology Division, and then in 1988 became the Information Engineering Directorate (IED). During 1987 the Trade and Industry Select Committee, whose role was to examine the expenditure, administration and policy of the DTI and associated public bodies, decided to conduct an inquiry on Information Technology. This began in December 1987. A lot of formal written evidence was collected and then a number of people were invited to give oral evidence. Or perhaps summoned is a better word, because there was really no choice, especially for the people who worked in the DTI. The oral evidence was taken in public. There were also informal discussions with many people, and the Committee visited the USA and Japan.

Prior to the DTI's oral evidence, and in the usual way, a memorandum on IT was submitted by them on 29 January 1988, and a further memorandum was submitted on 1 February. The oral evidence was taken on 10 February 1988. Note the short timing between the written and oral evidence. Sometimes the first written evidence results in extra questions, and so a second set of written evidence is not unusual. It was a very senior group from the DTI who appeared to give the oral evidence: Alistair Macdonald was now the Deputy Secretary responsible for the work, and there were three Under Secretaries: Dr John Thynne who was head of IT Division, Dr Tim Walker who was the head of the new IED, and Dr Pamela Denham as Head of Quality, Design and Education (QDE) Division. IT Skills were an important part of the DTI's policy for IT, and that responsibility rested with QDE Division. Software quality was important too, as part of an enthusiasm for quality in general.

Soon afterwards the House of Commons Public Accounts Committee also took an interest in the Alvey Programme, following a critical report by the National Audit Office (NAO). For this Committee it was the Permanent Secretary, Sir Brian Hayes GCB who led the DTI team, comprising Alastair Macdonald as Deputy Secretary and Dr Tim Walker as Under Secretary. Their oral evidence was taken on 4 May 1988, and also published. The Alvey Programme had independent academic evaluators from SPRU at the University of Sussex and PREST at the University of Manchester. Although their full Evaluation Report was not published until 1991, there was an interim evaluation report published in 1987. Evaluation was just one of the NAO concerns; the lack of proper financial information procedures was another. The NAO view was that there had been no central financial information systems; the monitoring of budget and spend was inefficient and incomplete, and financial reporting was irregular. These were hard criticisms and Sir Bryan Hayes agreed. He said it was a simple matter of fact. The explanation was that attempts to put in a computerised system had failed, several times. One of the problems was the way in which the three parts of Government were doing separate financial accounting. With hindsight it would have been easier for all the budgets to be given to a separate organisation, and be spent under a central system. But this was a new and novel programme and for obvious reasons each of the three partners, the DTI the MOD and the SERC, wanted to make sure that their budget contribution went towards achieving their objectives, not towards the objectives of a different organisation. Other NAO criticisms, also accepted as facts, included haphazard filing, where important documents could not be found. This was said to be caused in part by having industrial secondees who were not familiar with traditional Civil Service practices. In combination these two Committee investigations were not good news for the Alvey Directorate, and their whole way of working had to change.

While all these exciting policy discussions were taking place I had been sitting happily at Kewill Systems plc, so I had a lot of catching up to do when I arrived at the IED. On my arrival in post, no-one spoke to me about any of this. It was assumed that I already knew about the problems of the past. I began by reading a paper on Software Policies and Activities, written by my predecessor in September 1988. It was a very useful description of a wide range of activities in support of Government policies relating to software. The staffing for my group was very similar to my previous job, with a mixture of permanent staff and consultants. I was pleased to find that I had my own office staff, I did not have to share administrative support, and everyone I met was very good. I knew it could be difficult moving into a new area when some permanent staff might be more suitable than others. I knew I was very lucky.

I found I was also very fortunate with my predecessor's choice of the consultants and organisations who were already working for the DTI in the area. Firstly there had been a study of the computing services industry commissioned from Coopers and Lybrand Associates, and published in April 1987. It identified the likely major developments in the key sectors of the industry over the next ten years, and was widely discussed. Secondly, the National Computing Centre (NCC) was very actively involved. On my arrival I was given a copy of the Technical Report 'What is Quality', written by Alec Dorling of the NCC and published in 1988. Although the starting point of the book was quality in general, it very quickly focussed on the problems of quality in the software sector. There was a need to begin with proper definitions of quality - a high quality software product satisfies user expectations, conforms to its requirements and design specifications, and exhibits an absence of errors. There were also studies undertaken for the DTI by Price Waterhouse and Logica which showed that purchasers, users and suppliers of software suffered as a result of problems with software quality. It made journalistic headlines when Price Waterhouse reported that UK users and suppliers incurred unnecessary costs of at least £500 million each year, due to bad software quality. Everyone repeated the numbers, and they became an assumed fact against which to carry out new policies. Both the Logica study 'Quality

Management Standards for Software', published in April 1988, and the Price Waterhouse study 'Software Quality Standards: the Costs and Benefits' concluded that quality management systems might help to improve software quality but effective and appropriate use of software engineering methods and tools was needed too.

These publications gave powerful evidence to justify a programme of work for the next few years. I began to read everything I could find about software, software engineering and software quality. It was a joy to be able to go back to the technical areas with which I was familiar from my IT career. Much of the work had been done on defining the problem, what was now needed was someone who would move it all forward and make something happen. This job was exactly what I needed.

One successful aspect of Lord Young's Enterprise Initiative was the new Managing into the '90s programme. It aimed to provide practical information and advice to help firms adopt a strategic, integrated management approach to some of the key factors which influenced commercial success. One such factor was quality, where the programme aimed to promote and help senior management achieve a 'company-wide' commitment to quality. Indeed much of the written material which was made available to industry and commerce followed the developments in quality and standards in the UK since the publication of the White Paper 'Standards, Quality and International Competitiveness' in 1982.

Under the umbrella of the Managing into the '90s programme, the DTI produced a wide range of material explaining major aspects of quality achievement, one of which was 'Getting to grips with Quality', published in 1989. This booklet contained a list of videos and publications available about quality management. Topics included quality, quality improvement, statistical methods of product and process control, Quality Circles, and Quality Management Systems particularly the British Standard BS 5750. Active organisations were listed and included the British Standards Institution (BSI), the Institute of Quality Assurance, the British Quality Association, the Association of Quality Management Consultants, the National Accreditation Council for Certification Bodies (NACCB), the Association of Certification Bodies, and the National Measurement Accreditation Service (NAMAS). Many of these organisations were newly formed in the 1980s, as a focus for different stakeholders in the quality arena. Policy work here was the responsibility of Dr Pamela Denham and her Branches in the DTI's Quality, Design and Education Division.

The general situation on quality control, quality assurance and quality management systems was thus well organised, but then what should be done about the special case of software quality? Everyone knew that software was different. Software quality was an issue of major concern to both users and suppliers. Here there were extra organisations involved with the technology for software quality, including the Institution of Electrical Engineers, the British Computer Society, the National Centre for Information Technology (NCC), the Centre for Software Reliability (CSR) and the Centre for Software Engineering (CSE). I would soon get to meet everyone who was involved. I was privileged to have direct access to the expertise of the very best people in the UK, many of whom spent time each week with me in the DTI offices.

The recommendations of the ACARD report 'Software - a vital key to UK competitiveness' in 1986 had provided a useful basis for a plan for action within the DTI, and for coordinated efforts with our colleagues in other Departments. The DTI had always worked with a variety of Advisory Boards, and the IT Advisory Board (ITAB) was established in 1988 by the DTI and the SERC to provide advice to both organisations about their support for IT under the Joint Framework in Information Technology (JFIT), which followed the Alvey programme. Within ITAB several DTI/SERC committees were set up, including the Software Engineering Committee. Its members were a mix of academics and industrialists, and I became secretary for that committee. Each Branch of IED had a Director, and Professor John Buxton was Director of the Software Engineering Branch. The Inter-Departmental Committee on Software Engineering (ICSE) was also set up, chaired by Dr John Thynne who was our Under Secretary, and I was the secretary for this too. ICSE had the aim of agreeing on common approaches and use of standards in Government IT procurement; reviewing technical developments required for future systems; ensuring that the underlying R&D is carried out but not duplicated; and providing a forum for discussion of common concerns.

On 3 February 1988 Lord Young, Secretary of State for Trade and Industry, and Kenneth Baker, Secretary of State for Education and Science, had announced a new initiative to encourage collaboration between the scientific community and industry. It was called the LINK programme, and aimed to boost industrial R&D and to make scientists and the business community more aware of the potential for profitable exploitation of science and technology. The LINK initiative 'Bridging the gap between science and the market place' had been announced by the Prime Minister on 10 December 1986, and was now a reality. The main objectives of LINK were:

> to foster strategic areas of scientific research directed towards the development of innovative projects, processes and services by industry;
>
> to stimulate a real increase in industry's investment in R&D;
>
> to help industry exploit developments in science and make scientists more aware of industry's needs by strengthening the links between industry, higher education, the Research Councils and other research establishments;

to develop technologies which cross the boundaries of industrial sectors and scientific disciplines.

It was expected that £83 million would be spent on the first five programmes, of which the Government would provide up to half. These five programmes were molecular electronics; advanced semiconductor materials; industrial measurement systems; eukaryotic genetic engineering; and nanotechnology. Over the following five years it was expected that further programmes would start, taking the total Government and industry spending on LINK to at least £420 million. The overall LINK Secretariat was based in the DTI, but the secretariats for individual programmes were divided between the DTI and the SERC at Swindon. A LINK Steering Group was set up, to advise on the selection of programme areas, which was chaired by Bob Malpas the Chairman of Cookson plc, an industrialist. Other members represented industry, Government Departments, Research Councils and higher education.

The LINK programme was open for traditional eligible organisations: companies and publicly funded research organisations. For the first time it was allowed that Research and Technology Organisations, who were usually only able to participate as industrial partners, could be eligible for consideration as science base partners. This was in recognition that in some circumstances they might be uniquely placed to offer a basic science input. The arrangement was that proposals for topics for new LINK programmes were approved by the LINK Steering Group and then each programme could fund a number of different projects within its agreed priority topics. As Secretary of the DTI/SERC Systems Engineering Committee, I was soon looking at collaborative research projects to which were applied the LINK rules.

IT Division had established a programme of work on Open Systems Technology Transfer, with which I had been involved in my previous job on MAP/TOP/OSI, having published a booklet on Open Systems in Manufacturing which was intended as a simple introduction for senior managers. It was part of the overall Enterprise Initiative. In 1988 a programme of work on standardisation had been recommended to supplement this work. I was therefore responsible for two programmes, one about Software Quality Technology Transfer, and the other for Standards Making.

An important part of the technology transfer programme was the STARTS programme, originally Software Tools for Application to large Real Time Systems, and launched in 1982. It was an awareness activity whereby senior people from industry and government came together to describe and agree a statement of best practice. Their joint advice was then made available widely across the UK to help other companies to purchase and supply better quality software.

STARTS came in two distinct flavours. The first was RT-STARTS (Real-time STARTS) which concentrated on the production of a STARTS Guide which described methods and tools which could assist suppliers in producing software for complex real time systems, and a STARTS Purchasers Handbook, describing best practice for purchasing real-time systems. The Handbook provided forms of words concerning the level of software engineering expected in tenders. The experiences when introducing software tools and methods into organisations were being collected by a questionnaire and interview, and these results were disseminated too.

In 1987, the STARTS initiative was expanded to cover a wider range of business systems. This was IT-STARTS, which also aimed to improve the quality and use of information systems, and addressed its message to senior managers. In 1989 there were three parts:

1. The IT-STARTS message to Senior Management. This was intended to help senior management understand how information systems are used as management tools.

2. Developing systems together - a handbook for users. This helped people who were having information systems developed for their use to understand the development process. The little red booklet was written by the NCC, in simple words, with jolly cartoons. It began with the lifecycle - planning, design, implementation, and maintenance. Then it described the roles of those involved - the users, the project controller, and the developers. There was then a lot of discussion about building the system, working towards the user requirements document which is the basis from which the system is designed. The systems analysts then produced a description of the new system in business terms, in order to show the design and make sure that everyone understands it. Technical design followed, and once the programs were written and documented and the hardware was available, implementation began. Installation and testing was carried out, and the system was accepted. Subsequently, maintenance involved corrections, extensions and alterations to the systems. All this was the expected best practice in those days, and the principles are still very valid now.

3. The IT-STARTS developers' guide. This promoted the use of software engineering methods and tools among systems developers.

STARTS main objectives were therefore to accelerate the uptake of best software engineering practice and methods.

STARTS was delivered through four mechanisms:

1. Providing guidance on best practice to in-house developers and external suppliers, with information about, and assessments of, the best available software engineering activities

2. Promoting the use of best practice amongst purchasers and users when procuring and specifying systems

3. Promoting coordinated and constructive demand from purchasers for suppliers to use the best software engineering practice

4. Involving the user more productively in the development process and increasing awareness amongst senior management

The Standards Making programme had three parts: improvement of the UK participation in standards making; preparation of guidance on the application of these standards to the business needs of industry; and establishing the new Software Sector Certification Scheme. I was back into attending meetings of standards makers and I represented the DTI on the BSI Committee which was responsible for software quality management systems, named QMS/2/2/7 and part of the QMS/- family of quality management standards committees.

First it was necessary to develop understanding among independent software suppliers and in-house data processing departments about how to build quality into IT systems for different applications; how to apply the generic quality management standard (BS 5750/ISO 9001/EN 29001) to IT/software; and how tools and methods could support quality management and other software standards. The naming convention was that BS was the British Standard, ISO the International Standard and EN the European Standard.

Once they had this understanding, the next step was to encourage UK software producers to put in place quality management systems which met BS 5750/ISO 9001/EN 29001 and to apply for assessment and certification. But first a Software Sector Certification Scheme in which users and suppliers have real confidence had to be set up. This scheme promoted the use of standards to improve the quality management of software development. Its importance was that it was the only scheme involving certification by accredited bodies and which had been specifically designed for software development and delivery. The certification procedures required third party certification of the quality system to be carried out by accredited certification bodies, using auditors who have direct experience of the software industry and its processes. There were three certification bodies, from memory they were BSI QA, Det Norske Veritas and Lloyds Register QA.

Government was seen to have a unique and important role here in its public purchasing role. The next step was to develop a common approach to the use of quality management standards for Government procurement of IT and to make a public statement that all Government IT suppliers would be expected, at some future date, to meet ISO 9001 as a condition for contracts. Finally there was training. There needed to be training courses for quality assessors and to ensure that consultants providing a service to help firms put in quality management systems for IT were up to date with technical developments.

One early challenge was to find a suitable name for the scheme, so I ran a little competition between the people I knew. It was Cameron Low who came up with the suggestion of TickIT. The logo was a tick symbol, followed by the words IT. It was simple, gave an obvious visual message, and there was no doubt that it was the perfect name for the scheme. Cameron was an eminent member of the IT community, having been a member of the Alvey Committee when he was at PA Communications and Telecommunications. He was a Fellow of the British Computer Society (BCS) and asked if I would like to be put forward to upgrade my membership of the BCS from Member to Fellow. I had a recognised computing qualification, with my DPhil in Numerical Analysis from Oxford University, so I agreed and I became recognised as a chartered engineer at the same time. I was then entitled to use the letters FBCS denoting that I was a Fellow of the British Computer Society and CEng meaning that I was a Chartered Engineer. It all gave extra credibility in my dealings with academics and the DTI paid for my subscriptions as part of a general scheme for encouraging engineers to get professional recognition.

One corner of my group was a small team responsible for software security. That meant that I was required to be positively vetted before I was able to read all their papers which came across my desk. In the traditional manner I was interviewed about my life style, and any skeletons from the past. It was a short discussion because there was very little to discuss, but there is always a detailed desk exercise as well. I had previously seen the positive vetting process because my husband had needed to be checked when he was working in the Ministry of Defence, and some years later he had been a referee for a friend who was working in the MOD. It was by that unusual route that we discovered something about the name of our house, the Courts of the Morning. We had not named the house ourselves, but we discovered it was the name of a house which had been used as the base for a fictional attempt to overthrow the Government in South America. Needless to say, we went out and bought the novel, which was written by John Buchan. It is surprising how much the ladies and men with size 10 boots looked at what seemed to ordinary people to be unimportant and trivial details.

Meanwhile I was able to continue working on safety critical systems policy, but without seeing the specialist papers on software security. Safety critical applications of software were making policy inputs even more urgent; flying for the first time as a passenger on an early Airbus A320 brought the reality of the problem to me. The A320 had the first digital fly-by-wire flight control system in a commercial aircraft. There was a problem and we were delayed on departure while a new printed circuit board was flown out on the next flight from London. This was the only instance when I experienced serious delays, although delays were common leaving Brussels, Amsterdam or Paris in the evening, and I used to find myself running between the check-in desks of British Midland and British Airways to make sure I got a seat on whichever would be the next flight home. I only ever carried hand luggage and even then I usually managed to carry some local produce, for example French cheeses and salami from Paris, as well as a change of clothes and the papers for the meeting. The weight limits for hand luggage were less strict in those days.

The policy approach with safety critical systems was to find out what was going on, then to think about the DTI policy position, and how best to have an influence for the benefit of UK industry. So there was a study, done by a Working Party set up jointly by the Institution of Electrical Engineers (IEE) and the BCS, which I was funding on behalf of the DTI. The study was to identify current regulations for safety critical systems, and to consider new techniques and procedures, including certification of products, processes, companies and individuals. The Working Party delivered its report during 1989, and I had lots of discussions with Bob Malcolm who was working for me as a consultant and also involved in the work on behalf of the IEE.

Several parts of Government had a passion for safety critical systems. In the DTI we were working closely with all of them, but specifically the Health and Safety Executive and the Ministry of Defence. ICSE decided to set up a small Task Group on Safety Related Software (ICSESRS) to develop a strategy for safety-related software. That Group met for the first time in 1988, and for the second time in April 1989. Subsequently a Press Release was issued in June 1989, announcing the objectives and the priority tasks. I became the secretary of this group too, and was now the secretary of three different committees. In this case, the secretariat work was done jointly. I was responsible in the DTI and Ron Bell and Keith Wickes were responsible in the Health and Safety Executive. Unfortunately Ron and his team were based at the HSE offices in Bootle near Liverpool, so much of our discussions had to be done by the fax and telephone.

Four extensive studies of safety related systems had been carried out by the Ministry of Defence, the HSE, the International Electrotechnical Commisson (IEC), and the IEE jointly with the BCS. The findings of these studies, together with draft MOD and IEC standards, had each been published. One of the tasks of the ICSESRS working group was to review these documents in order to establish a common UK Government approach to the use and certification of systems containing safety related software. This consolidation would be undertaken in consultation with industry, professional institutions and other interested organisations.

There was an initial discussion of what would go into the strategy paper, and how the work would be shared. The main sections were to be:

A section setting out the advantages from a standards position of why there was a need to develop such a strategy.

The aims of the strategy with respect to the UK from both safety and economic viewpoints.

A section that set out a technical framework showing how it was necessary to adopt a systems approach in order to rationally develop a software strategy.

A section setting out a detailed strategy for the development of safety-related software. It was felt that the HSE study on Safety-Related software would constitute this particular section.

A section setting out a standards strategy based on the ideas and arguments developed above.

A section dealing with the training implications arising from the proposed software strategy.

The systems approach used the concept of the Safety Lifecycle and the necessity of using a systems approach, using arguments that had been developed elsewhere, including the IEE and BCS Report on Safety-Related Systems. This gave an overview of the concept of safety integrity and developed the ideas relating to safety integrity levels for both systems and safety-related software. There were a number of documents which already had these ideas, including the joint IEE and BCS Report, various drafts of standards in IEC/SC65A/WG9 and 19, and the STARTS Guide. And there are classical ways of achieving quality software, including the lifecycle project management, quality assurance, documentation etc. The intention was that this would all develop into a conceptual model, which would indicate what 'inputs' we have to the software development, and under which we have control, for the desired 'output'. The details of the conceptual model would then be explained in terms of the techniques and software development characteristics. Finally the conceptual model had to be shown to be implemented in practice. What integrated package of measures was suitable for software integrity level 2, for example? There were going to be four integrity levels.

Many new organisations had been set up in the early 1980s as a consequence of the developing problems and opportunities with software.

One of these was the Centre for Software Engineering Ltd (CSE). Based in Flixborough, a town near Scunthorpe made famous by the explosion at a chemical plant in 1974, CSE was launched in November 1983 to carry out assessments of safety-critical systems. The Chief Executive was Dr Phil Bennett, and he soon introduced himself to me.

Another source of useful technical input came from the Centre for Software Reliability (CSR) where Robin Bloomfield was also a regular contributor to DTI policy. CSR was a strictly non-profit making organisation that was established in 1982 by a group of specialists in order to provide a focus for the reliability, safety and security of computing systems. CSR worked with two research centres, one at the City University in London and one at the University of Newcastle-upon-Tyne. Robin was based in London. CSR had three main objectives:

1. to promote and participate in research and development;
2. to provide and support technology transfer by means of courses, workshops, seminars and literature;
3. to develop advisory services to government and industry in the planning, management and review of relevant programmes, projects and standards.

The prime topic of interest to CSR was clearly software reliability. To obtain reliable software, techniques were needed to avoid making design faults, to remove those which are nevertheless introduced, and to tolerate the residual faults which still slip through. To measure and predict the reliability of software required the definition of metrics, the collection of appropriate data, and the analysis of credible reliability models. Issues such as safety, security, system development, project management, quality assurance and control, metrics, formal verification, were all relevant to software reliability.

Some of my policy work could not be done jointly with colleagues in other Departments, and had to be done solely on behalf of the DTI. In July 1989 I was responsible for preparing, and later publishing, the DTI policy statement on the draft Interim Defence Standards 0055 'Requirements for the procurement of safety critical software in defence equipment' and 0056 'Requirements for the analysis of safety critical hazards'.

A DTI policy statement sounds a serious heavy publication, but here it was only two pages of A4. The essence of the DTI comments was that the wide ranging consultation from the MOD was welcomed. There were many standards initiatives, and there was a need for harmonisation. The aim, as always was the preparation and use of recognised international standards. The MOD policy statement proposed that the use of formal methods be mandatory. Within the DTI this gave us some concerns on behalf of our industry, and it was recognised that there were many research issues as well as a need to define and publicise current best practice. The latest edition of the STARTS Purchasers Handbook included a new chapter on safety related systems. Detailed technical comments were prepared at the NPL, where my old colleague and international expert Dr Brian Wichmann was responsible for the work.

July came and Lord Young went, to be replaced by Nicholas Ridley as our new Secretary of State. Fortunately nothing exciting usually happens during the summer holidays. Just after my positive vetting came through it was agreed that the area of computer security and computer mis-use was becoming sufficiently important that a new Branch was needed to deal with it. IED Branch 7 came into existence, and my little team moved across there, and I stayed behind. I never did see any of their classified papers.

As part of my responsibility for software engineering I learned more about the importance of formal methods, and had technical discussions with Martyn Thomas of Praxis in Bath, and complemented all this new knowledge by persuading the Mathematics people at the Open University that I knew enough about Software Engineering to tutor their brand new course, M355 'Topics in Software Engineering'. I suppose there were very few academics who knew anything about software engineering, and of those even fewer wanted an extra job tutoring for the Open University. I had the advantage that I had already been a tutor for other third year computing courses, and had a reputation as a competent, or even excellent, teacher.

Having been accepted as a tutor in the South Region for M355 I was shocked to receive the course material, some of which was written in a foreign language as far as I was concerned. I had to climb up a steep learning curve very quickly. Fortunately I had access to experts, and I had the winter to look at the course material; the course did not start until February 1990. My contact with the students was limited to marking their four sets of work, for which I had the solutions, so that was not too difficult, and doing three face-to-face Day Schools. Here it was quite frightening because I did not really understand chunks of the course material. I admitted to my students that I would have liked to be more expert. In addition, the first year of tutoring any new course is always challenging. I had done it before and many tutors deliberately avoid taking on the teaching of new courses in their first year. Fortunately for me and my M355 students the OU continued to provide excellent Day School material, with photocopied sets of questions for the students to work through, and solutions provided by the central academics. Professor Darrel Ince at the Open University was an expert, and he had prepared the course material for students and tutors. I clung to the tutor material as a life line for the year, and was reasonably successful. My students did well and they all passed. It extended my ability to talk as an expert about something that I did not know very well, whether that is a useful skill or not.

Meanwhile I was still teaching the OU technology course on Computer Aided Design, which I was enjoying. The extra burden of M355 was too much work, and I resigned from M355 at the end of the first year.

PART THREE: LEADERSHIP AND MANAGEMENT

Leadership sets direction and strategy, motivates and produces change.

The leader asks: 'Where do we want to be?'

The manager asks: 'How can we get there?'

From 'Leading for Quality', published by the Cabinet Office in 1994

'civil servants of the future will need to have both those skills particular to the profession of Government and the same commitment to performance and achievement found in the best outside organisations'

From the 1994 White Paper 'The Civil Service:Continuity and Change'

19 Promotion to Grade 6 in Engineering Markets Division

I was enjoying my current job, but since I started it I was very aware that I should look around for my next posting, hopefully on promotion. I had applied for several jobs at Grade 6, and then in July 1989 I applied to Engineering Markets Division, for the post as deputy to the Branch Head responsible for the engineering machinery and equipment industry. To my delight, and perhaps the surprise of my IED colleagues and my Personnel Manager, I was offered the job and this meant I was suddenly promoted to Grade 6.

Having arrived at the National Physical Laboratory as HSO at 24 I had been promoted to SSO at age 28. I was then promoted to Principal at 33 and now I was going to be Grade 6 at 37. For a scientist, this was good progress.

Having only returned to the DTI in January 1989, and with the annual reporting cycle being from April to April, I had no staff report on file which rated my performance while at Kewill Systems plc or in my present job, or my promotability. This had to be done quickly before I moved.

In the previous seven months I had obviously impressed my current boss and Reporting Officer, Dr Peter Wilkinson, because when he had to write the annual report he rated me as Fitted for Promotion to Grade 6, which was his grade, and Likely To Be Fitted for Promotion in the next 2 years for the more senior Grade 5. I wondered idly whether he would ever work for me. The rating of my actual performance in my job was 2, which meant I was significantly above requirements, on a scale of 1 to 5 where 3 was average. It was very rare for anyone to score a 1 because they would usually have been already promoted to the next grade. Since I had already succeeded in becoming promoted to Grade 6, it was no surprise that he marked me as Fitted for Promotion. If he had my sense of humour then he might have scored me as Exceptionally Fitted for Promotion, but he did not. Looking back I wondered why the report, given to me in September 1989, was an assessment only of my performance from January to April 1989. It would have been more sensible if it had covered the entire time from January to September.

In the normal way for the Annual Review Process, having been given a copy of my annual report to read I was invited to attend a Performance and Planning Review on 11 September.

These formal review meetings had five purposes.

1. To give a better insight into how performance and potential have been assessed
2. To give an opportunity to discuss the performance during the reporting period
3. To be given a better understanding of the job and what was expected
4. For me to put forward my ideas on the job and related points
5. To agree a forward job plan with objectives for the next reporting period.

This was a standard framework for all DTI staff, and I reported on my staff in exactly the same manner, using the same framework for discussion. In my case, much of the discussion at the Performance and Planning Review was about developing my skills for the next job at the higher grade. It was also an important opportunity to put forward my ideas on the current job and to make sure that my Forward Job Plan was agreed. It would be this job plan which formed the basis for the job description for my post when the vacancy was advertised.

Everything moved quite slowly and the vacancy notice for my existing job appeared on 7 November 1989. It was Vacancy Number 356 of 1989, which gives an indication of how many vacancies were advertised.

In the 11 months the job had not changed significantly. The purpose of the job was still to lead and manage a mixed discipline team of permanent staff and technical consultants in the development and implementation of awareness, technology transfer and standards activities in the field of computer software quality. I asserted that software development was said to be a black art which, through lack of discipline, led to poor quality and high costs. Yet some organisations were reasonably successful. An important element of the remit of my team in IED6 was to develop, to set up and to manage mechanisms which facilitated the spread of best practice from the few successful organisations to the many that could benefit from improving their approach. The main elements of the work included the establishment of a UK scheme for the certification of software quality management systems and the extension of this scheme into Europe. Systems and software safety was identified as an area of growing concern in which policies for developing standards and guidance material, and for disseminating the material, needed to be worked out. In addition, the Department was advised by a series of committees in the development and implementation of its strategies, and the job included running the secretariat for three of these committees. It was an interesting job, with many features which would appeal to good candidates. Being secretary of policy committees was good experience and dealing with software, although a technical subject, was not as messy as dealing with traditional engineering.

Time passed. People talked to me about the job and I was happy to let them know what was involved before they came for the formal interview. The handle turned, the process continued, I moved out and someone else came to sit at my desk and continue doing my job. It was interesting that my predecessor in my job had been a woman, and so was my successor.

What exactly was I going to do in my new job? The duties of the post were described as deputy to the Branch Head responsible for the engineering machinery and equipment industry. The coverage extended to equipment used in construction, mining and tunnelling, as well as most types of machinery used by manufacturing industry. Those were the days when Ministers had created a number of Market Divisions in the DTI, the idea being that civil servants should have a good understanding of the operation of both domestic and international markets within their sectors, and the performance of business within them. It had always been essential to have good contacts with industrialists, and the Market Divisions were to formalise that and also to promote the fashionable priority topics of the day - the Single European Market as well as the priorities from the White Paper of deregulation, quality and standards, and education and training. Action was also being taken to promote collaborative research; in the engineering sector my new area included responsibility for a LINK programme on the Design of High Speed Machinery.

The job sought someone with a mechanical engineering background supplemented by knowledge of electronics and IT. In my view, much of my previous experience was relevant, and I had certainly been closely involved with manufacturing industry. With careful drafting, a standard skill for civil servants, my c.v. was crafted to fit the job and to highlight my relevant experience. In my application for the job I wrote that the post brought together my experience and knowledge of manufacturing industry and IT, reinforced by my recent experience in software for manufacturing at Kewill Systems plc while on secondment, and my responsibility for software quality and standards. It built on my knowledge of the International, European and UK Standards worlds, and my previous responsibility for advanced manufacturing technology standards. As Secretary of the DTI/SERC Systems Engineering Committee, I had looked at collaborative research projects to which were applied the LINK rules. This seemed to address all the right words from the job vacancy notice. It must have worked, and I was invited for interview. I found that getting invited for interview was not difficult; it was the capture of the job at the interview which was the real challenge. I am not very spontaneous and I write much better than I speak.

I was interviewed by a panel which, as always, included my new boss. In this case it was Alan Conway. I had not met him before but the interview went well and I was told I had been successful in August, although I did not move until the October. I knew I was going to be able to work well with Alan, and he obviously thought the same about me. I was delighted to have finally got this promotion, and my annual salary took a leap to £27,547 which was an increase of over £5,000 per year. At the time I did not realise that the delay in my move was because there were serious plans in the wind to reorganise it all. There must have been serious consideration as to whether to move me into my new job while knowing that the Market Divisions were shortly going to disappear. My job would then be disappearing too.

As a Grade 6 for the first time I was allocated my own Personal Secretary, Barbara, although I only had a half share with another Grade 6. My arrival must have been rather a shock for my new colleagues. Women were rare in the senior levels of the Civil Service, and women engineers at my level were very scarce. Having been accustomed to his own secretary and then being required to share her with me was obviously difficult for the other Grade 6, not helped by his brusque manner in demanding his work be done. Barbara never complained but I was concerned for her. I had five sections, each headed by a Grade 7, and totalling 21 staff. Most of them were older than I was. It reminded me of when I started teaching for the Open University, when all my students were older than me. Alan Conway was very good in helping me settle down and introducing me to the rest of the Division.

I had more problems getting accustomed to the regular Branch Head meetings with the Head of Division, Christopher Benjamin, who I remember swore. Not that I am a sensitive soul. I am used to engineers and to visiting engineering companies, but I was so surprised. With hindsight, maybe it was the only technique which worked for him at those meetings to deal with the sheer frustration at the futility of what we were doing. In those days I tended to go into a new job, taking it at face value. I never did very much homework on the background of the people with whom I would be working, except for the immediate boss and the people who would become my staff. I now wish I had looked up Christopher Benjamin in Who's Who. Since leaving Oxford in 1976 I had been interested in aircraft, and I have always had a special passion for the Concorde aeroplane, from when I visited Paris as a child and saw the mock-up of the first French aircraft. One of the few regrets of my life is that I was not able to fly in it before it was grounded. In looking for information about Concorde recently I found the transcription of a programme 'Supersonic Dream' broadcast on January 18, 2005, and then available for purchase. Many important characters from the days of Concorde contributed, including the key Ministers: Roy Jenkins and Michael Heseltine, and the engineers and pilots. One key contributor was the same Chris Benjamin who had been Private Secretary to Roy Jenkins when he arrived as Aviation Minister in 1964. Chris then became

Concorde Administrator between 1971 and 1974. I wish I had done my homework better; we would have started our working relationship with a lot more interests in common.

Market Divisions were a new invention and civil servants had to go off and find out about 'their' industry. To give a flavour of the sort of work involved, in my area the PA Consulting Group had been asked to make an overview of the markets generated by activity in micro-engineering. The idea was to obtain an overview of current R&D, production and use of micro-engineering, identify products and systems where micro-engineered components can give competitive advantage and identify market opportunities worldwide for micro-engineered components. Micro-engineering was about the application of techniques developed in the microelectronics sector to the manufacture of components with tolerances in the region of 1 micron. Techniques such as photo-lithography, chemical etching, ion beam machining, and thin-film deposition formed the basis of this emerging technology.

The overview work included interviewing a number of people in Universities and companies, from the USA, the UK, Europe and Japan. There were 58 respondents in total. This may seem a slim sample on which to base policy work, but there was also a lot of desk research on centres of excellence worldwide, market potential, technical trends and current and near future applications. The report from PA arrived on my desk at the end of November. As might have been expected, their conclusions were not very positive, with limited activity in the UK, no centres of excellence, and constraints imposed by various lacks of design and manufacturing capability. PA said that micro-engineering was both an opportunity and a threat, which was again no surprise, and that more work needed to be done to properly audit the technology base and to review options for the provision of design and manufacturing capability. A discussion meeting was held at the end of December. In other circumstances this might have been a basis for further consultancy work, but policies were changing and this influenced the next steps.

The new emphasis on the Single European Market also meant that overseas visits were an important part of the job. I found I was expected to take part in a visit of senior staff to our opposite numbers in Rome, which had been organised before my arrival. In contrast to what people think, foreign business trips are usually quite hard work, with tedious flights and full days of meetings and discussions. None of my colleagues spoke Italian and we had to rely on interpreters for the meetings which made discussions slower. Rome in the winter was not very pleasant. It was cold wet and grey, although the Embassy had arranged for us all to stay at a reasonable Hotel in the centre of town, and our transport to the various meetings was all arranged for us. This made it easier to get our meetings done efficiently. Fortunately there were no problems with the budgets to pay for it all. It was my only overseas visit while I worked in Engineering

Markets Division, and I did not find it very useful for my own job, although others seemed to have more success with their meetings with opposite numbers. Because it had all been planned before my arrival, I had no choice but to go and do my share of the meetings. I spent most of my time with Chris Benjamin as he followed his own planned meeting schedule. On the flight home I wondered whether my costs had been good value. There were benefits for me in getting to know my senior colleagues better – everyone who went was at my level or above. But junior staff could have easily taken the notes of the meetings I attended.

I saw no need to learn Italian but I had continued with my French lessons, and now I was able to justify starting to learn German. I had my first lesson with the German teacher, Lotte Couch, on 4 December 1989. I already had some knowledge of the language, up to reading a menu and booking a room in a hotel, because of our visits to Mindelheim-Mattsies in West Germany to visit the Grob company with the gliding business. The lessons continued on a regular basis until Lotte died tragically in a car accident while visiting her mother in Germany in July 1995.

Returning to the office in January 1990, Chris Benjamin circulated an unattributed research paper 'Minute to an Unknown Economist' which rumours said he had written himself over the Christmas holidays. In those days I could not fully appreciate his discussion about the classic views of Adam Smith in The Wealth of Nations, which were fashionable with politicians at that time, so I just read the first few pages and then filed the paper. I knew that Chris Tame had provided a reading list for senior civil servants at the request of Sir Keith Joseph when he arrived at the DTI, and this list had included Adam Smith among others. However, older and slightly wiser, I decided to look again at the article recently. By coincidence it was in the context of writing some course material for a new course on Public Administration being produced by the Open University. And at the same time I came across the text of a lecture 'Technical Innovation and the British Economy' given by Professor Chris Freeman of SPRU, at the Rutherford Appleton Laboratory in May 1983. It was a dusty research publication which had been brought home in a box when Pete moved from RAL to the Meteorological Office.

Through both these I was introduced to the ideas of Friederich List, a German who wrote about the National System of Political Economy in 1841. Fortunately his original paper was translated into English, and published in 1855/1904. He was known then mainly as the advocate of protection of infant industries, but Freeman pointed out that a central part of his teaching is the emphasis on the role of technology in economic progress and international trade. In those times, Britain dominated most world markets for manufactured goods, and List insisted that Germany first had to catch up in terms of technology. The policy conclusions were summed up as a long-term national technology policy, closely linked to industrial and education policy. I repeat the seven fundamental points in defence of national technology strategies here.

1. The importance of intellectual capital. Here Professor Freeman quoted List 'The present state of the nations is the result of an accumulation of all discoveries, inventions, improvements, perfections and exertions of all generations which have lived before us; they form the mental capital of the present human race, and every separate nation is productive only in the proportion in which it is known how to appropriate these attainments of former generations, and to increase them by its own acquirements…'

2. The recognition of the importance of the interaction between intellectual capital and 'material capital'. List clearly recognised both the importance of new investment, embodying the latest technology and the importance of learning by doing from the experience of production with this equipment.

3. The importance of importing foreign technology and of attracting foreign investment and the migration of skilled people as a means of acquiring the most recent technology.

4. The importance of skills in the labour force.

5. The importance of the manufacturing sector for economic progress and the necessity for investment in manufacturing as a means of stimulating the development of the entire economy.

6. The importance of taking a very long-term historical view in developing and applying economic policies.

7. Finally, List stressed very strongly the importance of an active interventionist economic policy in order to promote long-term development.

The advantages which German industry and the German economy acquired through the development of their system of educating and training craftsmen, technicians and technologists was impressive, and was still admired in the UK. Meanwhile in Britain the method of training engineers 'on the job' contrasted with the German system based on deliberate professional development and on the recognition in cultural terms of the value of design and engineering. There was still a lot to be done, and I did not realise that my next job would give me a policy input, even if only for a short time, into this important area.

Chris Benjamin was able to use his own experience to add to this research. He had seen the advancement of Japanese manufacturing industry, as had Freeman. Since the Second World War the bureaucrats and advisers in the Ministry of International Trade and Industry (MITI) had established a long-term techno-economic strategy, based on technical efficiency and innovations in production.

Freeman had identified four main strands.

1. The ability to take a systems approach to design, and involving employees in systems changes. Their 'Quality Circles' were seen as an important innovation in management.
2. The capacity at national level to pursue an integration strategy which brings together the best available resources from universities, government research and private or public industry to solve the most important design and development problems. 1981 was the time of the start of the threat from the Fifth Generation Computer initiative in Japan.
3. The development of an education and training system which went beyond the German level, both in terms of the numbers of young people in higher education and also in the scale and quality of industrial training.
4. Early recognition that leadership in the new technologies would be decisive and aiming for world technological leadership. In the 1980s these key technologies were robotics, IT and computers.

Chris Benjamin had many comments and criticisms about the relevance of Adam Smith's arguments to the current international trade and industrial scene. Remember this was in 1990, and that Adam Smith had been writing one hundred and fifty years earlier. In those days there were issues of restraining imports and satisfying demands, money and financing, selling goods in the markets, pricing linked to supply and demand, and the treatment of labour. One criticism was the tendency for Smith to generalise from a single example, and in his times manufacturing industry examples were either about making pins or producing textiles, and the social context was very different. To quote Chris Benjamin 'It is open to question whether the essential Smith approach is still either an adequate account of economic activities, or a system necessarily conducive to economic efficiency and success... where there is any significant human involvement the Smith approach becomes progressively more vulnerable.'

Because of his knowledge of Japanese manufacturing industry, and his contacts with senior industrialists there, Chris Benjamin was able to add special insights into the situation in the 1990s, and explain how Japanese manufacturing industry was so successful. One example was given from the Chief Executive of Matsushita, who observed that people actually doing the task were in the best position to improve the process. Another example was Tokai who manufactured plastic cigarette lighters - the modern day equivalent of the pins described by Adam Smith. Greater efficiency had been achieved by the introduction of machinery with 24 hour working, but the staff on each shift had to be highly trained to keep the operation going. Adam Smith proposed the need to have a supply of stock, whereas modern Japanese manufacturing had good relationships with their suppliers and used just-in-time methods. Components were delivered at exactly the right time to be incorporated into the manufacturing process; there were no warehouses full of stock. Co-existence and co-prosperity between manufacturers and suppliers was common in Japan, each recognising that in the longer term they have a common interest, and there is a continuous drive towards improving efficiency and cost-cutting. This was indeed a long way from Smith's 'haggling and bargaining in the market'.

In the context of working in the DTI in those times, I just accepted traditional economic arguments, passed down from experts in the Treasury. I was no economist and didn't see any need to become an amateur one. Government policy was based on the doctrines of market pressures and market efficiency, as the main route to industrial competitiveness. Everyone accepted that trade statistics were produced too late to be useful, and junior staff were too busy to think about finding data that recorded with reasonable precision and currency what actually was going on in the economy. When I worked at Kewill Systems plc the most recent trade information was based on a survey in 1981, and this was being used by the company to plan for expansion into new markets in 1988. Large companies had their own teams who collected trade information but many smaller companies did not; Governments were failing their industries by not providing timely data. Fortunately Kewill Systems plc could augment the data with their own insights into new markets.

In 1990 Professor Michael Porter wrote his classic book, 'The Competitive Advantage of Nations'. I bought a copy and put it on show on the bookshelf in my office. The book is very heavy, but reasonably easy to read. Michael Porter tried to isolate the competitive advantage of a nation, defined as being the national attributes that fostered competitive advantage in an industry. The proposal was that to create and sustain competitive advantage in international terms there needed to be a high level of productivity and productivity growth in industry, and this depended on improving quality and greater efficiency. I did exactly what the author advised against; I read Chapter 1 'The Need for a New Paradigm' and then went straight on to the end of the book and read the Agenda for Great Britain, one of eight national agendas. I wanted to know what was seen to be special about Great Britain. The agenda is just 3 pages long, which was a disappointment, but at least it was just longer than that for Switzerland, but not as long as Germany.

The main themes were not a surprise: educational policies were trying to improve standards but there is still a lot more to do; R&D was high as a percentage of GDP but too much of it is in the defence sector; there was too much corporate complacency which needed to be replaced by vigorous domestic rivalry; and there was a need for a faster rate of new business formulation, with the added benefit of increasing employment while established industries are reducing staff as part of their growth in efficiency. There was nothing new here. Everyone who was involved knew the situation already, but sometimes it can be useful for an independent outsider to send the same message.

It had been rumoured that there were going to be changes and finally it was announced by Nicholas Ridley on 21 February that it had been decided to close down the Market Divisions.

Roy Williams, my Deputy Secretary and Chris Benjamin's boss, held a lunchtime party for Market Division staff at Grade 6 and above on 29 March. The diary details surfaced much later on the Internet else I would not know about it. I must have been too new to be invited, and I did not mind. It seemed that the Market Divisions had been an experiment and the time had come for a change. There was a philosophy that people worked better when things changed frequently, but it is not an approach that I agree with. However I can understand that new Ministers want to shape their own Departments.

My job and those of everyone around me ceased, and junior staff were dispersed. I was told to go on 'gardening leave' but I decided to spend the time in my office waiting to find a new job, and being seen around the Department. I had an annual season ticket, so it cost nothing to continue travelling to London, and sitting at home did not appeal. My secretary decided she preferred to come to work too. I took the opportunity to concentrate on my French and German lessons. Older colleagues were persuaded or pushed into early retirement. I had to give the retirement speech for my boss, Alan Conway, because no senior staff were left to thank him for all his work during his long career. Chris Benjamin retired too; his party was on 26 April but I wasn't invited. I suppose I had not been working for him for long enough either, and he must have expected me to be out of the office. He has published his memoirs too, in 2009.

Although it was a difficult time, I was fortunate that I had the six months at Grade 6, had carried out the work well, and was therefore unlikely to be moved back into a post at the previous grade. Where would I go next? Within the DTI there were few jobs at Grade 6, generally for specialists, and mainstream administrative civil servants would go directly from Grade 7 to Grade 5 when they are promoted. I had a lot of spare time so I made a list of all the Grade 6 jobs in the DTI, and matched them against my experience. This was not very promising. I was not yet judged as fitted for promotion to Grade 5, so I started to look around outside the DTI for jobs at Grade 6, including Head of Systems Engineering at the Rutherford Appleton Laboratory (RAL) near Harwell. The post had been held by Dr Rob Witty, whom I knew, and if I was successful then it would have been arranged as a secondment for me for five years from the DTI. It was also close to home, and I would swap the train journey to London for a short drive by car.

Just a few days before I was supposed to be attending the RAL for interview I had good news - there was a possible new post in Education and Training Policy, part of the Enterprise Initiative Division. I went and met the new Head of Branch, Evelyn Ryle, and we agreed that I would join her. Not only did I have a post, but I was able to bring my secretary, Barbara, with me, which was good news for her too. I was nervous because it was the first time I would be working for a woman, and Evelyn later admitted she was worried because she had never had a scientist working for her. One unusual question at interview was whether I could do several tasks at the same time. This caused a cough and a gulp, because I was so surprised at such a question. I had always spent my career doing lots of things at the same time and juggling with work in different areas. Maybe 'real' scientists can only do one task at a time. Or maybe women are different. It certainly gave me food for thought. I took up my new duties on 4 June, after just one month between jobs. I felt I was very lucky to have found a good job so quickly.

20 Education and Training Policy

The Secretary of State, the same Nicholas Ridley who had closed down the Market Divisions, had instituted a review between August 1989 and March 1990 of the role of the DTI in education and training. Certainly the DTI's interest was seen as being less central compared with the Department of Education and Science (DES), and the Department of Employment in particular its Training and Enterprise Division (TEED). DES had overall policy responsibility for education at all levels; TEED took the lead on training. The role of the DTI was to ensure that British business has access to an adequate supply of relevantly qualified people, and to secure recognition of business needs in the education and training programmes of the other two Government departments. The White Paper 'Higher Education: Meeting the Challenge' showed that this had met with some success. The review aimed to see whether particular activities or areas of responsibility of the DTI should now more appropriately be handled by either of the other main Departments.

The starting point seemed to be based around an assumption that everything could be moved, and a case had to be made for each area which we thought should remain. Ministers reached their conclusions quickly, and policy decisions had already been made by March 1990. Four programmes, with their budgets, would transfer to TEED by April 1991. These were Education Awareness in Teacher Education, the Teacher Placement Service, the Education/Business Partnerships (all three from the Schools area of the DTI) and the Management Charter Initiative (MCI).

Five key policy activities would remain with the DTI.

1. A High Level Group of senior (Grade 3) officials from DES, DTI, TEED and the Scottish and Welsh Offices to meet under the chairmanship of the DTI. This group would consider future proposals from the three main Departments that had a bearing on the other Department's interests.
2. To continue to have policy and programme work in training, especially involving the purchase of equipment aimed at alleviating skill shortages caused by the introduction of new technology
3. In Schools, to retain responsibility for the Enterprise and Education Initiative including the Work Related Curriculum.
4. To retain responsibility for engineering-related programmes, including the Teaching Company Scheme (which I used to

manage in 1982); to continue to have responsibility for training initiatives in support of its collaborative research programmes.

5. To retain Management Education as linked to business competitiveness including sponsorship of the British Institute of Management.

The meetings of the High Level Group were usually held in London, which meant that colleagues from TEED in Sheffield had a tedious journey commuting and usually tried to have several meetings while they were south. On some occasions we went to the Department of Employment offices in London and tried to use their technology instead and hold a meeting by video conferencing. The studios at the Department of Employment were specially installed to avoid the need for frequent travel by their own staff between London and Sheffield. While the technology may have worked well for small meetings with a focussed agenda, it was not a success when large numbers of people are involved at each end. There were maybe a dozen people in the studio in London, and a similar group in Sheffield. It was difficult to see what was going on in the other location; the camera concentrated on whoever was speaking, and this ignored much of the other side discussions. At times it all split into two separate discussions, one at each location, without any Chairman holding it together. Often it was impossible to identify who was speaking, for writing the minutes. I was not impressed with video conferencing and only used the facility once.

The overall reduction of activities meant that much of the past policy work continued in the DTI, but with a much smaller group of officials. At the time of the Review there were 42 staff, divided into two Grade 5 - led Branches, one Branch dealt with Schools, and the other with Further and Higher Education. Evelyn and I were therefore replacing Martin Stanley and Roger Brown respectively. Our boss, the Head of the new Enterprise Initiative (EI) Division, was Alan Titchener. Following the Review the two original Branches had been combined, and were now the Education and Training Policy Branch, Branch 5 in EI Division. The size of the new Branch was to be reduced from 42 staff to 23 staff by 1 April 1991. I knew that Barbara and I were expected to move out on 1 April 1991 too. Having just moved from Engineering Markets Division when that area died I had not expected to be found a posting which required me to reduce down another area. The top priority of my duties was to agree and implement a plan to reorganise and downsize the Branch. I was also expected to defend the budget figures in discussion with local Finance and Resource Management experts and input to negotiations with the Treasury during Public Expenditure Survey bilaterals. It had been agreed that budgets and work would be transferred to the Department of Employment and it was important that the right amount of resources were transferred, not too much.

The first task on arriving in my new job was to catch up with the current policy situation. I was given an academic paper, written by Roger Brown, which brought together what he had identified as relevant information and provided a rationale for what should be done on links between Higher Education and Business. When I arrived in post, Roger had not yet departed, and he tried hard to pass on much of his expert knowledge. Obviously the government policy on links between HEIs and Business was based on the green paper 'The Development of Higher Education into the 1990's' (published in 1985) and two more recent White Papers: 'Higher Education: Meeting the Challenge' (published in April 1987) and 'DTI - the department for Enterprise' (already mentioned in the context of my previous work).

Taking the various activities, Roger managed to summarise and categorise the types of links. The three main links were education and training; R&D and commercialisation of academic resources and know how, as well as a residual category of general links. Then Roger had looked at the benefits, and the costs as well as the extent, meaning how much of HEI's income was derived from business links. While information was variable in the UK there was no systematic information about links in other countries, and this was suggested as a topic needing a proper survey. Some attempt was also made at estimating factors preventing and promoting links. As a new entrant to this part of government I did exactly what a new Minister would do. I read the first page, looking at the Introduction carefully, and then skimmed through the detailed material about government policy. I already knew about the Green and White Papers. Then I flicked the pages until on the last page, page 11, I found the list of four main things that the government could do. I knew Roger and I was sure that his analysis was rigorous, so these recommendations would be worth reading.

It was stated that there were four main things that the Government can do:

1.   maintain pressure on HEIs to diversify their funding. This is probably best done by continuing to squeeze the percentage of their income from Exchequer grant;
2.   promote specific types of links eg the LINK scheme for promoting collaborative research between companies and HEIs, the Teaching Company Scheme, Integrated Graduate Development Scheme etc;
3.   continue to draw attention to the benefits of co-operation and encouraging others to do so;
4.   provide and/or help others to provide information about how to go about forging links.

Government is still doing exactly these things. The analysis offered in 1990 was not intended as a final neat report, but rather as a reference document for discussion within government. I recognised many of the programmes, although the statistics were new to me. I also recognised the difficulties of estimating the benefits and costs. I filed the paper away and got on with doing the work.

I learned a lot from working for Evelyn. In my previous job I was treated very much as a Senior Principal, whereas in this job I was the real Deputy to a Grade 5. It was a very different experience and one that I grasped and worked hard to fulfil. Evelyn's style of management was different to those I had seen before, and it worked well. There were Monday morning meetings of Section Heads, and everyone was expected to attend and contribute. It was a sharing of information, and a discussion of issues. I learned that our staff often had more flair than we had for finding the solution to specific problems, and that with good calibre staff leadership meant that we gave them the space to do their job. I was introduced properly to the style of Machiavelli. 'It must be considered that there is nothing more difficult to carry out nor more doubtful of success, nor more dangerous to handle, than to initiate a new order of things.' (extract from The Prince). Over ten years previously, a framed copy of the same extract had been placed on the wall of the Rayner Unit in Whitehall. And the concept of Elephant Traps was introduced, in relation to making sure that our Ministers did not accidentally trip over them. As in other posts, success in policy work was about credibility with Ministers and senior officials. I smiled at the cartoon image of my Minister being an elephant.

There were other simple things. I had purchased a nice Coalport china cup and saucer for my office, and my usual first action on getting to work was to make a proper coffee for myself. Barbara, tended to arrive in work later than me in the morning, and stay later in the evening. This suited me well because it meant she could complete dealing with any letters after I had gone home, but I did mean that I had to make my own pot of filter coffee, which I then stored in a Thermos flask. Evelyn had a different approach. She had arrived with an electric coffee filter machine which was set up early in the morning and was available to offer coffee to visitors all day. It made visitors seem more welcome, and I soon got my own machine, as well as a large tin of biscuits. I added a Royal Doulton tea set instead of the usual pottery coffee mugs, so that my office china matched that in daily use at home.

I found that two of my Section Heads were each doing a MBA by distance learning, and I wondered whether it was too late to benefit from this myself. I was still tutoring for the Open University, and there is a scheme whereby tutors are subsidised to study one course as a student each year. When I spoke about an MBA at home Pete's response was quick: 'Don't do an MBA; instead apply to the Open University to be a tutor for it'. This also had the advantage that I would receive a small income whereas studying an MBA as a student is expensive. Sue Pearce, one of the permanent OU staff in the Business School at Oxford arranged to meet me for an interview, and I soon became a tutor for 'Foundations of Senior Management', the one year foundation course for the MBA. It was a compulsory first course for all MBA students and started in the month of October, although my part of the course did not begin until January 1991. No single tutor was expected to be able to tutor all of it, with its mixture of marketing, human resources and finance.

The course had six parts, and they were paired for three different tutors. I was asked to tutor Part C: Accounting and Finance for Managers, and Part F: Strategic Use of IT. The strategic use of IT was easy, I had lots of relevant practical experience to offer, but the accounting and finance was more difficult in places. I did have some practical experience from looking at balance sheets and profit and loss as part of assessing companies for DTI funding. I remember that at one of my early tutorials I asked my students about their backgrounds, and found to my dismay that one of them was a qualified accountant. Fortunately MBA students are given a different type of tutorial to undergraduates. The Business School provided material for tutorials, and the emphasis was always on group working where the tutor facilitated the learning process. It was a nice contrast to the mathematics and technology courses which were mostly Question and Answer sessions, working through past exam questions. I was able to use the knowledge of the accountant, and that of the rest of the group, to generate an interesting discussion about the course material and apply it all to the example case studies. I always had a set of recent company Annual Reports, which matched those of the companies where we had shares, and these were very useful too. I continued tutoring the course until 1993, and then moved to tutor a different MBA course in 1994. I had just got to know the material well when it was time to change. Life in the DTI was very similar. As soon as I got to grips with the work there was a change.

Enterprise Initiative Division was a new Division, and the Divisional Work Programme for the year 1990/91 was only assembled in July 1990. Normally it would have been defined in the Autumn of 1989, stating the forward work programme from April 1990. As part of the annual budget cycle, each Branch had to make a presentation to their Deputy Secretary, in our case Elizabeth Llewellyn-Smith, to defend their work programme. It gave an opportunity for her to meet with her new senior staff. Deputy Secretary is the grade immediately below Permanent Secretary, and is very senior and powerful. Evelyn and I had only just arrived in post and approached the task with some nervousness. We were all worried about what this presentation would involve, and there was a lot of effort preparing the briefing material. We held a full scale rehearsal where we made the presentation to our staff, then made a few minor changes before we went to her office and made the formal presentation. In the event it worked well, and I was both pleased and relieved. My only previous contact with a Deputy Secretary had been to meet the Chief Scientist and Engineer, many years previously.

We found that Elizabeth Llewellyn-Smith was about to retire from the DTI in 1990, and would be replaced by Roy Williams, who had previously been in charge of the Market Divisions when I was working in Engineering Markets Division. I heard that she would be going to become Principal of St Hilda's College, my old college at Oxford. It seemed a good occasion to mention that I had been at St Hilda's College as an undergraduate and post-graduate student, so I wrote a short note to that effect and we met for lunch and talked about life at a lady's college at Oxford. Miss Llewellyn-Smith had been educated at Girton College, Cambridge. We met for lunch at the United Oxford and Cambridge University Club at 71 Pall Mall. I had continued as a Lady Associate member there, and I still use it as my home when I am visiting London. She was not a member. It was only later, in 1996, that ladies were able to be elected as Full Members, and many Heads of House from Oxford and Cambridge had resigned their membership until ladies were admitted on this equal basis. I was less worried about the principle of equality; I saw no reason to change and pay almost twice the price.

Dealing with the staff reductions in my Branch was urgent and my approach was to interview each member of staff individually, discuss the situation and identify their preferences. I asked 'open' questions and the interviews mainly involved listening. To my surprise and relief many staff were willing or even eager to move elsewhere and in addition a few staff were interested in early retirement or redundancy. This was a surprise to me. I thought it was going to be very difficult and that I would have the final responsibility to choose which staff would go and which would stay, but I did not have to deal with that situation. For those who wanted to move, it was important to discuss options with their Personnel Managers, but that was generally a constructive discussion. Our staff were all of good calibre and did not find it difficult to find new posts. Those who wanted to retire had to agree terms, but the formulae were well known, and there were no surprises. Staff training and development continued to be a priority, both for staff who would be remaining and for those who were moving elsewhere.

I was not going to be needed once the Branch was reduced in size, so I had to deal with my own situation as well. My Personal Development Plan for 1990 focussed on improving both staff and financial resource management. The Civil Service makes available a wide range of excellent courses, and I booked myself on to the course on Government Finance and Accounts. This was two days, on 20 and 21 November, and held at the Civil Service College in London. The aim was to explain the principal elements of Government Financial Planning, monitoring and reporting systems, covering key definitions, procedures, responsibilities and approaches, and to stimulate thinking about future issues. Other attendees came from a variety of Departments; of the 32 course members there were only 4 of us from the DTI. It made a nice change to attend a course and meet senior non-DTI people. It was a course designed for senior civil servants, and was one of seven courses which together formed the Senior Finance series. Two weeks before the course started I was sent a pre-course reading list, and it was suggested that I read Andrew Likierman's book on Public Expenditure, and the Cabinet Office/HM Treasury boxed set on Public Expenditure Management. Barbara was tasked with finding these for me, and she found the book but was not able to get the other material. I was told that there was just one copy in the DTI and it was not available for loan outside the senior finance team.

The course began at the beginning with a lecture on the history of the control of public expenditure, starting from the Magna Carta in 1217: 'No scutage or aid shall be imposed in the Kingdom unless by the common council of the realm, except for the purpose of ransoming the King's person, making his first born son a knight, and marrying his eldest daughter once, and the aids for this purpose shall be reasonable in amount.'

By 1822 the annual statement was first presented to Parliament, the Public Accounts Committee was set up in 1862 and in 1866 the Exchequer and Audit Act provided for an independent audit. Having set the historic context, it was then all downhill, as one might say. Lectures continued about the Public Expenditure Survey (PES), the role of the Treasury, the Public Accounts Committee and National Audit. I had already met these organisations in my previous posts.

In 1990-91 total public spending was expected to total £233.7 billion, or 39.5% of GDP. Within that, spending planned and controlled by central government was £180.6 billion. The timing of the course was important. Doing the course in late November we were able to look at the Autumn Statement, published in early November, which summarised the Government's expenditure plans from 1991-92 to 1993-94. In January or February individual departmental reports were published, and the Autumn Statement supplement set out these plans in more detail. It was crucial to know exactly how this all worked in one's own Department. There were lectures about Departmental reports, the duties of a Principal Finance Officer, Commercial Accounting and In-Year Monitoring. It was a good balance of looking at the big picture, and then making sure that money was properly spent within the individual Departments. There were a lot of lectures, and some excellent handouts were provided. I went back to my desk tired and with lots of reference material.

New courses for Boss and Secretary had just started, described as the Office Partnership Course, and Barbara and I went along together in February. Evelyn and her secretary had been on the course and recommended it. I had watched how Evelyn worked and it had already been suggested that learning to use dictation would be a good idea for me, instead of writing letters by hand for Barbara to type, and it would increase my output. It also gave Barbara an extra skill. We agreed to try it and see. Dictation is good if a speech is being written for Ministers because it forces the text to flow. Too often speeches are written which read more like learned articles, and the poor Minister has problems with the phrasing and grammar. This could even in its extremes lead to embarrassing improvisations.

Once the shape of the new Branch had been agreed in early 1991, it seemed an appropriate time to organise a Branch meeting to make sure that everyone knew what would be happening from April 1991 onwards. We therefore decided to organise an AwayDay. It was decreed that everyone in the new Branch would take part, and we hired a conference room for the day at the Scandic Crown Hotel, near Victoria Station, and just 5 minutes walk from the office. It was unusual to hold such meetings outside of the DTI buildings, because it is additional expense, but we made a successful case that it was important to get away for the day. It is impossible to take part at the same time as facilitating the event, and Evelyn employed a consultant to plan how we should spend our time, to prepare for the different tasks, to facilitate the event so that we achieved what we wanted to do, and to report back at the end.

There had been a lot of hard work done by our Section Heads before the AwayDay. A thick folder of papers was produced, starting with a one page Mission Statement and Objectives. The Branch aimed:

> 'To improve the business performance of the UK by making education, training and development meet the needs of industry and commerce.'

This was to be done by:

1. identifying and monitoring business needs and priorities;
2. helping business to articulate its needs, especially SMEs;
3. promoting awareness and commitment throughout business to achieve and maintain appropriate skill levels (including 'best practice');
4. demonstrating the links between education, training and development and performance/competitiveness;
5. monitoring progress;
6. encouraging improved understanding, cooperation/interaction between business and education, training and development;

7. being well informed about current policy, practice and infrastructure in education, training and development (in the UK and elsewhere);

8. influencing key organisations to take appropriate account of UK business needs.

The pack of papers was a good compilation of the relevant policy context within which we all worked. Lord Hesketh had arrived in the DTI in July 1990, with responsibility for design and education and training. The papers included the brief for the meeting held between Lord Hesketh and Alan Titchener on 13 September 1990, which was an introduction to the work of the Enterprise Initiative Division. Our Education and Training policy budget in the DTI was set to reduce from £30.4 million in 1990/91 to £14.7 in 1991/92 and to reduce slightly in succeeding years; this reflected the agreed transfer of work to the Employment Department. The Education and Training policy work was part of the overall Divisional Work Programme (DWP), and our current tasks fitted into the DWP for 1990/91, with its 6 main objectives:

1. To contribute to a competitive and open economy, and in particular to a more efficient market.

2. To facilitate the promotion of positive purchasing in the public sector as a means of improving supplier competitiveness.

3. To stimulate and cross-fertilise work on import substitution both within the Department and in the private sector..

4. To help business to remedy key skills shortages by supporting appropriate measures to match education and training courses more closely to business requirements.

5. To prosecute DTI and value for money objectives for EI Division budgets.

6. To secure efficient use of running cost resource allocated to EI Division.

My Education and Training Branch had detailed targets under 1, 4, 5 and 6.

In addition the Secretary of State had asked for a policy paper on Education and Training in November, which was completed and circulated just a few days before Christmas 1990. It was a useful example of what was involved in doing policy work; it was not simply a matter of someone writing a paper and sending it to the Secretary of State. The first draft of the paper started from a Principal, and was then discussed within the Branch. When we were happy it was circulated to colleagues elsewhere in the DTI, in key policy areas, for their comment. Many officials read and commented on drafts of the paper before it was sent to Ministers, and the procedure was that it was then seen by a junior Minister, in our case Edward Leigh, en route to the Secretary of State. The paper provoked a meeting between officials and Mr Leigh in the middle of January, and a covering letter was added by Mr Leigh on 24 January when the paper was finally sent to the Secretary of State. The paper was sufficiently important that copy recipients included the Permanent Secretary, three Deputy Secretaries and five Under Secretaries. The paper reviewed DTI policy towards education and training and its relationship with other departmental policies to encourage innovation and management development, and suggested possibilities for future action for the DTI. There were four problems identified:

1. British levels of education and training achievement do not compare well with those of our competitors.

2. Management seriously underestimates the skills required by itself and its workforce and does not invest enough in training, particularly in small and medium enterprises

3. The education system fails to understand and give sufficient weight to needs of its customers - future workers and those who will employ school leavers.

4. The vocational training system, fails adequately to cater for re-skilling the current workforce to meet the demands of increasingly sophisticated technologies and production methods used in modern industry.

Areas for DTI action included pump-prime funding of academic course material (already being done with a programme in advanced IT); an awareness campaign to target companies, especially small and medium sized enterprises (SMEs), about the link between competitiveness and training; encouraging larger firms to get their suppliers to improve links with education to address skills shortages; and establishing a new programme where small firms would be offered management assistance by local academics and their students.

A sympathetic junior Minister can often add a useful political sanity check on the views of officials. Mr Leigh said that 'he was clear that the DTI had a key role to play in influencing the educational and training framework laid down by the DES and the Employment Department, in persuading business of the need to invest in the training and development of its workforce at all levels, and in continuing to run a number of well-targeted schemes to help overcome market failures.' He liked the suggestion of an awareness campaign which could spread the important message of the link between training and competitiveness, recognising there were clear links between industry's ability to innovate and apply the results of R&D, on the one hand, and the skills level of its workforce, on the other.

All this comprised a very full and heavy set of key policy documents, which were the basis for the new Branch strategy, and everyone going to be in the new Branch received copies. By the end of the AwayDay, Evelyn had melded her new team, and it had been a successful working day. I moved out with Barbara in March 1991 having completed my work. My colleagues gave me a Good Luck card and a tapestry frame. They knew that I liked to do tapestry work and embroidery for relaxation. It was the first time I had ever been given a card and a gift on leaving a job and I was very moved.

I had been invited by Evelyn to complete my own scoring of my Staff Appraisal Report, which I found an interesting and useful challenge. This resulted in a discussion with her of my strengths and weaknesses, all done before the actual report was scored and the detailed comments were added. It was useful for me because there were then no surprises. My Annual Staff Appraisal Report for the year 1990/91 marked me Fitted for Promotion to Grade 5, with scores of 1 (outstanding) for Management, Drive, and Reliability, and scores of 2 (significantly above requirements) on everything else, except for Numeracy and Technical Competence where I scored a 3 which I still do not understand. I suppose it reflected the fact that the job did not require much numeracy, and there was no need for any special technical competence. Overall I was delighted with the report. Evelyn was my Reporting Officer; she was my immediate boss and wrote the part of my report which scored my performance in the job. In the Civil Service the promotion assessment is done by the Countersigning Officer, not the Reporting Office. So the marking there was not Evelyn's judgement, but rather the judgement of Alan Titchener, the Under Secretary, although he would obviously have discussed his assessment with her. He said 'Pauline's performance in the last year had demonstrated that she was more than ready for her own command as a G5. Her record speaks for itself: a first class manager who achieves results and the intellectual and judgemental qualities needed for all but the most testing of G5 policy assignments.' Being good at policy work was measured by how much I could be relied upon to produce sound advice to Ministers or senior officials. I was pleased that my efforts had produced results and that my skills had been recognised.

Although it was hard work, I enjoyed this posting, and was sad to move out elsewhere.

21 Longer Term Studies

In November 1990 I had a discussion with my Personnel Manager, and was hopeful for a new posting in April 1991 as I left EI Division. I had not then seen my report, so was content with another posting at the same level, which was Grade 6. There was a vacancy in the Research and Technology Policy (RTP) Division, in Branch 2 where one of the Grade 6, Brian Arthur, was due to leave.

It was interesting that this was the post previously occupied by Dr Andrew Wallard when he was Grade 6, and I had been rejected by him for a post of Grade 7 on promotion when I applied a long time ago to join the same group. So, it was back to the same part of the DTI where I had begun my policy career in 1981. This time my Under Secretary was Dr Colin Hicks. My previous Under Secretary in RTP had been Alex Williams, who then moved back to Teddington to become the Government Chemist, an interesting choice of job for someone who had been originally trained in physics! Dr Andrew Wallard had also gone back to the NPL, to continue his measurement career.

RTP Division was now based in brand new offices at 151 Buckingham Palace Road, abbreviated to BPR. The building was functional not pretty being entirely glass in a rectangular metal framework with a row of small shops on the ground floor and DTI offices above. It is next to Victoria Coach Station and there is a good view of it from trains approaching Victoria Station.

It was the furthest DTI building from Ministers, and seemed an unusual choice for locating a policy Division when it was well known that the most important officials are always close to the Secretary of State. It indicated to me and everyone else that maybe research and technology policy was not thought to be very important. As a platform from which to get my promotion to Grade 5 quickly it might not be the best area, although if I was really good then I might stand out there. My office was Room 342 on the third floor, working for Derek Howarth who was the Grade 5. I had 10 staff, divided into two sections, and a budget of just over £500k.

One of my responsibilities was that I was head of the LTSU - the Longer Term Studies Unit. Fortunately I was able to have a short hand-over period with Brian Arthur, who was still working in the post. Before leaving, Brian was completing a report on Technologies for the Future, which was a synthesis of a number of respected forecasters' views, together with personal observations and comment. He split technologies into three categories: Important Existing Technologies, Emerging Technologies and Future Technologies. I was reminded of the Central Aim of Norman Tebbit in 1984 when he identified the importance of awareness and adoption of key technologies as part of his innovation policy. The report was finally completed in September 1991. Brian and I had different styles of working. He certainly saw his role as adding his own expert view into policy making, whereas I relied on bringing together expert opinion. While I may be an expert in some areas I was definitely not planning to expand my personal expertise; using experts had always been my approach in previous jobs and that was not going to change now. Unfortunately, compared with previous jobs, in this job I did not have a very large budget with which to pay consultants.

In addition Derek Howarth had written a status report on the LTSU in February 1990, and this gave a history of the LTSU, a rationale for the work, and a strategy for the future. Long or longer term policy work in science and technology had been part of the work programme of RTP Division for many years. In the early 1980s there had been a Long Term Steering Group (LTSG). It was a committee of senior officials from the DTI and other Departments, which was serviced by a subgroup drawn from RTP and DTI's Economics Division, as well as the central Policy Planning Unit. The main task of this LTSG was to identify the trends which would, over the next 10 to 20 years, be the key influences on companies and the economy. Based on an appreciation of these trends, the LTSG aimed to challenge existing DTI policies so as to compensate for what they descried as 'the natural tendency of policy makers to concentrate on short term issues'. It was a well known problem and many academic papers were published at this time about the problem of short term thinking within Government. The work of the Steering Group aimed to influence the annual DTI budgetary discussions, at the so-called Sunningdale meeting, where the most senior DTI officials met at the Civil Service College at Sunningdale and decided how budgets should be divided.

By my arrival in 1988 long term work had been formalised by the formation of a Long Term Studies Group, confusingly also called LTSG. Note the change in title from 'steering' to 'studies'. In 1988 the LTSG had been a research group, and members were encouraged to publish academic papers. For example, Mike Porteous of the LTSG published a paper in the journal Scientometrics Vol 14 Nos 3-4 (1988) titled 'The Role and Development of Quantitative Indicators for Research and Technology Policy Making: Some Experience from the Department of Trade and Industry'. His article discussed quantitative science and technology indicators from the perspective of their usefulness in bringing longer term considerations into policy making.

He discussed three key problems.

1. Selectivity – How to identify the areas of research likely to underpin the longer term competitiveness of industry. The experience of other countries suggested that selectivity needed to

be thought of as a process of establishing a consensus between companies, government and the research community.

2. Collaboration – Following from the need to select priority areas of research, collaboration between companies and the research community was an important feature. In the UK, there had been a shift in emphasis from support for individual companies' applied R&D to more collaborative, pre-competitive research programmes. Looking overseas, it was hoped that S&T indicators would provide information on the research activities and expertise in potential collaborator countries.

3. Exploitation – Considering what the role of government should be in overcoming the barriers to innovation in firms, which could limit the exploitation of research.

The paper then looked at examples of current and prospective S&T indicators, including patent data, bibliometric measures and co-word analysis, and systematic monitoring of technical journals and other sources of up-to-date information.

The role of the LTSG was reviewed in 1988, and renamed LTSU with the word Group being replaced by Unit. As might be assumed from its name, the LTSU also carried out studies of longer term policy issues, which ranged from identification of the next generation of key technologies to specific studies for Departmental internal customer groups.

The work involved close liaison with independent University and Business School research groups with an interest in longer term strategic planning issues, and many studies were carried out by the three main centres - the Science Policy Research Unit (SPRU) at the University of Sussex at Brighton, the Programme of Policy Research in Engineering Science and Technology (PREST) and Manchester Business School, both at Manchester. As was increasingly the fashion, there was less work done in-house, and the skill of managing projects became more important than having staff with real expertise. Since the aim of the LTSU was to discuss the ideas with industry, the studies were usually published and distributed.

When I arrived in 1991 I found a filing cabinet full of these studies, neatly filed and collecting dust. My first step was to ask what had been done, and by whom. Barbara quickly provided a list of all 56 studies. The Longer Term Studies Group was only set up in 1985, and so their first studies dated from that time. With just one or two exceptions, which were studies which influenced DTI priorities, all the studies were freely available and often at no charge.

The list of 56 studies, from 1985 until 1991, are in Appendix D. I was surprised when I saw the full list. When I worked in Engineering Markets Division my Branch had benefited from funding for the LTSU Study on micro-engineering, but we had been unable to pursue the recommendations. Generally, it seemed to me that the LTSU had been publishing studies which were only read by a narrow group of policy makers and academics. The work did not seem to directly affect industry or influence industrial competitiveness. Most people in the DTI did not know very much about the LTSU, and I suspect cared even less, unless they were sponsoring a study using the LTSU budget. The budget was small so the studies were done by organisations and people who were not too expensive.

I had always liked to employ young DTI scientists on Short Term Experience Postings, and I was able to find someone from the Warren Spring Laboratory to carry out a study of the LTSU reports for me. One of his criticisms was that the reports were difficult to be interpreted by a non-specialist. My first question had been - What studies have been done, and by whom? On investigating the files, he found that the studies were a mixed bag of different quality, produced by different organisations in different formats. There was no consistent presentation, and many reports did not even have an Executive summary. As part of marketing its achievements, LTSU needed to have a house style, so I agreed a format for publishing future studies. This also involved labelling the study and wrapping it in a standard cream and blue cover, and making sure it was numbered as part of a sequence, so it did begin to look like each study was part of a series. Study No 58 on Remote Office Work by Surrey University was the first example which was printed in the new LTSU binding. A joint study by LTSU and CEST on Intelligent Packaging was in progress, and later was published in the same covers.

In recent years there had been many studies by post-graduate students at Manchester Business School, where Brian Arthur had agreed that their MSc students could do work for the LTSU on certain topics under supervision. I fully supported this approach. It was good value, and meant that studies were done on a guaranteed one year time scale. The results were also published, and so were directly in the public domain. This was the idea in the 1990s. We wanted to tell people in academia and industry about new technologies, not keep the information hidden in dusty files and told only to officials and Ministers. The problem with all these LTSU reports, and with the report on Technologies for the Future by Brian Arthur, was how to make it all useful and accessible to policy makers and Ministers. Much of the writing, being technical by definition, was opaque to normal people on the street. The main people who found it interesting were other experts. Something different had to be done to encourage long term thinking to be embraced by officials.

People from organisations who had carried out studies for the LTSU soon came to meet me, including Francis Narin of CHI Research Inc of the USA. When I saw the list of studies I had wondered about the organisation CHI because it was unusual in being from overseas. CHI had carried out two studies for the LTSU, and their expertise was in patents as an indicator of the linkage between science and technology. They had been asked to carry out the studies because they had a unique research expertise in the area. Although they were not a University organisation, CHI also published widely, including papers in the journals Research Policy, Research Management and Scientometrics.

Another important and very different contributor to long term thinking was the Advisory Council on Science and Technology (ACOST). It was the successor to the Advisory Council on Applied R&D (ACARD), whose reports I have mentioned earlier, and ACOST had an expanded mandate to look at science, not just R&D.

Formally, ACOST was set up to advise the Government on:

> Priorities for science and technology in the UK.
>
> The application of science and technology, developed in the UK and elsewhere, for the benefit of both the public and private sectors in accordance with national needs.
>
> The coordination in collaboration with Departmental Advisory Bodies of science and technology activities.
>
> The nature and extent of UK participation in international collaboration in science and technology.
>
> And ... To publish reports as appropriate.

The LTSU had a policy responsibility for emerging technologies and my predecessor Brian Arthur had been the DTI Assessor of the Emerging Technologies Committee of ACOST. With his departure I became the DTI Assessor in his place. The Chairman, Professor Len Maunder of Newcastle University, welcomed me to the Emerging Technologies Committee, and I tried to catch up where Brian had left off. I started by reading the file copies of recent ACOST reports.

The ACOST Report on Developments in Biotechnology was published in 1990, and was the fifth report by ACOST since their creation in 1987. It assessed the recent progress in biotechnology in the UK since the Spinks Report was published by a joint working party of ACARD and the Royal Society in 1980. Alfred Spinks was a founder member in 1976 of the Advisory Council for Applied Research and Development (ACARD), of which he was chairman from 1980 until his death in 1982. The present opportunities and the potential for the future were considered and the present UK position relative to our major competitors was appraised. Areas of strengths and weakness in the UK were identified, highlighting the possible impediments to successful exploitation, and a number of recommendations were made accordingly. Dr Ian Lawrence from my group was the DTI Assessor on the Life Sciences sub-group which carried out the work. This was normal; a suitable DTI scientist was allocated as

Assessor to the sub-groups, depending on the topic, whereas the Emerging Technologies Committee had an Assessor who was Head of the LTSU, ex-officio. Me.

The ACOST Report on Advanced Manufacturing Technology, the seventh report, was published in March 1991. My colleague Dr Mel Draper of Manufacturing Technology Division was the DTI Assessor on the AMT sub-group. The report concentrated on the contributions from those experts who had attended a discussion workshop in September 1990, so the report was able to be published very quickly. However there was a disadvantage in the workshop approach which was that the depth of the report suffered compared with other ACOST reports, and it was then criticised.

Then the ACOST report on Artificial Neural Networks, which was the fourteenth report, followed in 1992. There had been a discussion of experts in March 1991, which was attended by Dr Peter Rothwell of the DTI, and for this subject the DTI Assessor on the Neural Networks Working Group was Richard Tremayne-Smith of IT Division. The short Government response was published in 1992. I was interested in neural computing, and so kept my copy of the ACOST report and the published Government response.

In 1988, 1989 and 1990 there had been just 2 ACOST reports published each year, in contrast to 1991 when there were seven published. It was the time of a flurry of activity. I arrived as the new DTI Assessor to find that more new studies were in progress. One was on Human Factors. Its title was People, Technology and Organisations, and again Dr Mel Draper was the DTI Assessor, although I also attended meetings.

In response to a proposal from the House of Lords Select Committee on Science and Technology in April 1990, the Prime Minister had agreed that ACOST should prepare a strategic review of science and technology issues every three years. So in 1991 ACOST published the first strategic review, and its own programme of work. The report provided a strategic overview of global, European and UK science and technology issues. It also set out ACOST's proposed work programme for the next two or three years and suggested areas where work might be carried out by other organisations. It is interesting to reflect on their list of General UK issues, and remember that these were written in 1991.

'In order to generate a competitive technology-based economy in the 1990s and early 21st century, the UK needs:

a coherent framework of science and technology goals, strategies and policies, taking into account the international developments discussed above, and an adequate and well-directed national investment in science and technology activities;

positive public attitudes towards science and technology;

a supportive regulatory regime;

an effective system of education and training in science and technology;

a vigorous and excellent science and technology research base;

sufficient and effective industrial investment in R&D, in the exploitation of R&D and in innovation more generally;

an economic climate which encourages innovation, including sufficient economic stability to enable the risks and rewards of innovation to be sensibly evaluated;

effective mechanisms to identify and exploit emerging and generic technologies;

effective mechanisms to encourage technology transfer.'

While this list was all very true, what should I do with it? How could it influence my work on longer term strategy? Looking at it now, over fifteen years later, has there been progress? I enjoyed working with the senior members of the ACOST committees and trying my best to act as a bridge between their thinking and that of the DTI. It was not easy to suddenly arrive as a new official into such an established group and I was grateful to those ACOST members who helped me settle in. Unfortunately I never got to be involved with any ACOST publication from the start all the way through to the end, so was never able to make the sort of contribution for which a DTI Assessor is recognised. Looking at the ACOST publications now, the contributions of lots of other DTI people are listed, and it is as if I was never there. Did I have any impact? I know the answer to that question but not to the wider question of whether ACOST itself had an impact.

Developing strategy and leadership were acknowledged core skills for senior officials and when I saw a course on Strategic Leadership from 2 to 4 September at the Civil Service College I quickly registered. I have always been committed to improving my skills, and take advantage of any relevant learning opportunities. Of course, one of the main benefits of attending courses at the Civil Service College is the chance to meet senior officials from different Departments, as well as a few new colleagues from the DTI. Strategic Leadership was a course which was designed for officials at Grade 5, as part of their professional development, and so that they could develop their leadership skills. It was therefore perfect for me as a potential Grade 5, and I could measure myself against others who were already Grade 5.

So, what can be said about Strategic Leadership which takes three full days? The answer is quite a lot, even though it cannot cover the depth and breadth of an MBA course on Strategy which lasts a full year. The aim was to convey current thinking on principles of leadership and provide personal assessment and development of leadership strengths and skills.

The Content covered :

Introduction to leadership, with quotes from Tom Peters, Martin Luther King, The Queen, Henry Mintzberg and others.

Comparison between managers and leaders.

Diagnosing the Culture. SWOT (strengths weaknesses opportunities and threats) and managing cultural change.

Belbin and the chemistry of teams.

Formulating a vision and a mission statement.

Managing conflict.

Effectiveness of groups: forming, storming, norming, performing.

This is basic MBA material and I had already covered much of it, in theory as well as in practice, in my previous post. But sometimes it is important to be seen to do the right training, and skills developed on the job can always be honed. It also meant that I was better prepared to play the various management games. The course used industrial examples, and discussed Total Quality Management (TQM), about which I knew quite a lot already.

I was keen to work towards my own mission statement, and went back to my desk at the LTSU on 5 September with the following:

'Our purpose is to ensure longer term thinking contributes to all levels of Departmental policy making'

This was a fine mission statement, but there needed to be concrete aims and objectives.

'We (the LTSU) aim to achieve three things:

1. For the Secretary of State and Ministers to trust our advice
2. For the Chief Engineer and Scientist, and our Head of Division, to act on our advice on priorities
3. For senior and middle managers throughout the Department, working with us, to see for themselves the longer term pressures and trends which will be important in their area'

One of the problems discussed during the course was how to market the LTSU skills. It provoked the rhetorical question What is marketing? So I produced a short anecdote about the difference between advertising and marketing, which I had found in the Michael Bland's book 'Be your own PR man' when I was working at Kewill Systems plc.

> 'There is an old saying that if, at the end of a candlelight dinner, you tell a girl that you are fantastic in bed, it is advertising. If you tell her that she desperately needs a man and you are the right one, it is marketing. But if at the end of the dinner she says that she has heard you're a great lover, and please can she go to bed with you, that is public relations.'

At the end of the course we were each given a booklist and a book: Leaders. The Strategies for Taking Charge. The Four Keys of Effective Leadership by Warren Bennis and Burt Nanus. The book came with good recommendations and the idea was that we would read it when we got back to our offices. To give a flavour for the contents, the front cover had the quote 'Managers do things right. Leaders do the right thing'. This difference may be summarised as activities of vision and judgement, versus activities of mastering routines - effectiveness versus efficiency. I went through the text with a highlight pen and here are five phrases which chimed with my experiences in 1991.

1. 'The new leader is one who commits people to action, who converts followers into leaders, and who may convert leaders into agents of change.'
2. 'Power is the capacity to translate intention into reality and sustain it. Leadership is the wise use of this power.'
3. 'The business of making another person feel good in the unspectacular course of his daily comings and goings is the very essence of leadership.'
4. 'Leaders are masters at selecting, synthesizing and articulating an appropriate vision of the future. You are likely to be inundated with information about the future... it is in the interpretation of this information that the real art of leadership lies. Leaders require foresight, hindsight, a world view, depth perception, peripheral vision, and a process of revision.'
5. 'The role of a leader is much like that of the conductor of an orchestra. The great leader calls forth the best that is in the organisation.

This was what I wanted to do, but it needed a surprising lot of energy to actually deliver it in a real situation. Sometimes it seemed that I was trying to push against an enormous inert lump of jelly. At other times I had more success.

As an inspiration I stuck a list on my filing cabinet of 12 qualities needed by someone who will achieve their dreams. I sometimes needed to read some stirring words, and thought my staff might benefit from the words too.

Leaders who achieve their dreams:

They have confidence in themselves.
They have a very strong sense of purpose.
They never have excuses for not doing something

They always try their hardest for perfection.
They never consider the idea of failing.
They work extremely hard towards their goals.

They know who they are.
They understand their weaknesses as well as their strong points.
They can accept and benefit from criticism.

They know when to defend what they are doing.
They are creative.
They are not afraid to be a little different in finding innovative solutions.

This was also the time I started decorating my office walls with posters and pictures. I had been lucky throughout my career; I had never had to share an office. I got promoted to Grade 6 at the time when staff at Grade 7 and below who moved into new buildings had to work in open plan offices. 151 Buckingham Palace Road was the first of the new DTI buildings to be open plan. It was an economy measure and enabled more people to be fitted in the same area. There were benefits too in terms of managing staff and seeing what was happening. At Grade 6 I still had my office with four walls, a roof and a door, although the size was compact. When I was out of the office my staff used my room for confidential meetings.

I had a calendar which was of Birds of Prey. I liked the beautiful pictures and had been on a falconry course at Mary Arden's House near Stratford-upon-Avon. But the real reason for the calendar was the dual meaning of birds – emphasising progress for women in the Civil Service. I also purchased a nice print of St Hilda's College by Valerie Petts, a view of London from space, and a spectacular large photograph of Marlow Bridge on the River Thames. There was a good framing shop in Buckingham

Palace Road, Kemp and Co. They did all the framing for me, and also had a service which I used for framing my tapestries and embroideries.

Consideration of longer term issues does not always mean that new work had to be done. In many cases other organisations, public and private, UK and foreign, are already engaged in such work and publish reports. Maintaining awareness of all this work is important and I found I was already a member of the 6 Countries Programme (6CP) and the Business Futures Network (BFN). I immediately inherited from my predecessor a number of overseas diary commitments for the meetings of these two groups. I decide to attend two or three meetings and decide whether it was worthwhile.

22 Six Countries Programme

The Six Countries Programme (6CP) on Aspects of Government Policies towards Technological Innovation in Industry was an international study group which had been established in 1974, following a series of UNECE meetings. It was established at the instigation of Walter Zegveld of the TNO, in the Netherlands. TNO is a technical research organisation, based in The Hague, which supports Government policy making in the Netherlands. The 6CP was established as an informal group which was representative of government organisations, yet could examine and discuss freely policies and mechanisms to stimulate a higher level of innovative activity, especially in Europe. There were four countries represented at first, but this increased to six in 1976 and by the time I was involved in 1991 there were ten: the Netherlands, Germany, France, UK, Canada, Belgium, Sweden, Austria, Ireland and Finland. The Chairman changed regularly by rotation but the secretariat was fixed, located at the TNO. The name, the Six Countries Programme, remained in spite of the number of participating countries exceeding six. The Six Countries Programme was an international network and forum between experts and practitioners engaged in research in innovation and related public policies. The members were policy makers in Government and academics who researched policy making. It aimed at a better understanding of the innovation processes and their development, and at an assessment of the impact of science and technology on public policies and programmes.

Each year two major events were held on research aspects of innovation, and I was pleased to find the events were held in English. The spring meeting had a specific theme, formal presentations and discussions. The autumn workshop was more informal with keynote speakers to stimulate participation in interactive discussions. Attendance at these events was by invitation only, and each country had to nominate suitable speakers and attendees for each event. I relied on my DTI colleagues to make suggestions for attendees, as well as discussing ideas for speakers with well known British academics. A report or book was published eventually after each event. These books were usually quite academic in nature, were difficult to read, and this made their circulation limited. I inherited a row of these books and wondered what to do with them.

In the 1980s there had been much discussion at meetings of the 6CP on whether there was such a thing as an innovation policy, and whether it could be articulated as a formal government policy and implemented in formal programmes. The outcome was the definition of 'the systemic approach' which recognised the intensive interactions between all elements of society and the strong interdependencies between technology, economics and politics. Innovation policy if it was to be successful must take these into account. It must be not merely an articulated policy but an attitude of mind pervasive of all those formulating what are the implementing policies and programmes – research, education, industry, information, environment, manpower/employment, local government and finance. An innovation policy by creating a common attitude would become the coordinating instrument, enabling each institution to perceive its role within the wider framework and creating a climate within which each can more favourably carry out its role.

The focal point of a 'systemic' innovation policy is the entrepreneur. It is his or her investment in industrial innovation which creates economic wealth. Government can pick neither innovations nor projects nor winners. It cannot itself create wealth and there is no linear progression from research to innovation, from tax relief to creative use of technology or from other mechanisms to those entrepreneurial decisions which productively create wealth. These discussions about innovation policy had generally taken part between a limited number of experts and policy makers. In 1985, to celebrate the 10th anniversary of the 6CP, the evidence and some of the thinking was published to expose the ideas to a wider public. In the UK, Ministers were ready to embrace the idea that Government could not pick winners, and that responsibility for wealth creation rested with industry.

The UK was a very active participant in the 6CP and well respected for its contributions. From 1989 to 1990 my predecessor Brian Arthur had been Chairman of the Six Countries Programme, and the meeting in the spring of 1990 took place in London. The locations of the meetings were not fixed, and each country took turns to host them. London was a popular venue because it was so easy to get there from all the other participating countries. It was made clear to me that being Chairman was an honour awarded to an individual, and was something which I would have to earn. It was not something that I inherited. When Brian moved on and I arrived the Chairman became Asje van Dijk from the Ministry of Economic Affairs in The Netherlands. For a while both Brian and I represented the UK on the Steering Committee, until the demands of his new job meant that he could no longer take part. Most national participants in the Six Countries Programme seemed to spend their entire careers working in public policy, technology forecasting, foresight and scenario planning, whereas I saw my participation as just another jigsaw piece in a more diverse career. Perhaps it was for that reason that I had been brought in to the job and Brian had been transferred to another area. I visited Asje van Dijk and his team in The Hague several times, to compare notes on policy work in our two countries, and to talk about future Six Countries Programme discussion topics and potential speakers.

After my first visit to The Hague I decided to stay overnight in Amsterdam in future. It was easier to fly to Amsterdam after work in the evening, and then go to The Hague by train the following morning for meetings. I also preferred staying in Amsterdam, although the standard hotel which was recommended near the Railway Station could be noisy at night. When we went to Amsterdam on holiday we preferred to stay at one of the many little hotels on the banks of the canals.

The first 6CP meeting I attended was the 31st meeting, the autumn workshop on Technical Competence and Firm Strategy, held in Stockholm in November 1991. I remember the conference dinner was held at the Vasa Museum, which had only been opened in 1990. It had a large hall where the warship Vasa, the only intact 17th century ship in the world, was preserved.

I next attended the 32nd meeting, on the subject of Lean Production. It was the spring 1992 meeting and held in Stuttgart. I had just organised the purchase of a HP95 palmtop computer, which I used to make my notes and then transferred them across to Barbara who sorted out the spelling and grammar. Although I had intended to do more dictation work, I found that using the palmtop was more convenient. Typing with one hand on a little qwerty keyboard was prone to errors, but it was so much more efficient for me to do the notes imperfectly in real time, instead of spending hours at my desk afterwards.

I enjoyed the optional conference visit to the famous Mercedes Benz car manufacturer, based in Stuttgart. Having already some knowledge of manufacturing techniques, and an interest in engineering, I found the meeting added insights to the use of the technology and I could contribute something from my own background. Everyone was encouraged to participate personally, not to bring a formal brief representing their official Government position. Although lean production was seen as a management technique for manufacturing companies, many of the basic ideas were translatable into a service environment, and this included the Civil Service.

Then I attended the autumn workshop meeting on User-Producer relations in the Innovation Process which was held in November 1992 in Helsinki. I cannot imagine why the Steering Committee agreed that a meeting in Finland should be held in November. The problem was that participants from Finland wanted to hold a meeting in their own country, and no-one else could offer an alternative venue in the autumn. There was good advance warning of the trip and I remember that I had previously purchased a heavy green Austrian Loden coat, during a business trip to Vienna, and I had a warm boating hat with ear flaps, as well as good winter boots and gloves. The temperature outside in Helsinki in November was well below freezing point. Fortunately the meeting was held at the Technical Research Centre of Finland (VTT) at Espoo, near Helsinki, and accommodation was provided on the campus so there was no need to commute from a central hotel. I arrived at Helsinki airport, then caught the airport bus and went straight out to the meeting. I remember seeing a white Arctic hare while walking through the snow on site to my room.

The Steering Committee and the organisers all met for dinner before the conference started, and we were taken to a Russian restaurant, which was very interesting. Speaking neither Finnish nor Russian I had to rely on colleagues to order the food. I need not have worried; it was all very enjoyable. The Russian food was good, although from what I glimpsed of the prices wines and vodka were expensive. I think we started with a glass of Russian Champagne, which sounds very expensive but would have been cheaper than the French equivalent. Of course, it was only a short trip across the water from Helsinki to Tallinn and St Petersburg, so I would expect a Russian influence. Our Finnish hosts organised a good meeting, with a fine conference dinner on the first evening. There was one small problem on the second day when the Chairman for one of the sessions did not appear and I was asked to take on the role, at short notice. I agreed and was surprised when I was later presented with a little iittala glass vase, made in Finland, for my efforts. I gathered that small token gifts were common for the session Chairman. It was only worth a few pounds but was a nice gesture.

After the conference ended there was a Steering Committee meeting to plan future events, so I was committed to stay an extra night on business which was a Friday. I still had not been able to visit Helsinki and I paid for one extra night myself in order to see something of the town. I therefore had the whole of Saturday to look around and flew home on Sunday. Pete said that he was definitely not interested in a weekend in Finland in November and preferred to stay in the warm at home. In spite of my warm clothes, I was not prepared for the temperatures, and planned my exploration depending on the location of nice warm buildings. Churches were well heated, and in one I found a choir practising for a concert later that day. I did no shopping, and anyway the shops closed early on Saturday. I simply wanted to look at the sights. When I got all my photographs back I thought the camera was broken. All the pictures were in black and white, and everything was a dismal grey colour. Then we noticed that the brake lights of the cars were red and the pictures were really in colour, but there was no colour in the scenery. Leaving Finland I bought a Duty Free reindeer skin rug at the airport. It only stayed in the house for a year because it moulted, then I passed it on to a charity shop. The local sweet red cloudberry liquor was a better buy, and lasted longer.

23 Business Futures Network

Geoff Woodling set up the business futures practice within the Stanford Research Institute (SRI) in the USA, and then he set up the Business Futures organisation in 1988 with Jim Smith when they left SRI, and this included the Business Futures Network (BFN).

I was invited to replace Brian Arthur and take part in the BFN, which comprised a group of corporate executives from international companies who contributed to a scanning process. It was a very different type of group to the 6CP and I was the only civil servant present. In order to take part in the network meetings, and to gain the benefit of the conclusions, I had to contribute information. During the year I read a lot of interesting articles as part of my job, and those which seemed to me to be a potential signal for change were copied and filed. My contribution was sent to the Business Futures secretariat, as were the contributions of all the participants. The difficult task was then for them to take all this material, and to identify the issues and develop scenarios, especially those which had business implications of changing values and lifestyles. Scanning based disciplines have been the core activity of Business Futures, and enable the identification of the potential sequels of long-term issues and trends. They have been employed over many years to develop a valuable long term record of signals of potential change.

The results of the scanning process were disseminated at the BFN meetings, which were held twice each year, but were not published. The results were strictly confidential to participants although I circulated a note to my DTI colleagues. The first meeting I attended was held in Vienna. I stayed in a cheap hotel, the Pension Nossek, which was conveniently in the pedestrian part of the centre of town, and close to the cathedral. It had been recommended by the DTI travel people. Everyone else stayed at the hotel where the meeting was being held, and I vowed that I would do that for the next meeting. BFN had negotiated a special cheap conference rate and it was not much more expensive than paying day rate at the conference and then overnight elsewhere. It was just around the corner to the Pension Nossek that I found a shop which was selling the heavy winter green loden coats. I knew that I would be attending the 6CP meeting in Finland in November, and I had nothing suitable to wear for the winter weather. I had to limit the amount I paid because Austria was not then part of the European Union; they joined only in 1995 and so I was limited by the duty free allowance. Pete had never been to Vienna and so we decided that I would stay after the meeting, and he would join me for the weekend.

As part of the conference I had already seen the evening performance of the wonderful Lipizaner horses of the Spanish Riding School. I had enjoyed it very much and managed to get two tickets so we could both watch the Saturday morning practice to music. The breeding of Spanish horses in Austria dates from 1562. In 1991 it was the only place where the Classical style of courtly riding was still performed. There were a series of spectacular aerial exercises, including the levade where the stallion raises both its front legs, and the capriole where he leaps into the air and kicks out with his hind legs.

At the end of the BFN meeting it had been agreed where the next meeting would be held, and with the unification of Germany it was proposed that the meeting should be held in Berlin. Everyone agreed, and when the invitation arrived I found it was going to be held at the famous Kempinsky Hotel in old West Berlin. I found it in my Michelin Guide, and worried about the costs. To my surprise the conference package deal was not very expensive and I contacted the hotel and arranged that I extended my stay over the weekend at my own expense. Pete wanted to come and visit Berlin once the meeting had finished. My hotel room was large and so there was no problem with him sharing it and I did not need to move room.

As the date of the meeting, around 9 April 1992, got closer we found it was going to clash with the date of the General Election. John Major was Prime Minister and had inherited a large majority when he replaced Margaret Thatcher. It was clear from the opinion polls that he was going to lose a lot of seats at the election, but the question was whether we would also have a change of Government. It was my first experience of being involved in preparing briefing papers for an election. There is a protocol about briefing a new Government, and different sets of briefing have to be prepared in advance for each of the possible winners, taking account of their manifesto promises. To my surprise the Conservatives won, but with a much reduced majority of 21.

I went out to the Berlin equivalent of Selfridges and bought a box of 6 German cut-glass Champagne glasses. Pete arrived at the Kempinsky Hotel having bought a bottle of champagne as he came through the duty-free shops at Heathrow airport, and we toasted the new Conservative Government. Of course, our joy was not a political statement. It was purely financial. We expected that an incoming Labour Government would increase income tax, and everyone remembered the times when Harold Wilson raised the top level of income tax to 98%. Our joint salaries were high and this level of taxation would have been a serious problem for us.

We continued with an excellent weekend holiday, walking around the centre of Berlin, marvelling at the remains of the Berlin Wall, visiting the Zoo and listening to a group of South American buskers playing Pan Pipe music in the shadow of the ruins of the cathedral. We ate far too much, having discovered a basement beer cellar which also did solid Bavarian food. Their speciality was schweinehaxe - a whole roasted pork knuckle each.

For meetings of the 6CP and the BFN it was important to maintain language skills, so I continued to fit in weekly individual language lessons in both French and German.

24 Developing a Longer Term Strategy

Whereas there had been some contact with Ministers in previous posts, when I arrived as head of the LTSU there was none. Indeed it was initially thought that Ministers would not want to have a group of officials looking at long term policy; it might be seen as a threat. Then Dr Geoff Robinson arrived as Chief Engineer and Scientist, on secondment from IBM, replacing Dr Ron Coleman. After being Deputy Director at the NPL, Dr Coleman had been Government Chemist before becoming Chief Engineer and Scientist, so he had spent his career in the scientific Civil Service. Dr Robinson came from a very different background having spent his career at the IBM research laboratory at Hursley. They did have something in common, they were both eminent scientists. Dr Robinson requested that longer term thinking should make a greater contribution to DTI policy-making.

My boss Derek Howarth retired and he was replaced by Ian Downing; Ian had worked with the Club of Rome and was interested in strategic planning. The LTSU remit was extended so we were tasked with increasing awareness of longer term pressures and trends and promoting skills in longer term thinking throughout the DTI. It matched well with my earlier mission statement, and the concrete aims and objectives which went with it.

The Innovation Advisory Board (IAB) had been set up late in 1988 to advise the DTI on matters of innovation policy. The Board was chaired by Lord Chilver of Cranfield, and comprised an unusually eminent mixture of senior people from industry, commerce and academia. Innovation policy had suddenly become a very important policy topic. There was now an agreed definition of innovation. It was emphasised that innovation was not limited to R&D. Innovation was the management of change, and that occurred anywhere in the cycle from invention to post-production servicing. Comparisons of international performance, especially the work of Professor Michael Porter, matched with the analysis of the IAB in its paper 'Innovation: City Attitudes and Practices' and the results of the conference on 'Innovation and Short Termism' which took place on 25 June 1990. This conference was very well attended with many extremely senior participants. I did not attend, but was given my own copy of the proceedings. The participants listed from the DTI included the Permanent Secretary, Sir Peter Gregson, and Dr Ron Coleman the Chief Engineer and Scientist. Oscar Roith, a past Chief Engineer and Scientist now retired, was there too, as well as the Chief Scientific Advisor of the MOD, and Deputy Secretaries from the DTI and the Treasury. There were Chairmen and Chief Executives of very prestigious companies. The opening address was made by the Secretary of State for

Trade and Industry, Nicholas Ridley. In his conclusions he had only two points to make. The first was that there was little conclusive evidence one way or the other about City short-termism. There did however appear to be problems in the relationship between industry and the City, particularly in relation to communication. The second point was that these problems needed to be tackled from both sides. Nevertheless they represented only one factor influencing corporate performance and companies must still take responsibility for decisions on innovation.

Other organisations were also involved with raising the profile of long term thinking. An important example was the input from the Confederation of British Industry. One example was their work during 1990, in cooperation with the management consultancy Sciteb, which resulted in publication of a report 'R&D Short-Termism? Enhancing the R&D performance of the UK team'. This work involved confidential interviews with 32 directors of major UK industrial companies, 15 directors of major investors and a number of knowledgeable observers. It also involved collation and analysis of statistical data on companies from the UK and worldwide, looking for evidence of relationships between R&D expenditure and stockmarket value. The conclusions were that UK industry does under-invest in R&D, but there are substantial sector differences, especially between chemical-based industries and physics-based industries.

From all these contributions came proposals which were published by the IAB in October 1990 for a programme of action. The programme would be directed at gaining more recognition of the importance of innovation and at stimulating more innovative activity, and also at encouraging the longer-term attitudes and practices necessary to secure the prosperity of UK companies and of the UK economy. There were three areas for action. The first area was Communications. The second area was Corporate Management and Shareholder Relationships. The third area was Investment Management Objectives. It was the first area of Communications which was going to influence DTI's innovation policy.

The general objectives in Communications were to make industrial management more aware that their innovation plans should rank with their international competitors; to help such managers improve the presentation of such plans; and to make analysts and shareholders more responsive to them. There was a long list of specific actions:

> press home the IAB message that 'Innovation is vital for profitable and sustainable growth' through a targeted campaign;
> encourage the introduction of an 'R&D Scoreboard' for the UK;
> press for the definition and disclosure of other intangible investments, including training and design;

draw up guidance for better company presentation of innovation plans to analysts, shareholders and the Press;

confirm with institutional shareholders that they are encouraging companies to bring forward innovation plans for discussion;

discuss with analysts and institutional shareholders any steps to ensure that their awareness of technological issues compares well internationally;

work with the economic and financial Press on developing a culture based on innovation-led growth.

The Innovation Unit was established in the DTI in 1991, headed at Grade 5 by Dr Alistair Keddie, with offices in the new DTI building at 151 Buckingham Palace Road. I was asked to help with the initial stages, before Alistair arrived in post. According to the OECD Frascati Manual, innovation was defined as follows:

'Scientific and technological innovation may be considered as the transformation of an idea into a new or improved saleable product or operational process in industry and commerce or into a new approach to a social service. It thus consists of all those scientific, technological, commercial and financial steps necessary for the successful development and marketing of new or improved manufactured products, the commercial use of new or improved processes and equipment or the introduction of a new approach to a social service.'

This was too long and was unsuitable for practical purposes and the DTI snappy definition of innovation was 'the successful exploitation of new ideas'. This definition was later expanded by the CBI.

'Innovation is the process of taking new ideas effectively and profitably through to satisfied customers; it is the process of continuous renewal involving the whole company and is an essential part of business strategy and everyday practice'.

The aim of the Innovation Unit was to bring about a significant change in national attitudes towards innovation and to promote market driven innovation as the key to competitiveness and sustained wealth creation. A key feature of the Unit was that it was not staffed with career civil servants; it included many senior managers seconded from industry whose role was catalytic. They were to develop activities and partnerships between business, professional, education and other bodies.

The IAB set up an Action Team on Communications (IAB ATC), chaired by Dr Peter Williams who was a member of the IAB and Chairman and CEO of the Oxford Instruments Group. Progress with the R&D Scoreboard was rapid. The first UK R&D Scoreboard was produced by Company Reporting Ltd and Sheffield University Management School, and published by The Independent newspaper on 10 June 1991. It ranked UK companies by R&D spend, listed the Top 10 UK companies by R&D spend, and then made an international comparison of R&D spend by the Top 100 R&D spenders. In the Preface the Secretary of State, now Peter Lilley, welcomed the report and noted that although R&D spend was rising UK firms were not doing enough compared with their main competitors in other countries. He said that spend on R&D for many sectors and companies was crucial for innovation, and companies must give greater priority to their innovation plans. The UK R&D Scoreboard was published annually, and was followed by the publication of a European R&D Scoreboard. Often good ideas from the UK are copied at European level.

The first UK Innovation Lecture, sponsored jointly by The Royal Society, The Fellowship of Engineering and the DTI was delivered on 6 February 1992. It was given by Mr Akio Morita, who was one of the two founders of the Sony Corporation in 1964, and was then the Chairman of the Board. He had been personally associated with many innovations in the electronics market. The lecture, attended by an audience of 300 invited guests, was part of a DTI initiative to raise awareness of the importance of innovation in all sectors of the business and education communities as well as among the public at large. The title of his talk was 'Science alone is not Technology. Technology alone is not Innovation'. He asserted that true innovation was made up of three key elements: creativity in technology, creativity in product planning and creativity in marketing.

He also had very strong views on one of the most important problems facing the UK. When asked by the Prime Minister, Mrs Thatcher, when she visited Japan whether he had any advice to give the UK he responded 'please change your society's concept to make people respect engineers as they do solicitors or chartered accountants'. A sentiment I fully agree with.

It took longer to make progress with an Innovation Plans Handbook. Prepared by the IAB ATC with help from consultants Arthur D. Little and published in January 1993, it was titled 'Getting the Message Across. Improving communication on innovation between companies and investors'. The handbook addressed four topics: the vital importance of innovation; the link between innovation and business strategy; how companies can communicate their innovation strategy to the investment community; and how investors can evaluate this strategy. It included two checklist cards.

The Manager's checklist asked five important questions:

1. Are our plans for innovation consistent with our business strategy?
2. Are we confident we have the skills to achieve the desired results?
3. Do we have an appropriate balance of innovation activities?
4. Have we got the best balance between low and high risk and short and long-term projects?
5. Have we calculated the net financial impact?

There was also the Investor's checklist, again with five questions.

1. Is the company using innovation appropriately to support its business strategy?
2. Are the company's plans for innovation workable?
3. Have risks been realistically assessed?
4. What will the net financial impact be and is it accounted for properly?
5. Do the risks and returns translate into long-term shareholder value?

Dr Colin Hicks was budget holder for the Innovation budget and for the Measurement and Technology and Standards budget, in his role as head of the Research and Technology Policy Division (RTP). He decided to ask for 5 Year Forward Looks (5YFL) from users of these budgets as an input to priority formulation and budget discussions. Research Councils had produced Forward Looks for many years, and it was deemed time for the DTI to do so too. It was a good idea and this new work was a high priority for me and my group in the LTSU, and I welcomed the increased and interesting workload. Barbara scheduled bilateral meetings for me with all of the spending Divisions to discuss their 5YFLs and it was expected that there would be an increase in the number of long term studies carried out, as my staff in the LTSU would also be asked to help their spending colleagues identify the longer term pressures and trends in their areas. My colleagues elsewhere in the DTI looked with shock at the problem of producing these 5YFLs. It had been a serious shock when they had been required to write ROAME statements, describing the Rationale, Objectives, Appraisal, Monitoring and Evaluation for every new programme of work, some years earlier.

This requirement for everyone to provide a 5YFL resulted in a flurry of work, and contracts were placed by many Divisions with suitable consultants. I went to a presentation by one of these, Dr Roy Farmer, who had been asked to manage a study to 'Define what it is the DTI's

Information Technology Division should be doing in the area of IT standards to ensure that the UK IT infrastructure is in good shape in 5-10 years time'. It became called the UK IT Futures Study, because it was much more extensive than just IT standards. The work began in July 1991, with the final report made in May 1992.

One aspect was to identify the 'gap' i.e. the areas which needed to be addressed more effectively. The approach had four main stages. The first was to identify the IT trends and the business priorities. Technology and application trends were listed and clustered, resulting in 16 clusters which were identified as applicable to business objectives. Twelve key economic sectors were identified and a profile was developed for each; from this fifteen common business objectives emerged. The second stage was to draw a box diagram, or matrix, of technology trends against business objectives looking for intercepts, and answering the question: 'Which of the technology trends was a high priority towards a particular business objective?'   For each high intercept, the drivers and inhibitors which will affect the take-up of potential were identified. Finally the key drivers and key issues were obtained.

I was interested in the use of scenarios for getting insights on the future, instead of reading through boring long lists of unpronounceable technical jargon. While I could cope with most areas of new technology, it is well known that stories have a much more long-lasting effect on people, and scenarios are basically a number of alternative stories about the future.

The Shell Group and its operating companies had been using scenario planning for some 20 years and Dr Oliver Sparrow, then their Chief Strategist, produced a discussion paper 'Management Matters - scenarios for Britain'. The paper encapsulated a number of ideas and insights distilled from discussions and seminars. He produced two scenarios. The first was called 'Layers and Pockets', where the key elements were that Europe has little relevance to the bulk of the population, and professionals form an over-arching layer of consensus of good practice. Change is achieved in a managed, tolerable manner, and standards and regulation become harmonised. The second and alternative scenario was 'the Fraternal State'. Here problems were created because the less educated and integrated in society do not feel a part of what is happening. Political response was piecemeal and resulted in a 'Europe of the Regions'. For companies this meant conflicting tiers of regulation and local pressures, with emphasis on the consumption of wealth rather than its generation.

I met Oliver for the first time when he gave a presentation on all of this to officials. I knew he was by background both a scientist and an economist, and was the Chief Strategist at Shell. I attended the discussions without having the chance to read the paper in advance, and so it is probably no surprise that I rejected the two scenarios in my own mind, and wondered whether it was all too academic to be useful. It would probably have been better to have been involved in the construction of the scenarios, but I was not. The problem was not about the content or the detail but about how the material was communicated to us.

In 1993 the Group Planning team at Shell produced 'Global Scenarios 1992 – 2020', which represented two different futures. These stories were created to serve three different major functions. Firstly they helped prepare for discontinuities and sudden change. Secondly they created a common culture, or language, through which the future can be imagined. And thirdly they challenged the mental maps we hold.

The first scenario was 'New Frontiers' and was a story of growth, turbulence and change. Liberalisation, both economic and political, creates enormous upheavals as markets and societies dismantle long-standing barriers, and poor countries begin to claim a larger role for themselves on the world stage. The four key aspects are Shift to the Poor; Business Challenged; New Priorities in Rich Countries and High Energy Supply and Demand.

The second scenario was 'Barricades' where people resist liberalisation because they fear they might lose what they value most – their jobs, power, autonomy, religious traditions and cultural identity. This resistance leads to an increasingly divided world of rich against poor, region against region, insiders against outsiders, and ethnic and religious groups against their neighbours. The four key aspects are Politics of Identity; Poor Marginalised; Energy is Bad and Constricted Markets. People can react with hope, and seize the opportunities of 'New Frontiers', or as in 'Barricades' they can react with fear and try to erect barriers to liberalisation in order to protect what they value. The strategic question is: Which reaction will dominate?

At about this time I joined the Strategic Planning Society (SPS) on behalf of the LTSU, and started to attend their meetings. There were not many Government Departments as members then, although later this changed. The SPS published a magazine and also offered a number of seminars and courses, from their base in London. I subsequently attended a course on scenario planning which enabled me to contemplate using scenarios as a management tool, but it still did not help me break the ice with discussions with expert economists. The SPS course on scenarios began with a slide by Gareth Price which said 'Those who claim to forecast the future are all lying even if, by chance, they are later proved right.'

At the same time I was reading a publication 'Global Trends in 1992', which also looked forward for 10 years, and was prepared by the PA Consulting Group. This I could understand, and I recognised their four influences on business - institutional and political developments, long-run and conjunctural economic trends, social and demographic shifts, and advances in technology and organisation. I had to look up the meaning of conjunctural in a dictionary. Although this volume was also written by economists, it was a much more enjoyable and interesting to read, and therefore had more influence.

The LTSU had also contributed towards the costs of a major study by the Policy Studies Institute (PSI), 'Britain in 2010' which was interesting. There were nine members of the consortium: Joseph Rowntree Foundation, Employment Department Group, DTI (LTSU), IBM UK, Glaxo, National Westminster Bank, Inland Revenue, Unilever, and the Department of the Environment. We numbered it in our series of studies as Long Term Study No. 51, although it was published by the PSI and had their ISBN. Led by Jim Northcott, the project was organised through a group of eight PSI researchers, with additional papers on health care, Europe and the USA being commissioned from experts. The report discussed the World in 2010 then focussed on Britain in 2010. Economic forecasts and three scenarios were provided by Cambridge Econometrics.

The first scenario illustrated a market-oriented approach, with lower income tax, reduced government spending and supply-side changes to improve the efficiency of the market and raise labour productivity. The model suggests this scenario would be likely to give a faster rise in consumers' expenditure; a slower fall in unemployment; an earlier improvement in the balance of payments; and total economic growth over the two decades to 2010 similar to that in the main forecast.

The second scenario illustrated a more interventionist approach, with higher income tax, higher government spending on social services, and expansion of R&D and training schemes to improve productivity. The model suggests this scenario would be likely to give a slower rise in consumers' expenditure; a faster fall in unemployment; an earlier improvement in the balance of payments; and, as with the first scenario, total economic growth similar to that in the main forecast.

The third scenario illustrates a more environment-oriented approach, with a major investment to improve water quality, measures to reduce industrial pollution, and a carbon tax to cut emissions of greenhouse gases, with offsetting cuts in VAT. The model suggests this scenario would be likely to result in major structural changes, with much higher prices for water, electricity, petrol, gas and coal, but lower price for many other categories of expenditure, particularly health, education and most recreational services. While structural shifts would be considerable, total economic growth would be likely to be much the same as with the main forecast.

By exploring these scenarios the report aimed to get the best available view of what was most likely to happen, so as to provide a considered context for people who have long term decisions to take. The other, and perhaps more important, purpose is to identify the potential areas of choice and illuminate the issues involved. The overall findings of the study were unexciting, but that was justified because the previous two decades had been steady and unspectacular. So why should the future be significantly different?

My more general policy role did sometimes involve some substantial briefing for Ministers. The views of members of the IAB were well respected. I recall being asked to deal with a proposal to the Secretary of State from Lord Chilver in November 1991 that there should be an elite qualification, a Diploma in Engineering. There had been a meeting between Lord Chilver and the Secretary of State in July 1991, where senior officials had been present but I was not, and then I was expected to follow up the meeting and provided detailed advice, with a reasoned argument on what to do, to the Secretary of State. It was not done in isolation; as part of preparing my advice to Ministers I went to discuss the proposal with Lord Chilver, but by then the idea had cooled and no action followed.

Another topic where I made an input was the definition of the terms research and experimental development. The definitions used in the UK were derived from the Frascati Manual, published by the OECD in 1981, and under revision in 1992. The definition of R&D covered three activities: basic research, applied research and experimental development. It was standard terminology used for international comparison and to justify Government funding. However, several very senior Government advisors proposed a different classification. The issue was to compare the two definitions, and in this case, explain the difficulties with adopting any new classification.

Unexpected ideas from Ministers always provided a challenge and we had to respond quickly when Ministers expressed interest in replicating the best of industry/education schemes operating overseas. Two schemes were launched quickly - the Industrial Units and Technology Audits. The scheme to assist in the strengthening and establishment of industrial units at higher educational institutions was intended to provide support for a broad range of activities which would enhance their overall performance, chiefly for the employment of additional personnel, enabling units to employ 'in-house' professional and commercial expertise. The scheme was conceived to improve the UK's performance in technology transfer between higher education and industry, and so was focussed on science and engineering faculties. £4 million was made available with a limited budget for each scheme. Thirty six industrial unit projects were funded.

The other new scheme assisted HEIs in conducting technology audits, in order to identify in a systematic way their scientific and technological capabilities, which may be commercially exploitable. Again the motive was to encourage further the exploitation of the UK's strengths in academic research. Total funding here was £2 million and 44 technology audits were approved. Both schemes accepted applications from 1 October 1991, and applicants were notified by 30 March 1992. Success here was by competition; the best proposals were funded, up to the budget limit.

25 Emerging Technologies and Technology Foresight

One of my staff had the lead for the UK in the Monitor programme, a programme of the Directorate-General for Science, Research and Development within the Commission of the European Communities. This programme sought to contribute to R&D policy and consisted of three activities: FAST (Forecasting and Assessment in Science and Technology), SAST (Strategic Analysis in Science and Technology) and SPEAR (The Supporting Programme for Evaluation of Applied Research). It was a tool for the analysis and assessment of EC Research and Technology Development (RTD) policy. Monitor was different to most other EC programmes because the Commission initiated studies, and contracts were awarded after a restricted call for tender. We wanted to encourage wider participation from the UK, aiming towards 'Juste Retour' (our fair share of the contracts), as well as influencing EC policy. It was not a task for officials and so we established a national Node, run by PREST at the University of Manchester.

There were already projects in Europe on long-term R&D objectives and priorities, sponsored by FAST. FAST highlighted prospects, problems and potential conflicts likely to affect the long-term development of the Community, with an orientation towards defining alternative courses of Community R&D action likely to help to resolve forthcoming problems and exploit opportunities. The programme included research projects, conferences, workshops and network activities.

FAST sponsored a study on key technologies which was published in 1987 and was carried out by VDI/VDE of Germany, the professional bodies for engineers and technicians. It was translated into English as 'Key Technologies. Turbulent Changes in Industry as a Result of Innovative Dynamics' by Heinrich Revermann and Philipp Sonntag. Recent technological developments were assessed to identify the critical areas for Europe, and determine those most significant for the future. Key technologies were defined as those which, when effectively controlled, offered keys to economic success and to significant social change. The suggestion in 1987 was that they comprised information technology, microelectronics, software, lasers, new materials, plastics, metals, energy, and biotechnology, and the most significant key technology of these was microelectronics.

The ability to apply key technologies was deemed to be a decisive factor in determining economic success. Example applications were sensors, actuators, the integration of details into new processes, robots, communication networks, changes in organisation, telecommuter work and flexible production leading to CIM. The potential effects of the key technologies were described in five industrial sectors: microelectronics, metalworking, textiles, machine construction and the motor industry.

As well as working within the 6CP and the BFN, which were mainly European discussion groups, I was watching what was happening in the USA and Japan. Here it was very useful that the UK had Science Counsellors in the British Embassies in Washington and Tokyo because they noticed the importance of the various surveys and White Papers, and quickly posted copies to us in London. It also helped that I knew both these Science Counsellors from previous jobs.

In the USA in 1990 both the Department of Defense and the Department of Commerce were active. The Department of Defense had begun to identify Critical Technologies, as an approach towards strategic thinking about new technologies. They gave a detailed list of 20 technologies and it obviously overlapped with the thoughts in the paper which had been written by Brian Arthur. The Department of Commerce also published a survey in 1990 which listed Technical and Economic Opportunities. They defined an emerging technology to be 'one in which research has progressed far enough to indicate a high probability of technical success for new products and applications that might have substantial markets within approximately ten years'.

At the same time, staff in the British Embassy in Japan had become aware of a major consultation exercise by the Ministry of International Trade and Industry (MITI), especially following the White Paper 'Trends and Future Tasks in Industrial Technology' published in 1988. In Japan, MITI had designed a survey to identify the key trends in science engineering and technology for the next 25 years.

The French were also publishing lists of what they called Inevitable Technologies and I spent some time in discussion with Thierry Gaudin, the head of the prospective group in the Ministry of Research and Technology and a past Chairman of the 6CP. His work concentrated on scenarios for the future, but they were written as science-fiction stories suitable for public consumption, and were based on his own observations. They were so interesting that I had them translated into English, at great expense. My knowledge of French was not good enough to do the translation, and I needed the text in English so that I could more easily share the ideas with colleagues.

Developing a new mechanism for identifying emerging and generic technologies was too important for my small group in the DTI to carry forward alone and an Inter Departmental Working Group with representatives from all major science and technology spending departments was established to explore ways in which a list of generic technologies of importance to the UK might be compiled. Lists had been published by the USA and Japan, but our list might be different; the UK strategic view of importance was unlikely to have criteria which exactly matched those in the USA or Japan. We come from a different industrial situation with different strengths and weaknesses. The Secretariat, always a powerful position to influence the work, was held jointly. I and a colleague from the Office of Science and Technology (OST) in the Cabinet Office shared the responsibility.

The first step was to identify a methodology capable of producing a list, preferably in order of priority. The Secretariat was charged with taking this forward, which meant that I and my colleague from the OST were going to have joint responsibility and must work together. The Inter Departmental Working Group then wished to pilot this methodology and explore options prior to making recommendations for a possible full scale exercise during 1993.

First we needed to catch up with what was going on overseas. In 1984 there had been a book published by John Irvine and Ben Martin, 'Foresight in Science: Picking the Winners' which reported on the findings of a study for the UK Government concerning the use of foresight to set research priorities in the USA, France, the Federal Republic of Germany and Japan. Subsequently another study was commissioned by the Netherlands Government which extended the coverage to include Australia, Canada, Norway and Sweden and proposed a framework for successful research foresight. Note the emphasis on research, with its base in the scientific community, whereas my policy interest in the DTI was much broader. Distinctive national characteristics were an important feature of their analysis, and whilst a consensus process had advantages, there were observed risks of politicisation of longer-term planning which limited the scope for making strategic choices regarding selective support for R&D. Again carried out by John Irvine and Ben Martin, this work was published in 1989 under the title 'Research Foresight'. Even if I was new to the subject, it was abundantly clear we already had a lot of knowledge about foresight in the UK.

An invitation to tender was sent to a number of consultants and academics, who we knew had relevant expertise. Many organisations applied to tender for the work, and were interviewed. We were impressed, in different ways, with the ideas from PA Technology, PREST at the University of Manchester and SPRU at the University of Sussex at Brighton. When approached, they agreed to work together. A series of background papers were produced in July 1992: Ben Martin of SPRU did a review of overseas experiences in the identification of emerging generic technologies, PREST looked at the identification and prioritisation of emerging generic technologies, and Hariolf Grupp of the Fraunhofer Institute for Systems and Innovation Research in Germany contributed a paper on the methodology for identifying emerging generic technologies - in Germany, Japan and the USA. PA Technology took all this information and made it into a useful presentation, including the strengths and weaknesses of each of the different countries approaches, and flowcharts showing the steps in their processes.

In parallel, economists from the DTI and OST, again working together, produced a paper on Criteria for Assessing Generic Technologies. At the first level there were three ultimate policy goals: Industrial Competitiveness, Quality of Life and Security. Scoring of the technologies would be done by looking at the potential benefits and how they could be captured, the cost of technologies, technical feasibility and our capacity for science and technology. It was hoped that this would produce a list of Significant Technologies, from which those to be considered further could be chosen. Finally these were measured against criteria for Government support. It was a neat theoretical recipe.

A presentation was given by PA Technology to the Inter Departmental Working Group on 9 September 1992, discussing methodologies for the prioritisation of generic technologies. The Secretariat, myself and colleagues in the OST, had spent a lot of time working with PA Technology, and so their presentation did not contain any surprises. Indeed as part of the process there had been a Workshop for DTI and OST officials on 1 September, and then another for representatives of the Inter Departmental Working Group on 2 September.

The proposed methodology first involved the identification of experts and the initial technical focus. Then the expert body would generate two questionnaires. There was to be one questionnaire for the opportunity/needs forecast and another for the technology forecast. The completed questionnaires would be collated and these outcomes would be used to illustrate a subsequent pair of questionnaires. This was the so-called Delphi iteration where responders were able to modify their opinions once they had seen what everyone else had to say. This was all finally combined in the Information Integration Phase, when the Needs and Technologies were ranked, and the UK strengths and weaknesses, obtained from desk research were incorporated. A final priority list of technologies was then obtained, which would be disseminated and comments and feedback welcomed. Much of the perceived benefits of the approach were about the consensus building and the discussions which it would provoke across the UK.

Prior to conducting a full scale study, a pilot study was carried out in late 1992, based on an iterative questionnaire approach to elicit expert opinion. The subject chosen for the pilot study was Information Storage and Retrieval Technology. It was chosen because it would be of interest and relevance to a broad cross-section of people and organisations. Some 140 questionnaires were distributed to Government departments and advisory bodies.

The exact procedure was included in a paper written by Ken Guy of SPRU, and presented at a meeting in Brussels on 26 January 1993. There were three distinct activities. The first was to test the co-nomination activity, which is described later, as a means to identify the members of an expert panel. The second was to test the questionnaires used to probe expert opinion on specific technology areas and provide information on which to prioritise generic technologies. Writing the questionnaire was itself a challenging task, but at least we had the Japanese questions to inform our thinking. Originally the German approach had used a questionnaire which was just a straight translation of the Japanese one. Finally there was a questionnaire to elicit opinion on changing social and political trends, new markets and applications and opportunities and future social needs. Together with my colleagues, I filled in my own views in the questionnaire. There were 23 topic areas within Information Storage and Retrieval. For each of these I had to score my degree of expertise, the degree of importance of that topic, the time when the technology will be realised, and the constraining influences on realization of the technology (choosing between social, technological, economic, ecological or political).

In December 1992 it was reported to the Inter Departmental Working Group by PA Consulting Group, in collaboration with PREST, that the overall process had proved robust. The pilot study had shown that the questionnaire approach was usable.

The Advisory Council on Science and Technology (ACOST) was working in this area too. Their Standing Committee on Emerging Technologies had been replaced by a Working Group on Emerging and Generic Technologies in July 1992, chaired by Professor Mike Brady the Head of Engineering Science at Oxford University. Professor Brady had been persuaded some years earlier to come back to the UK, having established himself as an eminent professor in the USA. Membership of the Working Group included Professor Michael Ashby of the University of Cambridge, Professor Derek Burke of the University of East Anglia, Dr Keith Mansford formerly of SmithKline Beecham plc, Professor Stan Metcalfe of PREST at the University of Manchester, Professor Michael Mingos of Imperial College, London, Dr Alan Rudge of BT, Professor Brian Shackel of the University of Technology at Loughborough, Dr David Smith of BP, Professor Colin Webb of the University of Oxford and Dr Bob Whelan of CEST.

Their role was to review UK mechanisms for the identification and promotion of emerging and generic technologies in general and of particular technologies when such detailed study is warranted. They also were to consider what factors inhibit the development and exploitation of such technologies. This work was about technologies, not research. I was the DTI Assessor on the Working Group, together with Philip O'Neil from my LTSU group. It was exciting to be involved at such a formative stage in the development of such an important strategic programme. The ACOST report was completed on 28 July 1993 and used to influence the new Technology Foresight Steering Group, which would be chaired by the Chief Scientific Advisor, and based in the Cabinet Office.

In March 1993 a comprehensive report on Research Foresight and the Exploitation of the Science Base had been published by HMSO. The author was Ben Martin of SPRU and that report provided a very useful explanation of what was happening in the UK as the foresight programme rolled steadily forward. Note that this report was still about Research Foresight, whereas my policy interest was in technologies and Technology Foresight. Note also that the Technology Foresight Steering Group was chaired by a very senior scientist, the Chief Scientific Advisor. The science base and the Cabinet Office had got themselves organised and assumed the responsibility for taking forward the work. Given that much of the emphasis was about exploiting the science base, it was perhaps understandable.

Three Task Forces were set up. These were in biotechnology, catalysis and telecommunications. The Task Forces were asked to comment on whether foresight had been carried out successfully in those areas, either in industry or in government, and the extent to which it had meshed with Government policies and programmes.

Our discussions with colleagues overseas and our travels around Europe had created a lot of interest with other policy makers and it was soon proposed that the UK should Chair a sub-group of the Ad Hoc CREST Working Group on Emerging Generic Technologies. I attended the first meeting which was held on 15 February 1993, in Brussels. CREST was the Committee for Research and Evaluation of Science and Technology, and was involved with deciding on priorities for the allocation of funding in the EC Framework programme. In 1993 the Framework IV Programme was just beginning, as its predecessor Framework III ended. In order to start from the right terminology, Ben Martin of SPRU was asked to prepare a paper clarifying the meaning of what is meant by the three words: generic, emerging and technology. We had already seen lists of emerging, generic, pervasive, critical and strategic technologies. What was the difference between them all? A generic technology was defined as a technology which, when exploited, would yield benefits for a wide range of sectors of the economy and society. There were different approaches to technology foresight in different EC member states and in Australia the USA and Japan, and each country had a different set of national criteria for prioritising across the technologies. All this was described and discussed.

Then the Government White Paper 'Realising our Potential: A Strategy for Science and Engineering' (ROP) was published in May 1993. The Conclusions for action were that the UK should be :

> developing stronger partnerships with and between the science communities, industry and the research charities;

supporting the science and engineering base to advance knowledge, increase understanding and produce highly-educated and trained people;

contributing, according to the UK's strengths and interests, to the international, and particularly European research effort;

continuing to promote the public understanding of science and engineering;

ensuring the efficiency and effectiveness of Government funded research.

This led to a number of proposed reforms :

Departmental Mission statements and Forward Look to be published.

Technology Foresight will be used to inform Government's decisions and priorities.

ACOST would be developed into the Council for Science and Technology.

Technology transfer schemes to be developed.

Renaming and some re-shaping of Research Council priorities.

There would be easier access to support for SMEs.

Improved coordination between the Office of Science and Technology (OST) in the Cabinet Office and the Department for Education with respect to dual funding.

There would be further scrutiny of Government research establishments.

Improved cross-Departmental coordination on S&T.

Improved Government coordination across European programmes.

Emphasis on doing the MSc degree prior to working for PhD.

A campaign to spread (better) understanding of S&T.

By the middle of 1993, much of the framework for going forward with the very first Technology Foresight exercise in the UK was in place. The Technology Foresight Programme had been announced and a number of 'Focus on Foresight' seminars took place across the UK - the first was in Edinburgh on 13 September, followed by London, Birmingham, Manchester, Belfast, Newport, Swindon, Wilton and Southwell. It was an interesting list of different places to go. I think the Chief Scientific Advisor, then Professor William Stewart, must have wanted the first seminar to take place in Scotland. The meetings discussed the objectives of foresight, and how Technology Foresight should be organised. There were a flurry of publications as academics and policy makers saw that this was going to be a key part of future science policy, and wanted a slice of the action. The smiling face of William Waldegrave, Minister for Science, appeared on booklets and publications. A Technology Foresight Steering Group was established to oversee the work of the panels of experts who were tasked with providing input on how market opportunities were changing and how science was moving. Day to day management of Technology Foresight was done by a new team at the OST led by Mrs Helen Williams, and the lead for the next stage was firmly with them.

We were some time behind the Japanese Foresight project, which by 1993 was in its fifth year. Duplicating their approach, a number of Sector Panels were needed to do the work and the first stage was to find out who knew what in the UK. This was done in a systematic way. People in the field were asked and their recommendations and suggestions were combined. The process was called co-nomination, to identify those who are widely considered by their contemporaries to be the most knowledgeable. These people are 'The Pool' from which individuals are chosen to join the expert panels which were to conduct the detailed studies of future market and technological developments. There was a risk that this would develop into a collection of established people, who contributed only the same old ideas, and so young people who might have exciting new insights were deliberately chosen too.

The aim was to set up the 15 Sector Panels during February and March 1994, ready for work to begin in April. These were

> Agriculture, Natural Resources and Environment
> Manufacturing, Production and Business Processes
> Defence and Aerospace
> Materials
> Chemicals
> Construction
> Financial Services
> Food and Drink
> Health and Life Sciences
> Energy
> Transport
> Communications
> Leisure and Education
> IT and Electronics
> Retail and Distribution

Twelve of the Sector Panels had a senior DTI official as member. Everyone worked very hard. It was the most extensive consultation of industrial and scientific opinion ever in the UK. It all culminated on 22 May 1995 with the publication of the Technology Foresight Steering Group's report, which drew together the results of the year-long process to identify key market opportunities for the UK, together with the underpinning technological opportunities needed to realise them. The report provided guidance, to Government and Industry, on future priorities for science, engineering and technology and made a number of recommendations on standards, regulation and skills. The key foresight topic areas were:

> Telepresence, Multimedia
> Bioinformatics
> Genetics and Biomolecular Engineering
> Software Engineering
> Management and Business Process Re-Engineering
> Sensors and Sensory Information Processing
> Communication with machines
> Security and Privacy Technology
> Environmentally Sustainable Technology
> Health and Lifestyle
> Optical Technology

It was the perceived lasting benefits of technology foresight which ensured the Government's continued enthusiasm for the process. Firstly there would be the formation of commercial and academic strategies to promote innovation. Secondly there would be the creation of lasting networks between industry, Government and the science and technology community. Thirdly there would be the emergence of coherent visions within their communities on complementary developments in science and technology.

I continued to receive regular letters from the head of Personnel Management, congratulating me that the Permanent Secretary has approved the inclusion of my name on the list considered ready for promotion to Grade 5. He wrote initially on 20 November 1991, when the first list was established, and subsequently on 4 December 1992 and 20 December 1993. Although I was not promoted, I was performing well in my present job, and earning performance increments. For example, on 1 July 1992 I received my first performance increment in consequence of my Box 2 markings awarded in 1990/91 and 1991/92 annual reports. Then on 20 October 1993 I received another performance pay increase for 1992/93. My salary was then £40,882.

26 Personal Disaster in Stratford-on-Avon, while boating

We went off on holiday with our narrowboat as usual in May 1993, and agreed with my parents that we would be going to Stratford-on-Avon, and would meet them there. They came to join us by train. My father was 79 and was no longer allowed to drive, and I think they found the journey more tiring than they expected. From Lichfield it was necessary to go first to Birmingham, and then change trains. They were staying at the Courtland Hotel close to Bancroft Gardens and the River Avon. We all met in the afternoon on the boat, and had dinner and a glass of wine.

Very early the following morning we were awakened by the lady from the Hotel; my father had collapsed and she thought had died, on his way to the bathroom. I found my mother sitting in the hotel room with my father lying dead on the floor outside in the corridor. Their room was not en-suite. It had all only just happened and soon afterwards the ambulance came and pronounced him dead. My mother said her final goodbyes and we sat together quietly and wondered what to do next. I spent the morning and most of the next day dealing with the paperwork, spoke to the coroner and local Funeral Directors back in Burntwood, and then hired a car to drive her back home. We were all stunned with the shock. Meanwhile we negotiated with the British Waterways staff so that we could overstay our time on the moorings. They were very kind.

I spent some time with my mother while Pete worked hard, bringing the boat back up the Stratford canal on his own. Ownership of the canal had only been transferred from the National Trust to British Waterways in 1988, and the canal was not yet in good condition. From Stratford Basin to the main Grand Union canal at Lapworth there were 35 locks in 13 miles, and landing stages were still being built or extended near the locks.

When you are handling a boat alone you have to be able to tie up the boat, get off safely, then empty the lock and open the gate, get back on the boat, steer it into the lock, climb up the ladder if there is one, shut the lock gate, open the paddles until the water has filled the lock, then open the top gate, get back on the boat, steer it out of the lock, tie it up, walk back and shut the gate, and then go back to the boat and drive away towards the next lock. Sometimes Pete said there was nowhere to get off and he had to take the boat forward until it was touching the lock gates and then climb up the gates. Thankfully he did not have an accident, and it was only two days until I could join him again at the flight of locks at Hatton, near Warwick. What had been planned as a nice quiet cruise became a mess of logistics as we shared our time between my mother, going to work, and moving the boat.

To add to our problems the boat was broken into on two consecutive weeks while we had it moored in a marina near Napton. The thief was my size because he took a set of my waterproofs, as well as a few tins of food and bottles of wine. At least he didn't make a mess. We discovered later that he was well known to the Police, but was hard to capture. During the summer he lived outdoors, only stealing from boats when he needed. In the winter when it was too cold to live outdoors he walked into a Police station and admitted his crimes and tried to go to jail where he could be warm and fed, aiming to be released again the next spring. He liked David Piper boats because he preferred to get in through the top, through the hatches, not by breaking down the main doors. We had friends who had suffered from his attentions many times, and used to leave him notes for where the food and wine was. Another friend had actually been on board when he got in, and rang 999. The local Police helicopter came searching for him, but he got away over the fields.

In the middle of all this I got back to work to find that I was suddenly under pressure to move job. It was a totally unexpected change of circumstances and with my family problems my defences were down. On the very day I got back, two Under Secretaries came in turn to my office and spoke to me. Dr Colin Hicks, my present boss, was first. He understood the shock which followed my father's death and gave good advice on how I could help my mother cope with what had happened. He suggested that she would get practical and spiritual support from her local church. Colin has a strong Christian faith, and this underpins all his actions. My mother has a strong faith too, but she had stopped attending church services because my father no longer went.

To my surprise Colin then changed the subject and said he wanted me to move job immediately, to become Head of the National Measurement System Policy Unit (NMSPU). I immediately refused. I was enjoying my work as head of the LTSU. The NMSPU was a very small Unit, responsible for the budget spent with the National Physical Laboratory, the National Engineering Laboratory, the Laboratory of the Government Chemist, and a few other places. I saw it as a dead end posting, not a career step, and I was hoping that my next move would be upwards, not sideways into a job which I perceived was less interesting with less staff and responsible for big budgets doing narrow scientific research work. I wanted to do more of the broad policy work, and get more involvement with Ministers, and manage a larger group. I was told that the NMSPU would be moving from RTP Division to become part of the Environment Division, headed by Dr David Evans. David then came to talk to me. The tactics had obviously been rehearsed beforehand. It was hard to resist the concerted persuasion of two Under Secretaries and eventually they persuaded me to take the job.

27 Managing the budget for the National Measurement System

So, in May 1993 I became the Head of the NMSPU, which was yet another Grade 6 job but which reported directly to the Grade 3 who was the Head of Environment Division. At least I was not working for a Grade 5 again. It was a very different sort of job - I had just 6 staff, and a large annual budget of £42 million. Even after I arrived in post I still did not want to be the Head of the National Measurement System Policy Unit, and I never enjoyed the work. Maybe I was chosen for the job because I was unlikely to object if Ministers wanted to reduce the enormous budget spent on measurement, and equally I knew a lot about the laboratories and could understand their technology. I was very unhappy, but put my head down and got on with the work. In the circumstances, and after my father's death, it was a good idea to be busy.

In its previous position in RTP Division the NMSPU had been headed by a Grade 5, Richard King, but there the job also included aspects of international science and technology programme management and policy input to EC proposals. Only the UK part of this work was going across to me, and of his 26 staff I got to have just 6, and one of those was a vacancy which was fortunate because it meant I had a slot for my secretary. Otherwise I would have risked losing her, or having to fight for an extra post. It seemed to me that Dr Colin Hicks had managed to keep the bulk of his staff, and get rid of the boring work.

And then I had an idea. One possibility was that I take this previous responsibility as a fact, and I suggested my post should be graded as a part-time Grade 5, instead of a full-time Grade 6. For me it would have meant a reduction in salary because I had been told that the work represented between 2/3 and 3/4 of a fulltime job, but it had the advantage that I would finally have managed to break the glass ceiling which was keeping me at Grade 6 although everyone said I was very fitted to be Grade 5. The salary would be less, but we were already in a situation where the salary was less important than having the right responsibilities. The next step was for Dr David Evans to seek approval for the new post to be graded as Grade 5, which to his credit he attempted. Key factors which defined the choice of grade between 5 and 6 included the complexity, depth and breadth of thinking required in the job, the level of autonomy and the impact of actions and decisions taken.

I was still working in the area headed by Dr Geoff Robinson, whose job title had changed from Chief Engineer and Scientist to match the Chief Scientific Advisor at the Cabinet office; Dr Robinson was now DTI's Chief Adviser on Science and Technology (CAST). He asked for special focus to be made on giving Ministers the best assessment of the value of the National Measurement System (NMS), to look carefully at the validity of the current arrangements for tendering work, and assess the consequences for the Laboratories of their reduced workload. I was very new to the area, and in June 1993 I had not spotted that they were going to have a reduced workload, the details of which I would be implementing.

When I had left the NPL in 1981 I had taken a particular perception with me of my colleagues in the Division of Numerical Analysis and Computer Science (DNACS), and I am sure that they had an equally strong view of my defection to Headquarters. I think it was easier for career scientists to understand a colleague who was sent to HQ, then came back to science as soon as she could. When I left I made it clear that I was not coming back. If I did continue to do research it would be as an academic, even if I could not find a place in one of the better Universities. Then for over 10 years I had no contact with the NPL, except socially through Bernarr Hopkins who was now retired, and Alex Williams and his family. Now I was on the other side of the table to old colleagues, and not only from DNACS but for the whole of the work programme at the NPL, and the other DTI laboratories (LGC, NEL and WSL) as well. I was to be the proxy customer for all their measurement work.

As background, Dr David Evans had studied physics at Oxford University, and then gained his DPhil there. He was the same age as Pete, so just a few years older than I was. I soon found he was very bright. Instead of joining the Civil Service as a scientist he had chosen to take the fast-stream route. He had become Chief Scientist in the Department of Energy at an age when most scientists were still doing middle management courses and waiting for promotion to Principal. He then moved to the DTI on promotion as Under Secretary.

Having worked with people who listened to my opinions and trusted my advice I found that I was now working for someone who had very much his own ideas, and where we differed I was the one who had to change. It was firmly pointed out to me that the role of a civil servant was to serve Ministers and deliver their policy. Whether I liked it or agreed with it. I did not disagree and wondered why he had made a special effort to make sure I understood the official line. I had never found myself in conflict with Ministers in the past, but I knew of colleagues who despaired when Ministers acted against what was, in their opinion, sensible and justified advice.

When Dr David Evans became my boss this meant that Dr Geoff Robinson, the CAST, became my countersigning officer who signed off my annual report and made any recommendation for my promotion. He was supposed to get to know his staff, but in the first year he admitted he had not met me and in the second year he wrote nothing on my report. This was a disappointment because he had been very much my generation when he had studied mathematics and computing at Nottingham

University, and he then moved to the IBM organisation at the same time as I had chosen to go from Oxford to the NPL. We should have had a lot in common, but never managed to bridge the gap.

The Government's role in the National Measurement System had been defined in the White Paper 'Measuring up to the Competition', published by HMSO in 1989. The DTI had the responsibility for ensuring that the stated objectives were achieved, namely:

'To enable individuals and organisations in the UK to make measurements competently and accurately and to demonstrate the validity of such measurements.

To coordinate the UK's measurement system with the measurement systems of other countries.'

As other background, in 1990 the Central Unit had produced a Review of Research and Development in Support of DTI Regulatory, Statutory and Policy Functions (the customer-contractor principle). It had remarked that the Measurement and Technology Support budget was expected to total £68.5 million in 1990/91, of which the NMSPU spending was £39.6 million. The new policy involved a presumption in favour of competition for all the work, justified by the need to secure value for money.

I became formally responsible for my part of the Measurement and Technology Support budget, and my small team provided the Secretariat for the Standards, Quality and Measurement Advisory Committee (SQMAC), pronounced 'skew-mac', which advised on how the budget should be allocated. Set up in 1988, its Chairman then was Professor Peter Payne from UMIST, and it comprised a mixture of industrialists, academics and representatives of other Government Departments. SQMAC had quarterly meetings, annual priority-setting rituals and annual reviews. There were also a number of SQMAC Working Groups to look at particular measurement programmes.

The National Measurement System (NMS) contributed to the competitiveness of the economy under the headings of Trade, Innovation and Quality. Yet again I was reminded that there was the recent White Paper, 'Realising our Potential', published in 1993, which had a key theme of developing and maintaining the technical infrastructure. The NMS provided measurement standards; knowledge of measurement methods and how they may be used to obtain valid results; and the necessary organisation to ensure that there are practitioners competent to provide measurement and calibration services which pass on accuracy and traceability to their recipients. It was the core of this technical infrastructure.

The 5 Year Forward Look exercise which I had set up in the LTSU demanded that I had to write a 5YFL myself for the NMSPU, which was submitted to the LTSU in November 1993. This was less difficult than in many areas because there was a White Paper to justify the activities, and previous 5YFLs had been done in January 1992 and January 1993. The 5YFL produced in January 1993 had been reduced by Ministers by 30% in March 1993, and so it was against this reduced level of funding that I started to write the next 5YFL. Scientific Generics, a consultancy company based near Cambridge who had previously done work for the NMSPU, carried out a study to determine the cost to the UK economy of a 30% reduction in the fundamental mass, length and flow programmes. They looked at five mechanisms by which the NMS creates value for the economy and concluded that the loss in value-added was around a factor of two, as a result of the proposed reduction in funding.

The first part of my 5YFL was a Strategy Statement, which described the overall remit, the relation of the work to DTI policy, the Strategy and Delivery Plans, the Impact of the Strategy, the External Drivers, the Tactics for using external advice and consultancy, any Changes since the previous 5YFL in 1992, and Highlights for the Future. There were reasonable policy grounds for public funding of the NMS work, but criteria needed to be established to determine the allocation of resources.

The second part of the 5YFL described the formal planning and priority setting process. Scientific Generics had been working with SQMAC since 1991 to develop a priority-setting mechanism. Each NMS project is awarded a Policy Score which is an assessment of how well the project provides benefits, assessed against DTI policy criteria. SQMAC members were asked to rate projects on a scale of 1 to 7 against seven policy headings:

1. Innovation (0.97)
2. Quality (1.58)
3. Regulation (0.92)
4. Public Policy (0.71)
5. Trade (1.38)
6. User Distribution (0.82)
7. Standards Interdependence (0.65)

The values from different experts were averaged for each project, and the seven criteria were weighted by the given numbers before being added to give the Policy Score (PS). These PS values were then normalised by subtracting the lowest value from all the others. PS scores then ranged from 0 to about 20.

A second measure was provided by Scientific Generics, the Economic Importance Indicator (EII), which estimated the size/importance within the UK economy, of each sector affected by the project. Official statistics were used of the value of the various economic sectors, and the extent to which the economic activity was likely to be affected by the NMS work was estimated.

The combination of EII and the PS gave a measure of the benefit of the work. This benefit has to be balanced against the cost, and so, after much arithmetic, a list of projects ordered by the value of benefit/cost was obtained. Within a limited budget, this gives a list on which a line for funding can be drawn. Projects around the line are then considered, some changes are made and a final list is agreed. It was a time consuming process, and the list sometimes gave surprises which had to be discussed. Generally it was a very advanced decision making tool, compared with how other parts of the DTI prioritised their expenditure. It is never easy to choose between even two similar projects, and this was the only way to choose between what we described as apples, oranges and elephants - NMS projects varied very much in size.

While the 5YFL was being crafted there were many changes happening, and their consequences would have a major impact on the NMS and the 5YFL. Although the original version of the NMSPU 5YFL was submitted on 10 November 1993, the final version was not agreed until 7 April 1994.

On 4 May 1993 the Secretary of State and the President of the Board of Trade, Michael Heseltine, had announced that he had commenced a review of the options for the future of the DTI's laboratories. The review was carried out with the aid of KPMG Peat Marwick management consultants, and on 14 April 1994 he announced the outcome of this review. The decision was that:

> A trade purchasers of the NEL would be sought in 1995.
>
> The LGC should be established as an independent non-profit distributing company in the private sector.
>
> The NPL should have its management contracted to the private sector during 1995 which may in due course result in the NPL becoming ready to move into private sector ownership.

These were serious changes in themselves, but were more serious taken alongside the reduction in budget for the National Measurement System. In 1994 the NEL employed 331 staff and had a turnover of £14.3 million, the LGC employed 316 staff and had a turnover of £15 million, and the NPL employed 736 staff and had a turnover of £48 million.

I had provided the Secretariat for the review of the NMS. The review showed that the new levels of proposed expenditure were consistent and compared well with the spending by our European partners. Germany was the only European country which spent more than the UK; all the others spent less. This had been the case for many years. Ministers believed that at a reduced level of spending we would sustain a national measurement system which was still sound and fit for purpose. In July 1994 work began on identifying areas where UK metrology organisations might develop partnerships with other countries. Scientific Generics again was asked to produce a report on the opportunities for collaboration between the UK and non-European Union industrialised and developing nations on measurement standards and their technical infrastructure. A similar project looked at the opportunities for collaboration with nations of the European Union, but I think we were able to do that work ourselves. It was only necessary to update our existing information, and make some visits overseas. The work aimed to be completed by September 1995.

One casualty of all this reviewing was the NMS work programme on Mass, Length and Flow. The work on Mass and Length was traditionally done at the NPL, and it had been a three year programme which was expected to be renewed in August 1993. A submission had been sent to the President of the Board of Trade in March 1993. At that date, the KPMG study had already begun, and Ministers were not enthusiastic about committing to a further 3 years of work. For obvious reasons, the work could not be stopped. So it was agreed with the President of the Board of Trade in July that the work would be continued for a further 6 months. Once the KPMG report was completed funding for the remaining 2.5 years was approved. It was a similar situation for the NEL and their programme on Flow, although that was due for renewal one month later. I was pleased that the remainder of the programmes had finally been approved, but worried whether future programmes would be equally hard to persuade Ministers to continue.

On 20 May 1994 I wrote a speech for Dr David Evans, which he gave to the British Measurement and Testing Association. It is a neat summary of DTI policy at that time, and so is useful to repeat it here. He said:

> 'The Government's overall objective is to ensure that it is possible to make measurements which are valid and fit for the purpose. By this we mean essential for trade nationally and internationally; they underpin innovation; and their traceability ensures quality measurement systems.
>
> How does Government seek to secure a measurement infrastructure to meet the needs of UK industry? It does this in four ways :
>
> 1. by developing the market in measurement by providing choice for industry in measurement services (accredited laboratories);
>
> 2. through world-class metrology 'centres of excellence' which are well connected to industry and which disseminate measurement capability;
>
> 3. by supporting those areas where the market cannot support itself, the Government targets those areas where there is most benefit following the widest discussion with industry;

4.   through collaboration in Europe and globally, wherever it is practicable to do so.

This is done at the minimum cost to UK tax-payers, but we must maintain the range, quality, timeliness and long-term availability which is required.'

It is possible now to reflect on whether these reductions were indeed the right policies, and those still working in the area must have a view. I am not in a position to comment, but remark that the NMS Review in 2005 showed an annual expenditure of £60 million, well above the budget of £38 million which was recorded as spent in 1999. In 1994, and as a result of the 30% reduction, there was predicted a decline in funding for the National Measurement System. Dr David Evans was able to announce that the expenditure would be £36.2 million in 1994/95 and £32 million in 1995/96, which he compared with £42 million in the last financial year 1993/94. This was an enormous reduction in real terms, and David had to work hard with Ministers to deliver even this budget. They wanted less expenditure. The intention was to manage the reduced expenditure by having a greater focus on those activities which would lead to future industrial benefits, as well as increase international collaboration. Inevitably a large proportion of the budget went to the NPL who received 75% of the NMS funding.

In May 1994 I wrote the contribution about the National Measurement System which was included in the Briefing Notes on Current DTI issues. This ring-bound book was given to everyone in the DTI who needed to deal with topics outside their immediate area, which might arise in dealings with outside organisations or businesses. Companies treat any meeting with a DTI official as an opportunity to discuss any and all aspects of DTI policy, and often junior officials were not aware of the current policies in other areas. The briefing notes were intended to help reduce mistakes and included signposts to the appropriate officials. The points to make to business about the NMS were that the DTI's responsibility was to carry out the Government's policy, as stated in the 1989 White Paper. Its objectives, in 1994 updated form, were

To ensure that the UK is provided with an internationally harmonised National Measurement System infrastructure in an economic, effective and efficient manner

To commission, appraise, monitor and evaluate the programmes of work which provide the national measurement standards, their dissemination and calibration services

To act as the focal point in the UK for measurement and testing matters.

Defensive briefing was provided too. It explained that the DTI was committed to obtaining the best value for money by limiting reliance on traditional monopoly suppliers. To this end the Department:

identifies metrology work which can be carried out by other credible suppliers and encourages competition for such work;

recognises that the agencies are undoubtedly centres of excellence for certain areas of metrology work. The effect of the proposed privatisation of the agencies will have no effect on the delivery of the NMS, the current tender process will continue to be used and the former agencies will be free to bid for work as before;

has adopted a reduced level of expenditure, as shown by the 1994 Departmental Report, which still compares well with that spent by our European partners;

uses independent, expert, external advice to ensure that the NMS is sound and provides best value at minimum cost to the taxpayer through a full and effective dialogue with UK industry and others;

promotes collaboration with European partners to share limited financial resources, prevent unnecessary duplication of effort and to provide measurement services which UK industry cannot provide from its own resources.

Each of the 3 Laboratory Directors, for the NPL the LGC and the NEL, quickly provided new ideas on how the arrangements between the customer and the contractor could be improved. It was a topic which we knew the CAST wanted to take forward. The NMSPU developed its own thoughts in parallel, and the four distinct contributions were assembled in July under the title 'Getting Closer and Nicer - Partnerships for the NMS'.

Measurement had been identified in the USA as a critical technology. The UK Technology Foresight Programme had identified 15 sectoral themes, but measurement technology was not one of them. I commissioned a study to define a mini technology foresight initiative on measurement, based on the same methodology as the main technology foresight activity. The idea was to involve scientists, engineers, industry, academe and other organisations in the identification of areas of strategic measurement research likely to yield the greatest benefits to UK competitiveness. It gave an enlarged input compared with asking the views of the members of SQMAC. These results would then be used to contribute to discussions on the future NMS work programme. Hopefully using a fashionable technology foresight approach would ensure that the results were accepted by Ministers.

For many years NPL had been working in old buildings which were no longer satisfactory. It was agreed that a single new building, with 16 interlinking modules each two storeys high, was needed and fortunately planning and organising this was not my responsibility. However, I was asked to take part in meetings as the design of the new building progressed. It was important that, as a proxy customer for the work done within the NMS, I had the chance to influence at the design stage. When Bushy House and the adjoining land had been donated in 1899 for the location of the National Physical Laboratory there were rules about what work could take place on the site. In 1994 there were issues about the ownership of the site, as well as the design of the new building. It was to be a Private Finance Initiative (PFI) contract, and was one of the first. The planned cost of the new buildings was £96 million and the Department would pay £11.5 million per year once the buildings were complete. I knew it would be many years before a contract was signed, and much later before the NPL staff could move into their nice new laboratories. I expected to be retired before the building was completed. I definitely hoped that I would be well away from the NMSPU by that time. Indeed work started on the new building in 1998, with an expectation to complete the work by 2001. After an invitation to tender, the 25 year PFI contract had been awarded to Laser, a special purpose company jointly owned by the Serco Group plc and John Laing plc. The fixed price contract was for £82 million.

There were problems and the contract was eventually terminated in December 2004. The completion of the project was delayed by some five years. Having retired I joined the Glazebrook Association, named after Sir Richard Glazebrook the first Director at the NPL from 1899 – 1919, for staff who have worked at the NPL. Our meetings are held on the Teddington site and I can admire the new building.

In May 1993 Dr David Evans tried to get my post re-graded from Grade 6 to Grade 5, without success. I was even prepared to have the job graded as a part-time post at Grade 5, which could be justified because it had been carried out previously by a Grade 5 alongside other duties. I was very focussed on getting the next promotion.

If there were no opportunities for promotion in my present work, this meant that I needed to look outside my immediate area. While commuting to London I had met Charles Robson, who lived nearby and who worked as Head of the Chief Scientist Group (CSG) at the Department of the Environment, which was a Grade 5 post. His post was going to be advertised and he told me that in August 1993 he was moving to the European Foundation in Dublin. I applied for his job.

The Department of the Environment (DOE) had a smaller science and technology policy team than the DTI, and the Head of the CSG reported directly to the Chief Scientist, and was responsible for carrying through the commitments in the Government's recent White Paper on Science and Technology, as they applied to that Department. This included the Department's input to the Government's Annual Forward Look on Research, responding to the Technology Foresight Program, looking at research assessment of major policy areas and liaising with the Director General of the Research Councils on the representation of DOE interests in Research Council work, and similar policy work at European level. It was a busy and responsible job for a Grade 5. For comparison, the similar post in the DTI was at Grade 3 level, with the DTI Chief Advisor on Science and Technology graded as Grade 2. I had a technical disadvantage that I did not have a lot of experience about the five main areas of their research to support regulatory and statutory functions: environmental protection, construction, housing, planning and countryside and local government. I was interviewed on 26 October, but was not successful. I had caught a virus while on business in Germany and my mind stalled at interview. It was all very disappointing for me, and must have been a surprise to those who interviewed me.

In September 1993 I saw a vacancy as Grade 5 Head of Senior Training at the Civil Service College at Sunningdale. I would have liked to work there, but Senior Training was about working with the very highest grades in the Civil Service, and I was not confident that was my niche. If it had been training for more junior staff then I would definitely have applied. I wrote to the Director, then Marianne Neville-Rolfe, explaining my situation and outlining my experience, with the hope of preparing the ground for an application for another Grade 5 post later. I could point at 15 years experience with the Open University, of which the last three had been in management training within the OU MBA programme. Unfortunately none of this experience was recorded within my DTI career, and my various countersigning officers could not make an honest judgement on that part of my performance - except to note that I made excellent formal presentations.

Then in March 1994 I was approached about a Grade 5 post in the Office of Science and Technology (OST). It was to head the Forward Look and Wealth Creation Division, which would have been a very good match to build on my experience. There were three main functions of the Branch.

1. To work with Government Departments to develop overall Government policy for science and technology, feeding into the annual Forward Look exercise.

2. To work with Government Departments to secure an alignment of their policy objectives with the Government's general objective of using publicly funded S&T programmes to increase national prosperity

3. To manage and plan implementation of the Government's Technology Foresight Programme.

I was interviewed on 3 May. My Grade 3 would have been Mrs Helen Williams, Head of the Trans Departmental Science and Technology Group, and she was present at the interview, as well as the Head of the OST, Professor William Stewart. I knew that the job wanted someone with experience at Grade 5, so I was not optimistic, and was not successful. I was very disappointed because I really wanted the job and I knew that I would do it well. The time working on setting up the Technology Foresight mechanism had been one of the most enjoyable highlights of my career. But I had again failed to be the best candidate at interview.

I seemed to be spending all my spare time filling in application forms and chasing the elusive posting at the next grade. There are many different jobs at Grade 5, and the challenge was to sort through the lists and identify any serious possibilities. In July 1994 I was interviewed by the Natural Environment Research Council (NERC) at Swindon for the post of Director of Technology Interaction. The duties of the post included the development of strategies for NERC's partnerships with Government Departments, relevant industrial sectors and their user communities; playing a key role in NERC's technology foresight and technology transfer activities; the assessment of the needs of industry and other users for NERC trained scientists; development of NERC's involvement in industrial linkage schemes(such as TCS, IGDS and LINK which I knew well from the DTI); and the development of a framework for increased interchange of staff between NERC, its Institutes, the Universities and industrial companies. Through my work in the DTI I had already seen NERC's 1994 Public Expenditure Survey (PES) submission in February, so I was clear about their financial plans. I also had their 1994 Corporate Plan 'Excellence and Relevance through Partnership' published in March 1994 and which set out plans for 1994-1998. So I should have been well prepared for the interview. The job was advertised as a four year appointment, with the possibility of eventual permanent appointment. The interview was at Swindon, which was an easier commuting trip than going to London. The interview panel was chaired by Professor Krebs, and I was surprised to find the panel included my old boss from the DTI, Dr Colin Hicks. Again, I failed at the interview.

Maybe I needed to get special training in winning interview competitions.

Until now, I had always taken work home, or done background reading on the train. Now I started to read books and do knitting and embroidery instead. We had been married in October 1974 and so in 1994 it would be our 20th wedding anniversary. I saw a cross stitch kit which used the two characters from the Love Is series, designed by Kim Casali. The phrase, slightly modified from the original, was 'love is … 20 happy years together' My train journeys and lunch breaks were now spent with a needle in my hand. When framed it was a perfect gift for Pete for our wedding anniversary. Usually people wait to have a large celebration until they have been married for 25 years but we had decided to hold a party at our house for the 20th anniversary as well. We didn't see our friends very often and many of our College group from Oxford lived a distance away. There was a lot of work involved in organising the celebrations, with several weekends doing the cooking and filling the freezer, and getting suitable home-made fruit wine into bottles. We had planted apples, plums, greengages, gooseberries, blackcurrants, blackberries and cherries when we designed the garden, and we had a few bottles of Champagne too, for the toast when we cut a cake.

29 Promotion to Branch Head in Management and Technology Services Division

As well as watching for vacancies elsewhere I started watching for the movement of colleagues within the DTI and found that there was going to be a Grade 5 vacancy in the Management and Technology Services Division (MTS) headed by Dr Keith Shotton. In 1982 he had been Head of Marketing and Information Services at the NPL, as I started my career in the DOI/DTI having moved from the NPL in 1981. Later we had both worked in IT Division, again in different areas. Although we had never worked together we had a common background.

I approached him to say that I was interested in the post when it became vacant, and to explain why I thought I had the right experience and ability to do the job well. While he agreed with most of the things I said, he pointed out that I was too late. He had already agreed that someone else, an existing Grade 5, would take the job. However, my discussion obviously made an impression because he later contacted me to see if I would be prepared to accept a different Grade 5 job in his Division. Callum Johnston, whom I knew, would be moving.

I was delighted and on 27 September 1994 I was finally promoted to Grade 5. My letter from my Personnel Manager had 'Congratulations !' scribbled on it. We were both delighted that I had finally made the next step up the ladder. I had just celebrated my 42nd birthday. My salary as Grade 6 had been £44,361 and now increased slightly to £46,635. It was not the extra money which mattered, but the chance to finally lead my own Branch and the knowledge that there were a large number of interesting jobs at Grade 5 for future postings. After eighteen years in the DTI I was now Grade 5, and I still had a further eighteen years before reaching retirement age. I was optimistic that I had a lot further to go in my career, and that I could now start making the contributions to policy which had been envisaged back in 1991.

The difference between working in a post at Grade 6 compared with Grade 5 is not clear to anyone who has not worked in the Civil Service. What special characteristics did the brightest and best people at Grade 5 have? According to the official description of the post, a Grade 5 was responsible for high quality work involving:

> substantial contributions to the formulation of Departmental policies on a range of subjects;
>
> provision of coordinated advice to senior officials and Ministers;
>
> preparation of legislation;

consideration of and advice on the operational implications of proposed changes in policy or legislation;

initiation and coordination of development, research and experimental programmes within broad policy;

overall management of administrative, scientific, professional or technical processes arising from agreed policy or legislation.

Of these I knew I was not going to be involved with preparing legislation, I did not have that experience, but I expected aspects of anything and everything else.

The work certainly involved problem solving skills and decision making. There is responsibility for the quality of output or advice provided. I expected to be providing solutions to the most complex and difficult problems, and to be responsible for decisions about personnel, finance, organisation, methods, and work allocation in my area and to contribute advice for the Division as a whole. Most posts have the discretion to commit substantial expenditure. The management responsibilities for a Grade 5 can vary enormously from several thousand staff in a number of specialist establishments to a very small team with a high policy input or advisory role. Representation usually makes up a substantial part of most jobs.

I knew from my colleagues that senior civil servants, at Grade 5 and above, are able to belong to the exclusive First Division Association, FDA. The unusual original name for the trade union was chosen because when it was founded in 1919 it represented first division clerks, as opposed to the Second Division Association, which represented more junior clerks. Indeed, I later discovered that staff at Grade 7 and equivalent grades were able to join the FDA too, but most scientists and technical staff belonged to their own specialist trade union. At the NPL I had belonged to the Institution of Professional Civil Servants (IPCS) for a short time, and then resigned when I saw it was not useful.

When I first joined the Civil Service, the Open Structure comprised the Permanent Secretaries, Deputy Secretaries and Under Secretaries. Members of the Open Structure would expect to move between different Departments and have a wide range of responsibilities. It was truly an open structure. The structure below them is outlined in Appendix A and includes the Administration Group, with Assistant Secretaries (Grade 5) at the top, and their Senior Principals, Principals and executive staff below.

In 1993 I was given a folder 'Managing and Developing People in the DTI', with included a section on Personal Development for Grades 5 and 6. The performance profile which was used there had 6 management functions:

1. Self-management
2. Managing People
3. Strategic Management
4. Managing Work
5. Financial and Resource Management
6. Communications

This is a good list, to which was added Personal Skills and Behaviours – for example decisiveness, flexibility, vision, judgement, confidence and self-awareness. The folder contained a work book which encouraged self assessment. Its one weakness was the reading list, which was exclusively about management in organisations. It would have been an equally good reading list for someone working in a FTSE100 company. There was nothing about the Civil Service and its special situation and special values, or about working within a European and international policy context. The emphasis on management needed to take account of the context of the work, and that was missing.

I also listened to a presentation on management competencies, provided by Lim Soo Hoon of the Civil Service College in Singapore and Martin Barnes of the Civil Service College in the UK. It was a straightforward explanation of competencies, with an emphasis on the profile of an Agency senior manager, followed by a list of the new management competencies, which I think were going to be incorporated into staff reporting. These were divided into policy, process and people.

> Policy: conceptual thinking, analytical thinking and understanding the environment
>
> Process: seeking information, goal setting and measurement, planning effectively, process design and implementation, managing uncertainty, customer service
>
> People: gaining support of managers, staff, internal/external customers, contractors, empowerment, team management, coaching, teleworking

I found out later that Lim Soo Hoon went on to become the Permanent Secretary of the Public Services Division in Singapore, the first woman there to reach Permanent Secretary. She is about 5 years younger than I am. She is reported to have said: 'Success is not whether my voice is heard and my suggestion implemented. It is about the big picture and how I can contribute towards the jigsaw that finally forms the Singapore we want to build'. Those that have worked with her have told her that she speaks too fast for someone who asks many questions. Since then, she has learnt to speak a little slower. I smiled when I read this because I was told exactly the same in my staff report, when I was working in my last job as Principal in 1988.

Over the years there have been many different lists to define the performance criteria for senior staff. There were thus many ways for me to measure my success in my new role.

MTS Division was divided into four Branches and I was responsible for Branch 1. Typically Branch 1 in any Division was where the Head of Division looked for Divisional financial advice, and for assembling Divisional input to wider policy issues and the preparation of the Five Year Forward Look (5YFL). There was also a senior representational role, to represent the Head of Division at meetings and visits when necessary. It was not usually a post which would be given to a newly promoted Grade 5, and I was flattered that I had been seen capable enough to take on the work. In addition I was responsible for developing and implementing a Divisional marketing and publication strategy. This was intended to answer the very valid question: What is MTS Division, and what does it actually do? The title of the Division, bringing together management services and technology services made it sound as if we were a service function to the DTI. I would have liked to change the name but that was not in my power. In fact, MTS was part of the Small Firms command, and supported services that gave smaller firms practical help with innovation - particularly with management best practice, design and the use of technology. We published information, including a briefing pack on management best practice and technology transfer 'Today's support for Tomorrow's winners'. It included information sheets about benchmarking, best practice from overseas, business planning, financial management, managing information, marketing, product development, production management, purchasing, quality, and research and development.

From having just 6 staff in the NMSPU I now had 33.5 staff, which included an IT Strategy Team headed by a Grade 6 computer expert which was responsible for dealing with computer problems across the whole Small Firms command. My good professional IT credentials would have increased my suitability for the post. When I arrived the post also had responsibility for IT security and standards, but that was quickly transferred out and into a more suitable technical corner of DTI's Industry command. When I was positively vetted in 1989 it had been so that I could have responsibility for IT security, so it was a surprise to be responsible for the work again and then lose it so quickly a second time. Obviously it was not appropriate for it to be part of the Small Firms command.

My personal budget expenditure was £24.4 million per year, and I helped the Head of Division oversee and prioritise a Divisional budget of

£66 million. My title was Head of Technology Development and Adaptation for SMEs. Initial ideas were that we should sponsor and strengthen the technical infrastructure, especially the research and technology organisations (RTOs). I was asked to develop a new support programme to encourage the use of technology, which eventually became called the Focus Technical programme.

In July 1992 there had been a review of the technology transfer and awareness mechanisms used by the DTI. It had been carried out by the Assessment Unit, part of DTI's Research and Technology Policy Division, and led by Philip Hills who was a recognised international expert on evaluation. He was a colleague from when I ran the LTSU. Philip and his team took a large magnifying glass and poured over a range of DTI schemes. Technology transfer was defined as the process which enables technology developed in one place to be used in a completely different one. The results of his review were interesting, and were published as a booklet with a cover price of £5. The review examined mechanisms for the transfer of information such as seminars, demonstration projects and case studies.

Six general objectives for DTIs technology transfer programmes emerged from the analysis :

1. to raise the profile of a limited number of widely applicable technologies (specified in each case);

2. to encourage receptivity to new technological and managerial ideas especially in SMEs;

3. to stimulate provision of packaged information and advice in some specific areas with the prime objective of developing a self-sustaining, private sector, infrastructure for such provision (if practicable);

4. to create networks of personal contact between peers in related fields;

5. to encourage the development and extensive use of specified databases of technical information;

6. to help firms towards specific commercial decisions with desired economic effects.

Examples of suitable objectives for technology transfer were also provided. For example, 'to cause 50% of visitors/viewers to take a positive decision towards adopting the technology concerned within a specified timescale'. Finding out whether these types of objectives had been achieved was going to involve a lot of survey work.

In their conclusions, the recommendation of the kinds of area in which the DTI might concentrate were :

> stimulating receptivity to innovative technological and managerial ideas;
>
> general awareness of key technologies;
>
> packaging of some more specific technological information, especially for SMEs;
>
> offering disinterested advice or expertise to assist decision making in areas where it is not otherwise available.

All these thoughts were incorporated into the planning for my new Focus Technical programme. It would have been less than wise to ignore them. The ideas were sensible and remember the Assessment Unit was part of RTP Division and the Head of RTP was chairman of the ITS IPC, the committee which advised Ministers on funding for new programmes.

In addition, two important schemes to support R&D in small firms, SMART and SPUR, were being transferred to me from elsewhere within MTS, and I was pleased to be taking responsibility for them both.

SMART is the Small Firms Merit Award for Research and Technology. It was launched in 1986 and was an annual competition intended to help small firms produce outstandingly innovative ideas, but which are experiencing difficulty in attracting financial support to develop them. The awards were intended to allow these firms to take their ideas off the drawing board and into the market place. It is a competition in two stages. Stage 1 is for grants to assist in carrying out feasibility studies into innovative technology projects with commercial potential. In 1993 there were 1467 applications, from which 180 were chosen, with each awarded 75% of eligible project costs up to a maximum grant of £45,000. From 1990 there had been 180 awards each year. The project characteristics are that a technical and commercial feasibility study lasting between six and 18 months is supported, limited to technologies which are of interest to the DTI. Selection criteria are the quality and novelty of the proposal, the need for the grant, the track record of the personnel, the potential commercial significance and the exploitation proposals. Winners may apply for further Stage 2 funding of prototype development of 50% of eligible costs, subject to a maximum of £60,000.

SPUR is Support for Products Under Research, and was the only scheme still available within the DTI to fund new products and processes. It had survived only because it was targeted at small firms. General support schemes for new products and processes had been ended under the rules of the European Commission. The grant was fixed at 30%, and there was a maximum grant of £150,000. Each SPUR project had to involve a significant technological advance for the industry or sector concerned. Both SMART and SPUR were formally evaluated in 1994, and the reports were published. Both support schemes were an acknowledged success, and no Minister is inclined to chop something which is a success.

Getting together the Focus Technical programme was more difficult than I expected. My DTI colleagues were not convinced that there was a valid case for a new initiative, and I was not very enthusiastic either. I commissioned papers about technology transfer in France, Germany, and other countries in Europe. Ideas flowed in from a range of research and technology organisations. I commissioned a report from Pera International and Technopolis which studied the technical infrastructure which supports industry. It generated yet another new acronym – Business Support Organisations (BSO) which comprised those organisations within the UK infrastructure who provided technology-related services. These included, but were not limited to, the 36 Research and Technology Organisations (RTOs). There were also all the Universities. The principal conclusions were that the DTI should :

> Increase the effectiveness with which BSOs serve SMEs needs. This should be done through encouraging BSOs to develop more focussed strategies based on strong specialisms and via the rationalisation of the BSO structure.

> Create stability at the 'customer interface' between the technical support infrastructure and SMEs, to reduce the learning costs imposed on both users and suppliers by constant change in the infrastructure.

New DTI actions in the support infrastructure should therefore focus more on improving the capabilities of the existing infrastructure than on creating additional SME-oriented programmes. It was from this sentence that the name of the programme became 'Focus Technical'. The complete recommendations were that the DTI should develop initiatives which :

> improve BSOs' understanding of SME needs and the SME environment in general;

> benchmark BSO capabilities and performance, and use these benchmarks as a basis for focusing strategies;

> consider ways in which the BSO/SME interface may be improved;

> improve the access of smaller SMEs to the infrastructure;

> rationalise the use of resources and information within the system, for example by reviewing the geographic coverage of subsidised local deliveries and by organising necessary accreditation of BSOs at a national level, to avoid local duplication.

Once it was clear that there was going to be a new programme of support, many other stakeholder organisations wanted to add their ideas too. Brian Blunden, the managing Director of Pira International, had become the new President of AIRTO, the Association of Independent Research and Technology Organisations. He was soon organising meetings with me in London to submit their combined comments, made more powerful because they were on behalf of all 36 RTOs. He was speaking on behalf of 7,000 staff, most scientists and engineers, and an industrial client base providing income of over £350 million a year based on contracts with 25,000 companies each year, of which some 13,000 were SMEs. This extent of contract work with SMEs was a good effort, but it also showed there was a lot more which RTOs could do to help SMEs.

His own organisation, Pira International, was very active in technology foresight. It was investing in a new foresighting project entitled the Strategic Futures Forum, due to begin in July 1995. Industrial participants were invited to join and pay to become sponsors. Pira International had got its name as the Paper Industry Research Association and a number of study topics were proposed on packaging, printing, publishing and pulp, paper and board manufacturing. I was one of a group invited one evening to discuss the project, hosted by Professor Bain at the London Business School (LBS). Pira International was already sponsoring a programme for post-graduate students at the LBS. AIRTO and the CBI also organised a conference in October 1995 'Turning Foresight into Action'. This was not a technical meeting but involved the most senior policy makers in the UK. Keynote speakers included the Chief Scientific Advisor, Professor Robert May, and the recently departed DTI CAST, Dr Geoff Robinson. A DTI Minister took part in the panel discussions too.

It was finally agreed that the aim of the Focus Technical programme would be to re-focus the UK technical infrastructure on the needs of small firms, and improve the service which RTOs and Universities and other HEIs provided to them. It would involve change, reviews of working practices, learning about new markets, developing new product lines, and training and motivating their staff. After a difficult discussion at RTP IPC committee stages, the Focus Technical programme was finally approved and began in mid 1995. It was directed towards supporting the technical infrastructure, not the individual small and medium sized companies.

Proposed activities included:

Strategic reviews of how each RTO or HEI's technological capabilities, products and markets compare to the needs of small firms. These reviews will include analyses of organisational strengths and weaknesses, and the development of action plans to bring about appropriate changes.

Specific assistance to RTOs to develop new technology transfer activities affordable by small firms. For example to produce toolkits and packaged technology solutions which smaller companies can implement with minimum effort; introduce new marketing and sales techniques; offer short-term placements of staff to implement projects in smaller firms; or undertake specific technology transfer projects.

The programme had a target of conducting 85 strategic reviews – beginning by doing 35 with the RTOs and later starting 50 strategic reviews with HEIs. While RTOs were willing to introduce some new products and services for SMEs quickly, those products and services which had a higher commercial risk were delayed, hoping to get some DTI support from the second phase of the programme. The emphasis was to make better use of the science and technology base, and this was a recognised priority as part of support to SMEs. I had a team of staff who worked hard to discuss their proposals with each and every one of the RTOs.

There was also an existing successful technology transfer activity: 'Joining Forces', the National Programme for Technology Transfer in Materials Joining, which was a joint TWI/DTI initiative. TWI was the business name for The Welding Institute, one of the RTOs and based at Abington near Cambridge. The programme was specifically designed to help smaller companies, and provided an opportunity for a low cost, no risk appraisal of the use of materials joining and its impact on the company. Unlike the SFTES which I set up in 1981, this programme was not free for the small firms who used it.

The DTI awarded a contract for £5 million over three years to TWI, while the total programme extended to five years, with costs totalling £15.4 million, the bulk of these costs being supplied by income from industry. As was typical, funding was tapered with a reducing percentage coming from the DTI each year, perhaps 40%, 30% and 20% respectively for the first three years, then nothing in the final two years. The past funding programmes for Support for Innovation of a standard fixed percentage, originally 50% but later reduced to 30%, had long since disappeared. Tapered, reducing funding was the norm now. 'Joining Forces' gave an opportunity to access and evaluate best practice identified through TWI's worldwide networks.

It promoted the implementation of commercially beneficial joining methods through a range of activities including:

the Help Desk to supply answers and information quickly and efficiently;

Product & Process Reviews to establish needs and identify opportunities for improving profits and future growth;

feasibility studies to provide the facts to support decisions on improvements in products and processes;

the User Guide and supporting case studies to demonstrate the advantages of best practice;

visits to Demonstration Centres to show technologies in action using a practical hands-on approach;

briefings which examined business issues and commercial benefits;

workshops to explain how the technology can be applied to best advantage;

training to develop know-how and practical skills.

Other organisations were helping SMEs – particularly the new network of Business Links. In March 1995 there were 70 outlets open, with a target of 200 outlets by the end of 1995. Personal Business Advisors were employed in Business Links to help SMEs with start-ups, finance, taxation, training, exports, and issues from the Single Market. One of my DTI colleagues in MTS Division was supporting the appointment of Innovation and Technology Counsellors (ITC) in Business Links. These experienced senior business people were to provide long-term help and advice to client firms, but although they helped firms to locate technology they did little to effect the subsequent technology transfer.

Counsellors were encouraged to set up local networks of service providers, which we labelled NEARNET, and which they could rely on to offer high quality service to SMEs at a reasonable price. NEARNET could involve almost any external organisation that the ITC felt was necessary. It was expected that most enquiries for help from SMEs were likely to be handled through NEARNET. In addition colleagues in the DTI were also establishing a network of centres of excellence, SUPERNET, to enable ITCs to cope with more difficult cases. SUPERNET was managed for the DTI by PERA International. Launched in 1994, by the time of my arrival in MTS Division about 60 organisations were already members and it was expected that the majority of UK RTOs and HEIs would be involved in due course. NEARNET and SUPERNET were good initiatives and I would have liked to have been responsible for them.

The difficulty was how to position the Focus Technical programme when there was already all this existing activity, funded by my colleagues. I always like to see diagrams which simplify complexity, and my staff produced an enormous diagram which showed the interaction of all of the DTI's Innovation and Technology services. Centred on the Inventor/SME, the diagram listed all the DTI initiatives on technology access and use, best practice, technology transfer, innovation climate, awards, technology development and generation and then all the European schemes. This was a useful step forward because it highlighted where there were potential gaps and overlaps.

Another important player in technology transfer was the network of nine Government Offices and their regional staff. There were Government Offices in the East Midlands (GO-EM), Eastern Region (GO-ER), London (GOL), Merseyside (GO-M), North East (GO-NE), North West (GO-NW), South East (GO-SE), West Midlands (GO-WM) and Yorkshire and Humberside (GO-YH). Regular meetings were organised to update the Directors on current MTS activities, the relationship with other DTI activities, and to explore their role. The new Business Links were staffed with assistance from DTI staff in the regions, and the intention then was to base most DTI regional staff in Business Links in due course. A steering group was established to promote coordination and oversee DTI's activities on the use of technology. It was time there was better contact between MTS and the Government Offices and it is always useful to set up a steering group to exchange ideas.

We still took a regular winter holiday to the sun and in February 1995 we were going to New Zealand for 3 weeks. It was our second visit; the previous trip had been in 1993. Unfortunately Pete's Mom had fallen at home before Christmas, and broken her hip. She had not been well for some years and when she was in hospital in Bath they discovered that it was partly through having a limited diet. She liked to eat ham, and for over 20 years had a regular weekly order from her local grocer. She was not getting enough red meat and fish. The hip operation was a technical success, but her recovery was slow and difficult. Eventually she was discharged from hospital and we had to find somewhere for her to stay. It was obviously impossible for her to go home. Jennie, a grandchild who was also a GP, came down from Leeds when she could, to get involved with the treatment and the decisions on what to do next. Eventually a room was found in a nursing home on the edge of Bath, and we all breathed a sigh of relief that, for the moment, she was in safe hands.

She knew that we were off to New Zealand, and we were flying on a Thomson holidays charter flight. Their flights were much cheaper than flying with scheduled airlines and they only used a small aircraft with two engines, not the Boeing 747 Jumbos. We needed to land to refuel three times. Half way through the journey we landed at Singapore and were called over the loudspeaker system, taken to a quiet room and told that she had just died. We believed she had hung on until she knew we had left, and then given up. Everyone was very kind, and asked whether we wanted to take our luggage off and fly back to England. Before going on holiday we had discussed with the rest of the family what we would do if this happened while we were away, and had agreed that we would not fly home. So we continued onwards to Auckland, to stay with family there as originally arranged.

Pete's sister, who lived in Guernsey, dealt with all the funeral arrangements and started to sort out the details of selling the house and everything else. It was a long and tedious story, but eventually the house was sold. It was a nice house, one half of a large house which had been divided, and had lovely views across the River Avon on the west side of Bath. Unfortunately an early survey had suggested there might be recent movement in part of the building, which delayed the sale until the building could be measured and some repair work carried out.

Pete and I were both earning good salaries, and the extra money we inherited just added to the feeling that we were working very hard, increasing our savings, but not having the time to enjoy ourselves together. Our jobs were still both interesting and enjoyable so it was not an urgent problem, but we looked forward with more enthusiasm to retiring when Pete got to 50, as we had originally planned. This would be in 1998, three years later.

Each Autumn everyone involved in spending the DTI science and technology budgets took part in a prioritisation exercise. This was not unusual. The annual cycle of budget allocation had been in place for many, many years, and well pre-dated my arrival in 1981. In 1995 there were four distinct science and technology budgets: CARAD for Civil Aviation, the British National Space Centre, Non-nuclear Energy, and the Innovation and Technology Support (ITS) budget. In preparation for the large prioritisation exercise, some detailed work had been done comparing the four budgets, under the six headings of:

1.   The degree of Government obligation or commitment
2.   DTI's role as a prime mover in supporting the activity
3.   Nature of the benefits to the economy and/or quality of life
4.   Distribution of the benefits
5.   Degree of additionality
6.   Impact of the outcomes of the support

It was a careful and complex analysis. My interest was not in the balance between the four budgets, but in how the amount allocated to the ITS budget would be shared between competing programmes, mine included. MTS Division used the ITS budget, for which Dr David Evans of the Technology and Innovation Division was the budget holder. He had moved from being Head of Environment Division, and replaced Dr Colin Hicks who had previously been the budget holder. When I ran the LTSU I had been providing advice on the allocation of money to programmes spending this budget, so having been a gamekeeper I was now representing a significant group of poachers. Such is life. The authority for spending in this area came from the Science and Technology Act of 1965 and the Industrial Development Act of 1982, and the need for DTI support was very well-established. ITS expenditure was divided into five areas:

1. Climate for Innovation
2. Best Practice
3. Technology Access
4. Technology Development
5. Standards/Regulation

In 1995, and for the first time, the model used for prioritisation was based on the theory of decisions with multiple objectives and implemented in software developed by Dr Larry Phillips at the London School of Economics. The approach, called Multi-Criteria Decision Analysis (MCDA) has subsequently been used by other Departments, and recent examples in the public domain in 2004 include the MOD and the Environment Agency. The success of MCDA techniques within Government is said to foster better informed decisions, not only creating aligned commitment to the resulting plans, but also helping to facilitate new and innovative solutions. The idea has been used for over 10 years, which is a sign that it has some merit. It is a more independent approach than letting a group of very senior officials sit together and argue for their own share. I always supported the success of logic over oration.

In our case, discussion focussed on the strategies which indicate What and Why, not on tactics, operations or activities, which are concerned with How and When. The first meeting was held on 19 July; I attended the second meeting on 13 September. Both meetings were held in a conference suite at the Grosvenor Hotel, near to Victoria Station. I believe it was specially chosen so that we all got away from a DTI building.

Attendance was strictly by invitation, and papers were confidential to the named attendee. Most attendees were Grade 5 Branch Heads, although there were a few Grade 3 Division Heads. The overall purpose was to develop a collective view on the most cost-effective way ahead to allocate the ITS budget. Individual disagreements were discussed until a consensus was reached.

It was a numerical cost-benefit exercise, where the costs were known and the benefits were assessed against the four criteria of wealth creation; uncertainty and risk reduction; synergy; and prospect of success. Attendees were expected to use their judgement and expertise to evaluate the options against these criteria, and assess trade-offs between the different areas. Judgements had to be made about the relative contributions of each area's options to the four benefit criteria. In addition the relative importance of the criteria were judged to be 100 for wealth creation, 25 for uncertainty and risk reduction, 20 for synergy and 50 for prospect of success. All these numbers were poured into the computer; it was not obvious how everything would come together and that made it harder for interested people to force their own programmes to move up the priority list. There was then a break while the data was input, the handle was churned and the results obtained. A series of different results were produced because it was also important to identify priorities if either more or less total resource was made available.

The initial findings were that the DTI should be moving away from Technology Development (including my small firms programmes SMART and SPUR, as well as LINK programmes which involved collaborations between companies and academics) towards the other, softer options. This caused further exploration of the model and two subsequent portfolios of strategies were revealed. For a small additional cost they gave much larger relative benefits. Many sensitivity analyses were conducted, varying the weights, to see if these results changed significantly. There were changes, but nothing which affected the attractiveness of the two preferred portfolios. At least my major spending programmes, SMART and SPUR, were now finally safely included in the portfolios.

I always carry a small camera and I took photographs of the final results from the whiteboard, to share with colleagues back in MTS Division.

30 Striving for Excellence

In every job, some tasks are more interesting than others. Alongside developing the new Focus Technical programmes, I quickly took responsibility for creating the MTS Quality Plan. The first plan had been issued in May 1994. My predecessor, Callum Johnston, had been very active and during 1994 MTS Division held a number of workshops to establish what industry's needs were for overseas technology and best practice programmes. It was a good starting point for the quality journey. My journey into quality had begun much earlier, when I became responsible for software quality in 1989. The DTI had been explaining the benefits of a quality approach to industry much earlier, through the National Quality campaign which began in 1983 following the publication of the British Standard BS 5750 in 1979. It took time to apply the same tools to our own work.

The European Quality Award (EQA) had been launched by the European Foundation for Quality Management (EFQM) in 1992 for commercial companies. The first winner of the European Quality Award in 1992 was Rank Xerox, and I obtained a copy of their application which was published after they won. They explained that first they looked for good results displaying positive trends over 3 years. Second they looked for a clear link between the results and the processes which drove them. Where they had positive results and could demonstrate control of the process which delivered them, they investigated how pervasive they were throughout the company. Finally they compared their performance with their competitors or with the 'best in class'. It was the classic way of showing performance improvement, and I was sure that other organisations could learn from them, MTS Division included.

After the setting up of the EFQM and the launch of the EQA it was only a short time until the same framework was set up in the UK. The new organisation was set up in November 1992 and named the British Quality Foundation (BQF). Membership of the BQF Board was formally announced in December 1993, with Alistair Macdonald, DTI Grade 2 Deputy Secretary, as an observer. Applicants for the first UK Quality Award were invited shortly afterwards, with the first award made in 1994. A Guide to Self Assessment was also produced, with examples so that readers could develop their own self assessment process. Whether or not the reader applied for the UK Quality Award, self assessment helped achieve business improvements in competitiveness and effectiveness by identifying strengths and areas for improvement.

The European Quality Award and the UK Quality Award both depend on the Business Excellence Model. This assumes there are nine features of an excellent organisation. These nine elements are made up of four results criteria: Customer satisfaction, Employee satisfaction, Impact on Society and Business results, and five enablers: Leadership, Policy and Strategy, People management, Resources and Processes. To explain the way in which the criteria are interlinked:

'Customer satisfaction, Employee satisfaction and Impact on society are achieved through Leadership driving Policy and strategy, People management, Resources and Processes, leading ultimately to excellence in Business results'.

For each of the results criteria, the concern is what the organisation has achieved and is achieving. For the enablers it is how the organisation approaches each of the criteria. These criteria can all be scored, and the details are available from BQF or standard texts on quality. The very best companies, winners of an Award, will score over 600 out of a theoretical maximum of 1000. Ordinary companies struggle to score 200.

I had a team of staff who were responsible for quality, so I could rely on their expertise, but I decided to apply myself to become an assessor for the UK Quality Award. For those chosen, formal assessor training followed in April. Three days were spent at a nice hotel, usually a country house well away from anywhere. People were allocated to assessment teams, each comprising five assessors and a senior assessor. A Case Study was issued and a simulated assessment exercise was carried out. The Case study in 1994 was not produced in the UK but had been prepared for the 1994 European Quality Award Assessor Training Course, so any experienced people who were assessing both awards would go through the same case study twice. If the team works well together at the training session then it will be the same team working together to judge a real application. If there are too few applicants then sometimes two teams are allocated to the same applicant. Part of the benefit of this is to train new assessors, and they can compare their scores and assessment with another more experienced team. When I applied in the first year of the award I allocated the costs and time spent away on assessor training as part of my official training. I expected to do the reading and assessment work during the weekends at home. Each year the application process is repeated, and everyone has to go away on assessor training again. I was an assessor for four years.

In 1994 training the Case study was Aquanox - a fictitious medium sized chemical company based on five sites in Europe. Manufacturing industry was the typical applicant in the early days. In 1995 training the case study was the Essen Bank – a large, multinational provider of financial products and services. Then in 1996 there became a separate EQA award for the public sector. The case study for 1996 was the Spectrum Psychiatric Care Foundation, a not-for-profit organisation devoted to the care of elderly psychiatric patients and based on four sites. In 1997 the case study was Simon Valves which was a family owned engineering company, medium sized. One of the most persistent questions raised during assessor training concerned the worries about scoring a small organisation. From my policy responsibilities in MTS Division I was interested in small firms too and one of the applicants which I assessed for the UK Quality Award was a small firm.

Generally the process of assessment is that individual assessors read their application and make notes of strengths and areas for improvement. Provisional scores are made. It is all a paper exercise. Then the whole team meets, and under the guidance of the senior assessor compare their notes and scores. There is usually a discussion and then an agreed consensus score is reached together with a combined view of strengths and areas for improvement. This process often takes a full day, or longer if the application is contentious. A list is also made of Site Visit Issues. If the applicant is identified as a potential winner, the team will make a site visit. Finally the senior assessor, using contributions from the rest of the team, writes a Feedback report for the applicant.

In 1994 and 1995 I was privileged to work for experienced senior assessors, Steve Tanner and Norman Hughes respectively. Then in 1996, with Steve as senior assessor again for my team, it was planned that I would host the consensus meeting. The date chosen in July was while we were on holiday, cruising the canals between Chester and Ellesmere Port. Everyone decided that spending a day on our narrowboat would be good fun, and there were no locks to do. Pete spent the day steering while I and the others worked hard inside. In 1997 I was again off to Chester for the consensus meeting, but without the boat.

In 1994 Rover Group and TNT Express were winners of the first UK Quality Award and they were congratulated by the Prime Minister at a glittering evening at the Hilton Hotel on Park Lane. In June 1995 I attended the Award Winners conference, held at the Heritage Motor Centre at Gaydon near Warwick. The keynote speaker was Sir Iain Vallance of BT, followed by the two UK award winners: John Towers of Rover Group and Alan Jones of TNT Express and three European award winners: Paul Rafferty of ICL(D2D), Alberto Boiardi of IBM Semea Italy and Jose Manuel Cangas of Ericsson Spain. I was now able to justify attending the 1995 Presentation and Gala Dinner, held at Grosvenor House and with the awards presented by Ian Lang MP, the newly arrived President of the Board of Trade. It was an interesting and very enjoyable evening and I only just managed to catch the last train back to Reading. Staying in London was never an option because it was difficult to justify the costs of overnight accommodation. It was cheaper to take a taxi all the way back home than to pay for a night in a hotel. Even when I was no longer a current assessor I was still invited to the assessor meetings.

My last involvement with BQF was when I attended the assessor recognition day in November 2000. In October 2000 the Awards and Gala Dinner again took place at the Hilton Hotel on Park Lane, and the awards were presented by HRH The Princess Royal. In 2000 there were 200 assessors, 32 award applicants, 18 sites were visited leading to 10 finalists and 4 winners. For comparison in 1994 there were 120 assessors. Now the Award was well established being on the jury was still important for the DTI, but it was no longer a task for a Grade 2 Deputy Secretary. It was a task for a Grade 5 Director and my colleague from MTS, Dr Ken Poulter, became a member of the jury.

Improving quality meant satisfying the customers and my customers included the President of the Board of Trade and his Ministers. In March 1994 a glossy coloured book was produced: 'A Guide to Working with Ministers'. On the front cover was a picture of the actors from the 'Yes Minister' TV programme, showing the Minister, his Private Secretary and the Permanent Secretary. In the DTI, the President and his Ministers and their Private Offices had their own views on how their civil servants could better help Ministers achieve their objectives. The guide had been written following discussions with them and had been endorsed by them and by senior officials (presumably Deputy Secretaries and the Permanent Secretary). Obviously the various Private Secretaries had been closely involved with writing the guide. There was detailed yet clear guidance, in simple language, which included dealing with correspondence, creating submissions recommending a decision or action, preparing for meetings and visits, writing good speeches, and dealing with a variety of parliamentary business. The guide was well written and very useful to staff involved in policy work.

In June 1994 everyone received a leaflet 'DTI – The Way we Work'. It was intended to identify better ways of working and the leaflet was intended to be fixed on a filing cabinet or on a wall so that it was always visible. The aim, in banner headlines, was

> 'To operate in a direct and straightforward way, constantly seeking the most cost effective methods of working.'

The instructions here were more practical. Tighter working methods are basic to quality and contribute directly to the DTI's objective of providing a professional, high quality, accessible and responsive service. To streamline working methods we need to question how we do things and keep what we do direct and straightforward. This was a clumsy sentence but the actions were clearer. Meetings are expensive in people's time; a short note or a phone call may be more effective. Only put on paper what it is really necessary; think about more use of the telephone. With open plan offices and space limitations there was now an official personal storage limit of 3.5 linear metres per person, so much of the emphasis was on reducing unnecessary paper and sending files away to the file store. The emphasis was clearly on using the (rubbish) BIN, and this message went to everyone, including the most junior administrative assistants.

In May 1994 the MTS Quality Update newsletter had congratulated all the staff on making practical steps to do their jobs better. Quality was not just a buzzword for us. The drive for quality started at the top of the Division, with Dr Shotton and his Heads of Branch and the Quality Coordinators meeting regularly. Each of the four Branches had a named Quality Coordinator, and the Division Quality Manager worked for me in MTS1. Improving how we did our work was everyone's responsibility, and the MTS Quality Plan involved everyone from the Division Head down.

Examples of Quality Successes included streamlining the paper and electronic filing systems, improving service to the public by setting up a database to log and monitor written correspondence, holding a workshop to clarify the role and mission of one of the Branches, setting up a computerised system to keep track of programmes and projects, identifying gaps in IT skills of staff by comparison with a list of basic competencies, and devising and implementing a financial monitoring system to keep track of claims. Everyone received a personal copy of the MTS Quality Plan, and was exhorted to keep thinking about how they could do their work better.

My colleagues in the International Branch of MTS held a number of workshops during 1994, to establish industry's needs for overseas technology and best practice programmes. This was part of providing a Customer Focussed Service, and was praised in the DTI publication 'Results through Quality'. It was also very useful evidence for the needs for their work when they sought funding from the Innovation and Technology Support budget.

MTS was one of a number of case studies showing activities for implementing quality in the DTI. There were many different activities: Customer Surveys, Quality Teams, Staff Surveys, Quality Networks, Training in Quality, Quality Awards and Accreditation, Communications, Benchmarking, and having a Quality Infrastructure. All these approaches to achieving quality had been covered in detail in the DTI Quality Toolkit, and different teams were using different approaches. The DTI was in the lead across Government in establishing quality in policy areas. This was no surprise because the DTI had many years experience in promoting the message about quality to British industry.

By 1995 I had been an Assessor for the UK Quality Award for two rounds, and used this experience to push forward self-assessment within MTS Division, initially by preparing for discussion my own list of our strengths and areas for improvement. Described as a benchmarking questionnaire with 55 short questions it was actually an initial attempt at self-assessment using the Business Excellence Model, and I sent a questionnaire to Grade 2 Deputy Secretary David Durie, Grade 3 Dr Keith Shotton and the other Grade 5s. Everyone responded. It was too hard to ask them for rigorous scoring of the nine criteria and their sub-criteria, but I asked for a mark of either a, b, c or d depending on perceptions of the current situation. Scores of a are good, b is less good etc. Examples of the questions include under Leadership 'Our Senior Executives work together as a team' which everyone scored either a or b, and under Processes 'There is a formal quality system' which everyone scored as a. Other criteria did not score as well, especially those under the criteria of Customer Satisfaction. We knew there was some work to be done to get closer to our customers, although we did have customer satisfaction measures. Customers came in a number of different shapes and sizes, including Ministers. One of the benefits of a questionnaire approach was to share the joint scores between us all, and to discuss why some people had very different perceptions of what we were doing.

I was also invited by Alistair Macdonald, to give a presentation at one of his meetings with his senior staff, about the Business Excellence Model. I knew he had been through a short version of the assessor training, so he could take part in the jury discussions for the UK Quality Award at which the best applicants are chosen who will receive site visits. The award was about to be opened to the public sector and non-profit organisations, and this meant that the methodology became more useful for assessing quality in policy areas in the DTI.

MTS was also a member of the Policy Consortium established under the DTI Quality Task Force, and in January 1996 a booklet was produced which started to address the question of quality in policy areas. The management consultants KPMG designed the Policy Cycle, a diagram which separated a policy issue into two parts: doing the right things, and doing the right things right. On the one side there were objectives, options and appraisal leading to a decision. On the other side there was implementation, maintenance, evaluation and development. Many of the consortium members worked with KPMG to tackle quality, and there seemed to be a flurry of quality initiatives and activities.

I was still an active tutor for the Open University and a full list of my Open University teaching experience is at Appendix H. The MBA specialist course on Performance Measurement and Evaluation started in 1994 and I applied to teach it and became a tutor for the duration of the course. I also taught at several of the MBA Residential Schools. My close involvement with the UK Quality Award, alongside my enthusiasm for quality in my own area, meant that I could offer a lot of practical experience to the students. This led to a small consultancy contract to study the potential of the European and UK Quality Awards for quality improvement in the OU Business School. My work started in August

1995 and was to be completed by August 1996. It was an interesting task, carried out mainly at weekends.

The contract required two pieces of research work. The first phase was 'to review the content and process of relevant generic quality assessment frameworks, to identify where existing OU activities mapped onto the EFQM model, and to produce an outline report on the applicability of the model to the OUBS context and the potential or actual contribution of existing OU activities to quality improvement consistent with that model'. The second phase was to meet a range of OUBS staff and investigate self-assessment. Finally I was to decide on the desirability and feasibility of the OUBS submitting an application for the UK Quality Award. I decided it was better to give an honest answer and this did not seem to match with OUBS politics. A proper consultant would probably have played the game differently.

One consequence was that OUBS academic staff applied to become assessors for the UK Quality Award. I was pleased with this outcome. Being an assessor is a very good means to thoroughly understand the model. Reading about and judging the strengths and areas for improvement of the best organisations gives insights into the quality improvements needed back at home. I was sure that more influence was going to be made on OUBS quality when permanent academics had ownership of the EFQM model than when I praised it from outside.

In August 1995 I was circulated with information about the Government Study Fellowships, and while reading the rules I noticed that under the scheme two of the four awards available were specified as Senior Civil Service Fellowships. As the name implies, these were opportunities for senior staff, at my grade and above, to spend up to two years away on full pay carrying out a research project. I filed the papers but later as the climate around me changed, I reflected. There would be advantages in having 2 years away on paid secondment, and if the award started in 1996 then the timing would mean the Fellowship would end in 1998, and we would then be thinking seriously about retirement because Pete would be old enough to apply for early retirement. I was hopeful that the structure of the DTI would have settled down when I came back in 1998, and whatever the outcome the climate would certainly be different after the next election which was scheduled for 1997.

So, on 24 October 1995 I applied to carry out a project which I called 'Beyond Quality: Striving for Excellence in the Public Sector'. I had to choose a Senior Supervisor and I nominated Professor Roland Kaye at the Open University Business School. With hindsight I am sure I could have found a more suitable supervisor, perhaps at Oxford or at the London Business School, but I was concentrating hard on exploiting my existing contacts. The application had to be countersigned by my boss, Dr Keith Shotton, and first he asked me to draft some text which he could use. He eventually used most of my text and added a lot of words of his own, even more strongly recommending my application. I wrote and emailed lots of key people in the UK and overseas, including Dr Geoff Robinson, ex-CAST who had now returned to the IBM Laboratory at Hursley. Most people admired the proposal, said how useful the work would be, but warned me that I was proposing to cover a lot of the ground, and to reflect on whether it might be better to cover less area. The application went off and I waited to see what would happen next.

Of course, what happened next was that the whole arrangement for the Senior Civil Service changed, and at the same time we decided that we could afford to retire earlier than 1998.

31 The Competitiveness White Papers 1994, 1995 and 1996

Government support for innovation was well-established since the establishment of the Innovation Unit in the DTI in 1991. In August 1994, a leaflet had been produced which described the DTI's support for innovation.

> 'Innovation - the successful exploitation of new ideas – is essential for sustained competitiveness and wealth creation. Innovation does not involve R&D alone, but successful exploitation through good management, appropriate finance, skilled manpower and a supportive overall climate. Innovation is ultimately the responsibility of companies. Only they can bring together the resources, investment and skills for market success.'

The DTI aimed to help UK business compete successfully at home and in world markets. It acted as the voice of industry within Government and sought to ensure that there was effective communication between Government, the science and engineering base and industry. Its innovation activities included spreading awareness of innovation, encouraging best practice, simplifying access to sources of help and increasing the availability of all national and international resources. Activities highlighted in 1994, where I had been involved during my career, included the Technology Foresight programme, the annual Government Forward Look on science and technology, the Teaching Company Scheme, the SMART and SPUR schemes which support R&D in small and medium sized firms, and the LINK scheme. I had been lucky and I had contributed to many of the respected innovation support mechanisms, as well as to the definition of key strategic policy tools.

The Government continued to be committed to encourage innovation as a means by which UK companies can improve their competitiveness. The importance of competitiveness had been recognised in the White Paper 'Realising our Potential' (ROP) published in May 1993. As an example of the interesting things which happened as a result of ROP, the President of the Board of Trade had announced on 14 April 1994 that, following a review undertaken by KPMG Peat Marwick, the DTI laboratories should be placed under private sector ownership or management. He stated that this offered the best opportunity for the laboratories to maintain and develop the expertise and facilities which are most appropriate to the changing needs of both Government and industry.

The Laboratory of the Government Chemist (LGC) had been an Executive Agency of the DTI since October 1989, and had moved to new premises at Teddington, on the same site as the NPL. LGC was the focus for analytical chemistry within Government and the Government Chemist was cited in several Acts of Parliament as referee analyst. LGC also played a major role in the establishment of analytical chemical standards as part of the National Measurement System, and in the development of an international infrastructure to enable analytical data to be mutually recognised. I had funded some of their work as part of my portfolio of projects from the NMS budget. On 10 November 1995 it was announced by Science and Technology Minister Ian Taylor that the Laboratory of the Government Chemist was to be sold. There had been an invitation issued to bid, and the winner was a consortium comprising LGC Management and Staff, the Royal Society of Chemistry and the investment company 3i plc. The sale and purchase agreement was to be completed at the beginning of 1996. The relevant phrase in ROP which provoked all this was that there would be 'further scrutiny of Government research establishments'.

After ROP there followed the set of three annual Competitiveness White Papers 'Helping Business to Win' published in May 1994, 'Forging Ahead' published in May 1995 and 'Creating the Enterprise Centre of Europe' published in June 1996. The President of the Board of Trade, Michael Heseltine, was determined that there would be three White Papers, published each year. My colleagues who were tasked with delivering these had to work very hard to keep to his strict timetable. After the first two White Papers were published and with the third in progress he was promoted to became Deputy Prime Minister, and was replaced at the DTI by Ian Lang in July 1995.

Competitiveness is an important attribute. For a firm, competitiveness is the ability to produce the right goods and services of the right quality at the right price at the right time. It means meeting customer's needs more efficiently and effectively than other firms. For a nation, competitiveness is defined as the degree to which it can, under free and fair market conditions, produce goods and services which meet the test of international markets, while simultaneously maintaining and expanding the real incomes of its people over the long term. Success in the UK, and ultimately our standard of living, would depend on continuously improving all aspects of our performance across the whole economy.

I gave a number of talks about the work of MTS Division, and the current DTI policies towards small firms and innovation. This included a lecture at the University of Sussex in Brighton on 'Industrial Competitiveness: Winning, Forging and Enterprise' which brought together these themes. The Competitiveness White Papers had a number of important messages for small firms. The central message was that all firms, whatever their size, must strive to improve their performance.

Within this general message it was recognised that smaller firms were at a disadvantage compared to larger ones in some important respects, and special help was offered with a new package of support. In 1995 the vast majority of businesses were small firms; it was reported that 96 per cent of firms had fewer than 20 employees and small firms with fewer than 100 employees accounted for 50 per cent of employment.

Not all small firms were seen as potential recipients of DTI support. The policy was to focus assistance selectively on those firms with the potential and management will to grow. The main assistance was from Business Links in England, Local Enterprise Companies (LECs) and Scottish Business Shops in Scotland, and Business Connect in Wales. In May 1995 there were 103 Business Links either open or about to open, and the aim was to have over 200 by the end of the year. They would be the normal delivery mechanism for all DTI's business services from April 1996. Of the £206 million allocated over four years, £93 million was for new services for Business Links and £70 million was for management, technology and innovation. Business Links were based on a partnership between local organisations and delivered an enquiry and information service and were staffed by Personal Business Advisors supported by specialists.

There are particular problems facing the more innovative small business. These were recognised with new measures to raise the importance of innovation, spread best practice, improve networking, secure access to advice and technology and improve the prospects for smaller firms to develop successfully and bring to market technology-based products. My SMART and SPUR schemes were combined and simplified, and winners were encouraged to obtain business advice to progress their successful developments to full commercial exploitation.

Then on 11 March 1996 the Prime Minister announced a radical cross-Government review of the support which Government provided to business. At that time Michael Heseltine was Deputy Prime Minister and he continued in that post until the Conservatives lost the election in May 1997. The aim of the review was to set out proposals to:

> Ensure greater customer focus in Government-funded business support by delegating design and delivery of support wherever possible to business-led partnerships at local and sectoral level.

> Reward the most successful partnerships through the use of the challenge funding approach.

> Simplify remaining support, including through a significant reduction in the number of separate schemes.

I am sure that many of the older DTI civil servants smiled because we remembered exactly the same reasons for setting up the Support for

Innovation (SfI) scheme, all those years ago. It was intended to simplify and reduce the number of separate schemes. However the idea of business-led partnerships and challenge funding were new. The overall purpose of the sector challenge was to improve competitiveness and long term profitability by promoting a culture of business excellence and innovation through People, Technology, Markets and Finance. The essential features were that it would be a competition, with measurable outputs, and hands-off by Government. It was not just for larger companies: SMEs were a priority. The sector challenge bid process was that bidding rounds would take place twice each year. It would be a 2-stage process, with submission of outline bids and then full bids. Bids must be clear about what they would do, and how they would do it, and how they would measure success. There were output measures and evaluation criteria. There were nine evaluation criteria:

1. Impact
2. Strategic Fit
3. Relevance
4. Quality of content
5. Partnership
6. Value for money
7. Additionality
8. Financial viability
9. Credibility

This new approach to Government support was going to have an impact on UK industry. There was more emphasis on partnership, and the challenge approach. Government was now asking industry for ideas, and this included SMEs. It was intended to 'level the playing field' for support. The onus now was on lead organisations to propose good projects. This was not a totally new concept; for many years funding from the European Commission had been on the basis of a call for outline proposals followed by a beauty contest to decide which of these projects should be funded. There was much less work for civil servants, and with two competitions each year the work would arrive in two batches. The first round was due for decision by 12 February 1997.

32 The new Senior Civil Service structure in 1996

My first annual staff report as Grade 5 was due in April 1995, and I approached the activity with a mixture of nervousness and caution. My Deputy Secretary was David Durie, who later became Governor of Gibraltar. After my report had been completed I was invited to be interviewed in his office, where I found a large comfortable room which was very well furnished. I knew he had recently returned to the DTI after a posting as Deputy UK Permanent Representative to the European Union, based in Brussels. He was Dr Keith Shotton's boss and therefore my countersigning officer, and admitted that he had seen little of my work, but that I appeared to have made a sound start in the new post and grade. I needed to establish myself in the post before he could assess further potential. The flavour of it all was that I might be eligible for further promotion, but it was too early to tell. I realistically expected to have two or three different postings at Grade 5 before being considered fitted for promotion again, and that would be promotion to Grade 3. The promotion ladder does not involve passing through Grade 4. I knew I was already too old and never going to be good enough to achieve Deputy Secretary, Grade 2.

As a consequence of the two Civil Service White Papers, 'The Civil Service: Continuity and Change', which was published in 1994, and 'The Civil Service: Taking Forward Continuity and Change' which was published in January 1995, the DTI set up a Grading and Pay Review Team. This was not a special activity unique to the DTI; all Government Departments with 12 or more senior staff went through the same process. The review team included Dr Ian Thornley who was previously Personnel Director of Shell UK, and two DTI civil servants. It was a very small review team. By June 1995 the work of all staff at Grade 5 and above was being carefully inspected. I was interviewed, to find out what my group did, what my role was, and how I worked with my immediate staff. I recall at the end of the interview being left with the impression that there was a framework or model to describe the job of a Grade 5, but that there were difficulties doing the same for the grade above, Grade 3.

I was first to be interviewed in MTS so I reported back to my colleagues on my experience, and my notes identified a serious problem. For those of us who hoped to be promoted to Grade 3, it was bad news. There were clearly going to be many less Grade 3 posts, but there would be roughly the same number of posts at Grade 2 and Grade 5. In consequence, in future people at my grade might be working directly to someone senior like David Durie, at Grade 2. It was not something which I was pleased about, and I doubt it pleased other senior staff. We waited to see whether my instincts were correct, and what would happen next.

The DTI Grading and Pay Review team were also tasked to look at staff up to and including Grade 6. Their terms of reference are at Appendix F. Their task was to 'Examine the effectiveness of the present pay and grading structures, and consider and propose alternative arrangements which better meet these requirements'. A questionnaire was produced, and everyone was invited to complete it and give their views. There were twelve questions and I have grouped them so the style of seeking information about strengths/weaknesses/proposals for change is clear.

1. In your area of work, to what extent does the way that different tasks are allocated to people of different grades seem to reflect natural levels of responsibility for dealing with different types of task?

2. What changes could be made to working arrangements and/or management levels which would result in improved efficiency and performance?

3. What are the strengths of the Department's current grading structure?

4. What are the weaknesses?

5. What changes would you like to see made?

6. To what extent does the current grading system help or hinder career development?

7. What changes would you like to see made which would lead to improved development of careers?

8. What are the strengths of the present pay and reward system?

9. What are the weaknesses?

10. What changes would you like to see made?

11. To what extent are the current grading and pay arrangements successful in recognising and rewarding different levels of achievement, performance and responsibility?

12. Are there any other aspects of grading and pay or related issues in the Department on which you would like to comment?

Everyone who completed the questionnaire had the chance to take part in a discussion group. Certainly there could be no criticism that staff had not been consulted, but what junior staff offered in response to the questionnaire must have been very variable. Picking out useful ideas would have been difficult, but perhaps the broad changes had already been discussed, and the questionnaire was only being used at the level of details. Certainly Ministers seemed to know that they wanted change. I asked for a blank copy of the questionnaire for information, but was not expected to complete it.

In September 1995 the provisional Report by the Senior Management Review Team on Implementing the Civil Service White Papers in the DTI was circulated, followed in November 1995 by the glossy published version of the same document. The original Terms of Reference had been:

> to improve the organisation's effectiveness and performance;
>
> to continue the process of delegating authority and responsibility down the organisation to the point where decisions are most effectively made;
>
> to create more interesting and challenging management jobs within the organisation; and
>
> to make proposals for a senior management structure.

It was a thick detailed report, much of which did not relate to me or my area. The new structure, when it was announced on 15 November, had a number of interesting key features:

> leaner, flatter, management structures;
>
> fewer layers of management;
>
> work organised more coherently;
>
> team working given greater prominence;
>
> a new top management team.

At the time of the Review it was reported there were 196 posts at Grade 5 or above in the DTI, and there would be 170 posts in the proposed new structure, of which 152 would definitely be within the Senior Civil Service, with perhaps 9 of the remaining 18 also included depending on the outcomes of job evaluations. Chapter 11 of the report described the new Regional and SME Command, which included MTS Division with its 115 staff and the objective to promote management best practice and effective use of technology among SMEs. After April 1996 my post became Director of SME Technology, and still had my 33.5 staff. The work seemed to be the same but the responsibility was different because the post reported directly to the Director General. It was now acknowledged that the principle was to reduce wherever possible the number of posts at the intermediate level. Director would be the normal level for the new structure and sat between Heads of Section and the Director General who was the Head of Command. Where there had been staff in three levels, at Grades 5, 3, and 2, now there were only two levels: Director and Director General.

A minute was circulated to everyone in the Senior Civil Service, at my grade and above, asking whether they would like to consider taking early retirement, or severance. There appeared to be no strategic thinking in order to choose between those who were interested in leaving and a lot of knowledge and experience was discarded in order to simply reduce staff numbers and reduce the salary bill. We spent a few days at home doing careful sums and looking at our current and predicted expenditure against our income. I was only 43 years old, which was too young for early retirement, and I was therefore only considered for early severance on compulsory grounds – there would be no immediate pension but a redundancy payment instead. When I joined in 1976 it was possible to take early retirement at age 40, but the rules changed in 1987 and pensions were no longer an option before reaching 50 years of age. I filled in the forms and received written details of the various payments. There were no surprises and I suggested a date for leaving in April 1996, which was quickly agreed. The same offer of retirement or severance was made to junior staff, but some of those who applied were refused. I know of no-one in the Senior Civil Service who applied to go and was refused.

I found that many colleagues had also decided to retire early, including Dr Richard Hinder a Grade 5 colleague in MTS and my boss Dr Keith Shotton. Many others said that they would like to retire early, but the offer was not sufficiently attractive. Those with children still at school or going through University had no choice but to continue working; they could not afford to stop early. I was pleased that I was able to go, but worried that many of my other colleagues were left behind. If there was a change of Government in 1997, as was widely predicted, there was going to be a lot of work supporting our new Ministers and delivering their new policies. I had found it challenging to work with brand new senior secondees from industry and could imagine the problems of handling brand new Ministers. I hoped for my colleagues' sake that I was wrong about the problems ahead, and that those who remained would be able to handle the new challenges.

Over the years there have been many different lists to define the performance criteria for senior staff. It was not until core criteria were published in 1997 for those senior staff who would become part of the new Senior Open Structure that these criteria were used to measure a post. In 1996 it was necessary to have a means to find out whether a particular Grade 6 or Grade 5 job was sufficiently senior to be above or below the dividing line which distinguished the new Senior Open Structure. Some of the existing posts would fall below the line and others above it. Nine core criteria were defined, split equally between Direction, Management and Communication and Personal Contribution. The details are in Appendix E.

The rules for job evaluation of the new structure were not issued until March 1996. A glossy Handbook: 'Job Evaluation for DTI Jobs in the Senior Civil Service 'Majic'', was published. When I read the title my immediate reaction was to smile and think of magic, not majic, and I am sure I was not unique. In fact, Majic was an acronym for Managing People, Accountability, Judgement, Influencing and Professional Competence, which were the five factors used to score each job. The first four factors were scored on a scale 1 to 7, whereas Professional Competence was scored on a scale of 1 to 3. The overall score would help determine the pay band of the job. The lowest pay band, where my job would have been, was linked to scores of between 7 and 10 and salaries between £38,000 and £59,700. This matched exactly the current Grade 5 pay scale. I was never told my precise job score, but assume it was 8 or 9, matching my salary.

An important difference for the future was going to be the way in which people moved posts between one Directorship and another. In the past, promotion was to a grade, and movement up the salary scales was based on annual performance assessed in post. Transfer between jobs was a personal move and the salary, if the new job was at the same grade, did not change. Salary only went up; it certainly did not reduce if the post was less challenging. Grade 5 salaries had been negotiated by the Unions, like all the lower grades, but now they were part of the Senior Civil Service this would no longer be the case. Indeed as some jobs at Director and Director General were going to be advertised under open competition, it would be difficult to deal with changing pay levels as individuals moved around. It did have the advantage that the more challenging jobs could pay much higher salaries. I knew of instances when good competent people applied for their own job in open competition and did not win it.

One day I received an anonymous note in the post. Barbara always opened my mail but this was marked as Personal. She passed me the envelope and I found it was a poem, and when I asked my staff no-one would admit to having written it. It is an excellent poem and if the author would contact me then I will give him or her the recognition they deserve.

The Senior Management Review Lament

To go, or not to go: that is the question.
Whether it is nobler, in the flesh, to suffer the indignity of premature retirement
Or take up arms against the Senior Management Review,
And by opposing, end up dismissed?

Aye, there's the rub. What's a career worth, Horatio?

Look, here's a skull. Alas poor Colin.

I knew him well, Horatio.
Oft have those lips pronounced the knell upon my best ideas.
Oft has the IPC hung upon his every word.
Where now is that merry chuckle?
Where now his talent for management by walking about?

Heaven's full of ex-G3s.

So what of me?
Can there be life after this vale of tears?
Will my severance pay let me keep my Porsche?
What think you, Horatio?
For me, I say 'sod it all'. I'm only an SEO.

> Anon.
> (with apologies to William Shakespeare)

(The poem includes reference to Dr Colin Hicks as Chairman of the IPC, and Dr Keith Shotton who owned a Porsche.)

Although I would be leaving in April 1996, it was after the changeover date and I was still treated as if I was going to be working under the new structure. I attended all the meetings set up to explain what would be happening to those who were going to be part of the new arrangement. I was interested in what was happening, especially observing the process used for the management of change. While I remained in post I also had a responsibility to my staff to keep them informed.

This included attending a major conference 'Management in Government: The Future' from 16-17 November 1995 and held at the Queen Elizabeth II Conference Centre in Victoria Street. It was an expensive conference, costing £595 (plus VAT), and was held to celebrate the occasion of the 25th Anniversary of the Civil Service College at Sunningdale. Government Ministers, senior civil servants, management experts, academics and private sector leaders debated how tomorrow's Government could and should address challenges and challenging agendas as we moved into the 21st century. For my senior colleagues who attended it was an opportunity to network and discuss the changes which would have an impact on them in the coming years. My interest was more academic, having taken part in so many of the efficiency and quality experiments. My view was that many of the tools used to improve performance in industry would be of benefit to the Civil Service, but that it should be done in a thoughtful way not out of enthusiasm for playing with trendy new management techniques.

Two different sessions from the conference were memorable. Firstly, there was a presentation on the 'Levers for Efficiency', which described

Business Process Re-Engineering, the Balanced Scorecard and Benchmarking. These were fashionable management techniques at that time, and the DTI included information about them in its information to SMEs about best practice. Applying the same methods, as appropriate, to ones own work as a civil servant was not threatening, although it was unusual. Re-engineering is the fundamental rethinking and radical design of business processes to achieve dramatic improvements in critical, contemporary measures of performance, such as cost, quality, service and speed. In the Civil Service it was aimed at eliminating unnecessary tasks leading to less delay, a reduction in the production of paper, and less duplication of effort. There were quantifiable benefits from the reduction of storage and this was also facilitated by automation. Everyone had a desktop computer and worked with email. Unfortunately the key business processes need to be identified before they can be re-engineered and that often takes time and effort. The stated idea was that functional barriers would be removed and the complete redesign of processes would encourage the workforce to see themselves within the organisation as a whole, losing their hierarchical command focus. One consequence was the flattening of hierarchies, and this was a clear part of the agenda for the new Civil Service. Strategic direction was to be defined and measured using the Balanced Scorecard. This was another fashionable management technique, again widely in use in industry. The Government was committed to competition as a powerful means of improving efficiency and so Benchmarking was put forward as a tool for setting standards and targets when direct competition was not possible.

While teaching the Open University MBA course on Performance Measurement and Evaluation I had experience of explaining all these concepts to my students, many of whom worked in the public sector. I had become an Assessor for the UK Quality Award and therefore I was more interested in applying the Business Excellence Model of the European Foundation for Quality Management (EFQM) which measured performance against nine criteria: Leadership, People Management, Policy and Strategy, Resources, Processes, People Satisfaction, Customer Satisfaction, Impact on Society and Business Results. At the conference the South Yorkshire Police explained how they were using this same framework to measure their progress against goals. I had seen several similar presentations from my OU MBA students, including those who worked in the Civil Service, and including people who worked in the police force but not in South Yorkshire. I found that my students who worked in the police force, the NHS, and in schools all used the Business Excellence Model in very similar ways. Their business processes were similar although the actual work done was quite different.

In MTS Division I had used the same framework for a local benchmarking exercise, where I sent out a questionnaire to our Senior Management Team: David Durie, Keith Shotton and the other Grade 5s. I also had an excellent diagram which gave a guide to the various management tools, systems and sources of help and advice. We seemed to be suffering from too many imposed management tools without thinking which were appropriate and how they contributed to efficiency and effectiveness. In addition, all the MBA technical terminology and the alphabet soup confused junior staff.

The conference ended with the concluding keynote speech by Sir Robin Butler, Secretary of the Cabinet and Head of the Home Civil Service, the text of which was published by the Cabinet Office. I noticed many conference attendees arrived specially to hear him, and there was a lot of playing the game of 'Spot the Mandarin'. In June 1994 I had heard Richard Mottram speak about the Future Shape of the Civil Service, and knew that many of the levers for change were already in place, in particular the emphasis on quality of service and value for money within tight running cost controls.

Sir Robin Butler spoke about the establishment of the Civil Service College in 1970, and its subsequent expansion. But what everyone was waiting to hear was not the history of the past, but his views on what we should expect of today's and tomorrow's Civil Service.

The Civil Service would be expected to serve the elected Government by advising on public policy, and honestly and effectively administering the public services. The growth in size and complexity of those public services justified greater concentration on the skills of management. Management had become a major feature of Government, and while it was an important skill I could see a risk that the traditional skills in policy advice were becoming neglected. This obsession with management was also seen in Governments across the developed world, including examples given at the conference from the USA and New Zealand. There were common circumstances and influences at work. One was the conflict between the demand of the public for more and better services and the equal and opposite demand for lower taxes. There was pressure on the public service to provide better quality services at lower, or no higher, cost. This meant a constant quest for more efficiency. Senior officials must expect a movement in the demand for customised public service, and a complaints process for when standards are not met. Command structures and hierarchies were seen as overheads, to be thinned out, and empowerment meant bright young recruits should be given real authority. New technology could take the drudgery out of clerical tasks, and enabled work to be done where it was most cost-effective, even the other side of the world! (I added the exclamation mark here because I had real difficulties with the idea of foreign nationals doing clerical work for the British Government. Now my banking is outsourced to India.) The successful organisations of the future would be those which invest heavily in the people in their organisations, at all levels, and who will thrive on this continuing change.

Thankfully, there remained widespread agreement on the value of maintaining our Civil Service based on the traditional principles of political impartiality, accountability through Ministers to Parliament, objectivity, integrity and recruitment and promotion on merit.

During my career, the standards and ethics essential to the operation of the Civil Service had been described in various management documents and guidelines but it was only in 1995 that the first Civil Service Code was proposed. It was an Annex to the Civil Service White Paper 'The Civil Service: Taking Forward Continuity and Change'. In 1996 it became a formal condition of employment of all civil servants that they read the Code and conduct themselves in accordance with its provisions. The wording was subsequently revised slightly in 1999 to take account of the affect of devolution on the accountability arrangements for those civil servants working in the devolved administrations in accordance with the Scotland and Government of Wales Acts 1998. A new version of the Code was produced in June 2006 so that all civil servants have a simple, clear leaflet which defines the Civil Service values and the standards of behaviour expected of civil servants. The essence is that the Civil Service supports the Government of the day in formulating and implementing its policies, and in the delivery of public services. Civil servants are appointed on merit through fair and open competition, and can take pride in carrying out their role with dedication and a commitment to the Civil Service and its core values: integrity, honesty, objectivity and impartiality. The text of the 1996, 1999 and 2006 Civil Service Codes are at Appendix G.

The good news for my staff was that my post was to continue, and was there in the lists as part of the new DTI structure, but with no identified leader. I spent less time working in the office and I attended New Directions courses, aimed at helping those who were leaving to plan their next career. Then in February we took our usual 3 weeks holiday. Pete was ill while we were away and was taken into hospital, so we had to miss our flight back and stay abroad until he was well enough to be allowed to fly home. I had some annual leave which had to be used before I left, so an extra week away was not a serious problem.

In April 1996 I received a letter from Sir Robin Butler, welcoming me to the Senior Civil Service. All DTI staff in the current Grade 5 and above were to become members of the new Senior Civil Service, and so Barbara would be needed as Personal Assistant to whoever replaced me. I knew that my replacement would be Richard Allpress, and had already met him for a formal handover discussion. There were just a few days now before I was due to leave.

33 Celebrating the start of our retirement

With Keith, Richard and myself all leaving from MTS Division at the same time, we decided it made sense to hold a joint retirement party. We had many friends and colleagues in common and it was going to be better to have one large party rather than three separate smaller ones. It would also be a lot cheaper for each of us. The conference rooms in the DTI buildings began to be busy with retirement parties, and Good Bye and Good Luck cards disappeared from the local shops. Lots of wine and beer was drunk, speeches were made, and those leaving listened to a short version of the highlights of their career, and were able to thank everyone they had worked with. It was a very emotional time. There is traditionally always a collection to buy a leaving gift, and I used my leaving money to purchase an opal and diamond ring. My secretary decided to stay to look after my successor, although she was given the choice of a move if she had wanted. I gave her a present to thank her for looking after me so well for the 7 years. I hoped that Richard Allpress would appreciate her value.

The rules for severance were that the final salary used to assess the pension received eventually at age 60 is based on the best, and in my case the most recent, 18 months. This was perfect because it meant that my eventual pension was calculated only on my salary as Grade 5. When I left in April 1996 I had been at Grade 5 for 18 months and 10 days. I also received a substantial severance payment. I had worked continuously in Government Service since 1976 and therefore my terms and conditions were different to newer entrants. The concept was that the severance pay would be enough to generate the same income as I would have received if I had been able to collect my pension on the day I left. This lump sum was taxable, but at least I was able to limit the taxation bill by staying in the DTI for a few extra days and departing at the start of the 1996/97 financial year, instead of at the end of 1995/96. In May 1996 I formally completed my Senior Civil Service Performance Review, although I was no longer in post, and was awarded a small additional pay rise backdated to 1 April 1996, which gave rise to an even smaller rise in my eventual pension.

Meanwhile Pete was still working in the Meteorological Office, where there was the same scheme for early retirement and severance. He was not allowed to leave in April 1996 because he was representing the UK in some important policy meetings in Europe, but he was released in November 1996. His additional 8 months salary was useful for us, and gave me time to become accustomed to being at home. I was still doing some Open University lecturing, including tutoring the undergraduate course 'Innovation - Design, Environment and Strategy' and the MBA course 'Performance Measurement and Evaluation', together with some consultancy work, and teaching at OU Residential Summer Schools.

At the end of the year I took a 12 month sabbatical break from my Open University teaching. Then in January 1997 we set off with four heavy suitcases, to spend 3 months together touring New Zealand. We were finally going to take our tent and rent a little white campervan and pretend we were still students. Fortunately we enjoy being together, sharing the same experiences, and going to the same sort of places.

34 Epilogue

It was not until 2002 that I started writing my memoirs, and the two volumes have taken a long time to complete. I am not famous and despaired of anyone being interested in my childhood and early research career, so that part was written separately. I decided to publish it myself and I thereby learned a lot about writing and publishing. I produced the text file and the graphics for the cover; I paid professionals to do the typesetting and printing. The book has the title Quiet Quadrangles and Ivory Towers ISBN 978-0-9557163-0-0, and was published in November 2007.

If I had known at the beginning what was involved in writing and publishing my first book I may have abandoned the challenge. Because my research career included five years at the NPL from 1976 to 1981, which was then part of the Department of Industry, I had to seek formal permission to publish from the Permanent Secretary of the Department of Trade and Industry and the Cabinet Office. In the past it would have been the Director of the NPL who gave that permission, but things had changed. I duly sent the manuscript away by email on 24 May 2007 and received permission to publish on 13 August 2007. I was pleased there were no changes to make and the response, under 3 months, was quicker than I expected.

During 2007 the Department of Trade and Industry was divided and disappeared. The DTI Permanent Secretary, Sir Brian Bender, became the leader of the new Department for Business Enterprise and Regulatory Reform (BERR) taking with him some of his staff. The rest of the DTI went to the new Department for Innovation, Universities and Skills (DIUS). Colleagues with whom I had worked in the past were divided between BERR and DIUS. Those dealing with my manuscript stayed in BERR with Sir Brian Bender.

Having completed and published my first book I thought I now knew how to create the sequel, the manuscript of which was finished. My subsequent career in the Civil Service had been much more varied and interesting than doing research at the NPL and I was able to describe the working life of a civil servant, from arriving in the junior ranks and then moving upwards to achieve my career goal and become a member of the Senior Civil Service. I did not write a diary but I have a good memory, and this was augmented by access to published material. I enjoyed collecting together the highlights of each different job and explaining my contribution and achievements.

I sent extracts from the draft manuscript to many of my senior colleagues, and their reminiscences encouraged new cameos of life to emerge from the depths of my memory. It was also nice to make contact with colleagues again, most of whom were older and now retired. Some of the information gleaned from them was not suitable to be published, but very interesting nevertheless.

This manuscript was finally finished in November 2007, coinciding with the publication of the first part of my memoirs, and I sent it off to my previous contact in BERR to get permission to publish from Sir Brian Bender and the Cabinet Office. As my elderly mother often says 'So far so good'.

On 6 August 2008 I gave a lecture on the famous Cunard cruise ship, Queen Elizabeth 2, about writing and publishing memoirs, and sold copies of my first book in their bookshop. During that cruise I wondered why I had no news from BERR about the second volume of memoirs but I knew it was going to be much slower to read; it was over twice the length of my first book of memoirs and almost entirely concerned the DTI and the Civil Service. My rough estimate was a minimum of 9 months to deal with the second book, compared with 3 months for the first one. The only query from BERR was on 6 October 2008 and I was able to confirm that everyone I had worked with, who was mentioned by name and where comments about them had been made, had seen the manuscript and had no concerns. I was hopeful this meant there would be permission to publish granted shortly. Then in December 2008 my contact at BERR moved but this did not seem to affect progress and I was told the manuscript had been sent to the Cabinet Office.

Some confusion followed during 2009 meanwhile BERR and DIUS had been recombined into the Department for Business Innovation and Skills (BIS - a nice snappy name) and Sir Brian Bender retired in March. Now led by Lord Mandelson, the Department for Business, Innovation and Skills is 'building a dynamic and competitive UK economy by: creating the conditions for business success; promoting innovation, enterprise and science; and giving everyone the skills and opportunities to succeed. To achieve this it will foster world-class universities and promote an open global economy.'

Finally on 15 July 2009 I was informed by email that the new Permanent Secretary of BIS, Simon Fraser, 'has no objections to the publication of your book'. It had taken 20 months for the manuscript to be cleared for publication.

I have had an interesting career and believe that this gives me an interesting story to tell. Tony Benn, in a radio interview on 13 October 2006, asserted that 'every life is interesting… The theory that only important people are interesting is a load of absolute rubbish'. While I may not agree with everything Tony Benn says, in this case I am fully in agreement. If I had my life over again I would still make my career in the Civil Service. Working with Ministers definitely had its interesting and challenging moments.

APPENDICES

Appendix A The Civil Service Grades in 1982

Permanent Secretary

Deputy Secretary = Grade 2

Under Secretary = Grade 3

Scientists	Engineers	Administrators	Fast stream
DCSO	Director	A/S = Grade 5	A/S = Grade 5
SPSO	Assistant Director	Senior Principal	
PSO	PPTO	Principal	Principal
SSO	SPTO	SEO	
HSO	HPTO	HEO	Administrative Trainee(direct entry)
SO	PTO1	EO	

This is a simplified table which does not include Directors of laboratories.

In 1982 it was reported in the Civil Service Yearbook that a Principal earned £11,372 - £15,010, a Principal Scientific Officer (PSO) earned £10,398 - £13,448 and a Principal Professional and Technology Officer (PPTO) earned £12,121 - £14,154.

For comparison, in 1996 it was reported in the Civil Service Yearbook that a Grade 7 Principal in London earned £26,535 - £41,092, a Grade 6 earned £30,278 - £50,299 and a Grade 5 earned £39,031 - £57,978.

All the abbreviations and acronyms are listed separately at the end of the book.

Appendix B The Structure of DOI and RTP in 1981

DOI was organised into 6 areas under Permanent Secretary Sir Peter Carey:

1. Regional Development and Organisation: small firms;
2. Industrial and Commercial Policy;
3. Industrial Sponsership – Mechanical & Electrical Engineering, Industrial Raw Materials, Shipbuilding, Vehicles and Miscellaneous Manufacturers;
4. Industrial Sponsership – Aircraft, Posts and Telecommunications, Nationalised Industries Policy, Electronic Applications and Information Technology;
5. Research and Development (R & D);
6. Information.

R & D Division was led by Deputy Secretary and Chief Scientist and Engineer Dr Duncan Davies. He was responsible for:

The Council of the Research Establishments;

Research Establishment Management Division;

The research establishments (NPL, NMI, WSL, LGC and CADCentre);

Research and Technology Requirements and Space (RTS) Division;

Research and Technology Requirements and Perspectives (RTP) Division.

The Head of RTP Division was Under Secretary Alex Williams.
The Head of RTP Branch 2 was DCSO Dr T B Copestake.
The Head of the Technology Policy Unit within RTP2 was SPSO Dr G R G Lewison. I worked directly for Dr Lewison.

RTS and RTP subsequently merged, creating Research and Technology Perspectives Division (RTP), under Alex Williams. Much later it was renamed Research and Technology Policy Division and still retained its abbreviation RTP.

Appendix C List of Secretary of State at the DOI/DTI

Department of Industry

1981 September Patrick Jenkin (Lord Jenkin of Roding)

Department of Trade and Industry

1983 June	Cecil Parkinson (Lord Parkinson of Carnforth)
1983 October	Norman Tebbit (Lord Tebbit of Chingford)
1985 September	Leon Brittan (Sir Leon Brittan)
1986 January	Paul Channon
1987 June	Lord Young of Graffham
1989 July	Nicholas Ridley (Lord Ridley of Liddesdale)
1990 July	Peter Lilley
1992 April	Michael Heseltine
1995 July	Ian Lang

Appendix D Studies published by the LTSU

1985 1 The future of the UK domestic electrical appliance industry
      2 Future trends in manufacturing

1986 3 Technological trends and priorities (for Sunningdale)
      4 Long range planning by British firms by MBS
      5 The evaluation of technological priorities. Main Report by PREST
      6 The evaluation of technological priorities. A review of policy assessment.
      7 The Future of Health Care by the Technical Change Centre
      8 Priority products and enabling technologies
      9 Review of UK position and expertise in nanotechnology by PA
      10 Optimised materials selection in UK manufacturing industry by Quotec
      11 The public acceptance of new technology by Brighton Business School

1987 12 Protein engineering
      13 Opportunities for the UK pollution abatement industry by Ecotect
      14 The evaluation of technological priorities by PREST
      15 The evaluation of technological priorities case study by PREST
      16 Future patterns of DTI Science and Technology support
      17 Identifying areas of strength and excellence in UK technology by CHI
      18 FAST programme research on services by SPRU
      19 Research grant proposals as a data source for mapping research activities by the Technical Change Centre
      20 Priority products and enabling technologies
      21 Patent Trends Analysis: Aroma Chemicals
      22 Patent Trends Analysis: High Temperature Superconductors
      23 Services and the new industrial structure by SPRU
      24 The potential impact of nanotechnology in UK industry by Scientific Generics
      25 Matrix exercise: summary report, background and examples
      26 Barriers to the growth of small innovative firms
      27 The role and development of quantitative indicators for research and technology policy
      28 The evaluation of technological priorities: superconductivity

Appendix E Nine Core Criteria for the Senior Open Structure

These nine core criteria, split equally between Direction, Management and Communication and Personal Contribution, were published in 1997 for staff who would become part of the new Senior Open Structure.

Direction comprised Leadership, Strategic Thinking and Planning, and Delivery of Results.

1. Leadership

    creates and conveys a clear vision;

    initiates and drives through change;

    is visible, approachable and earns respect;

    inspires and shows loyalty;

    builds a high performing team;

    acts decisively having assessed the risks;

    takes final responsibility for the actions of the team;

    demonstrates the high standards of integrity, honesty and fairness expected in public service.

2. Strategic Thinking and Planning

    identifies strategic aims, anticipating future demands;

    demonstrates sensitivity to Ministers needs and to wider political issues;

    sees relationships between complex inter-dependent factors;

    makes choices between options which take into account their long term impact;

    translates strategic aims into practical and achievable plans;

    takes decisions on time, even in uncertain circumstances.

3. Delivery of Results

    defines results taking account of customer or other stakeholder's needs;

    delivers results on time, on budget and to agreed quality standards;

    demonstrates high level project and contract management skills;

    ensures that others organise their work to achieve objectives;

    knows when to step in and when not to;

    encourages feedback on performance and learns for the future.

Management and Communication comprised Management of People, Communication and Management of Financial and other Resources

4. Management of People
> establishes and communicates clear standards and expectations;
> gives recognition and helps all staff develop full potential;
> addresses poor performance;
> builds trust, good morale and cooperation within the team;
> delegates effectively, making best use of skills and resources within the team;
> seeks face-to-face contact and responds to feedback from staff;
> manages the change process perceptively.

5. Communication
> negotiates effectively and can handle hostility;
> is concise and persuasive orally and in writing;
> listens to what is said and is corrective to others' reactions;
> demonstrates presentational and media skills;
> chooses the methods of communication most likely to secure effective results;
> is comfortable and effective in a representational role (with EC languages where needed).

6. Management of Financial and other Resources
> negotiates for the resources to do the job, in the light of wider priorities;
> commits and realigns resources to meet key priorities;
> secures value for taxpayers' money;
> leads initiatives for new and more efficient use of resources;
> ensures management information systems are used to monitor and control resources;
> manages contracts and relationships with suppliers effectively.

Personal contribution comprised Personal Effectiveness, Intellect Creativity and Judgement, and Expertise

7. Personal Effectiveness
> shows resilience, stamina and reliability under heavy pressure;
> takes a firm stance when circumstances warrant it;

is aware of personal strengths and weaknesses and their impact on others;

offers objective advice to Ministers without fear or favour;

pursues adopted strategies with energy and commitment;

adapts quickly and flexibly to new demands and change;

manages own time well to meet competing priorities.

8. Intellect, Creativity and Judgement

uses intellect to offer insights and break new ground;

generates original ideas with practical application;

homes in on key issues and principles;

analyses ambiguous data and concepts rigorously;

defends logic of own position robustly but responds positively to reasoned alternatives;

encourages creative thinking in others.

9. Expertise

earns credibility through depth of knowledge and experience;

knows how to find and use other sources of expertise (including IT);

understands parliamentary and political processes and how to operate within them;

applies best practice from other public/private sector organisations;

understands how policy impacts on operations, staff and customers.

Appendix F DTI Pay and Grading Review 1995

The DTI Grading and Pay Review team were also tasked to look at staff up to and including Grade 6. Their terms of reference were that the review team should:

Examine the effectiveness of the present pay and grading structures in:

> Meeting the requirements of the organisation, management and conduct of the Department's work and the delivery of services;
>
> Motivating staff by rewarding and recognising different levels of achievement, performance and responsibility;
>
> Providing a clear structure of personal achievement;
>
> Maintaining the relative competitiveness of the Department in the market for good quality staff;
>
> Satisfying the requirements for the Department for particular skills and professional qualifications;

And consider and propose alternative arrangements which better meet these requirements and which:

> Improve the efficiency and performance of the Department overall;
>
> Promote delegation and personal responsibility;
>
> Permit flexible organisational structures which eliminate unnecessary layers of management and reinforce the cohesion and effectiveness of teams;
>
> Allow future changes to staffing, structures and methods of work to be accommodated and managed efficiently and with least disruption;
>
> Contribute to the better management and development of the human resources of the Department;
>
> Ensures that the business of the Department continues to be properly and effectively discharged consistent with Ministerial objectives and with due regard to value for money.

Appendix G The Civil Service Code : 1996, 1999 and 2006

1996: The first Civil Service Code

1 The constitutional and practical role of the Civil Service is, with integrity, honesty, impartiality and objectivity, to assist the duly constituted Government, of whatever political complexion, in formulating policies of the Government, carrying out decisions of the Government and in administering public services for which the Government is responsible.

2 Civil servants are servants of the Crown. Constitutionally, the Crown acts on the advice of Ministers and, subject to the provisions of this Code, civil servants owe their loyalty to the duly constituted Government.

3 This Code should be seen in the context of the duties and responsibilities of Ministers (set out elsewhere) which include:
   accountability to Parliament;

   the duty to give Parliament and the public as full information as possible about the policies, decisions and actions of the Government, and not to deceive or knowingly mislead parliament and the public;

   the duty to give fair consideration and due weight to informed and impartial advice from civil servants, as well as to other considerations and advice, in reaching decisions; and

   the duty to comply with the law, including international law and treaty obligations, and to uphold the administration of justice;

   together with the duty to familiarise themselves with the content of this Code and not to ask civil servants to act in breach of it.

4 Civil servants should serve the duly constituted Government in accordance with the principles set out in this Code and recognising:
   the accountability of civil servants to Ministers;

   the duty of all public officers to discharge public functions reasonably and according to the law;

   the duty to comply with the law, including international law and treaty obligations, and to uphold the administration of justice; and

   ethical standards governing particular professions.

5   Civil servants should conduct themselves with integrity, impartiality and honesty in their dealings with Ministers, Parliament and the public. They should give honest and impartial advice to Ministers, without fear or favour, and make all information relevant to a decision available to Ministers. They should not deceive or knowingly mislead Ministers, Parliament or the public.

6   Civil servants should endeavour to deal with the affairs of the public sympathetically, efficiently, promptly and without bias or maladministration.

7   Civil servants should endeavour to ensure the proper, effective and efficient use of public money within their control.

8   Civil servants should not make use of their official position or information acquired in the course of their official duties to further their private interests or those of others. They should not receive benefits of any kind from a third party which might reasonably be seen to compromise their personal judgement or integrity.

9   Civil servants should conduct themselves in such a way as to deserve and retain the confidence of Ministers and to be able to establish the same relationship with those whom they may be required to serve in some future Administration. They should comply with restrictions on their political activities. The conduct of civil servants should be such that Ministers and potential future Ministers can be sure that confidence can be freely given, and that the Civil Service will conscientiously fulfill its duties and obligations to, and impartially assist, advise and carry out the policies of the duly constituted Government.

10   Civil servants should not without authority disclose official information which has been communicated in confidence within Government, or received in confidence from others. They must not seek to frustrate the policies, decisions or actions of Government by the unauthorised, improper or premature disclosure outside the Government of any information to which they have had access as civil servants.

11   Where a civil servant believes he or she is being required to act in a way which is illegal, improper, unethical or in breach of constitutional convention, which may involve possible maladministration, or which is otherwise inconsistent with this Code or raises a fundamental issue of conscience, he or she should first report the matter in accordance with procedures laid down in departmental guidance or rules of conduct.

12 Where a civil servant has reported a matter covered in paragraph 11 in accordance with procedures laid down in departmental guidance or rules of conduct and believes that the response does not represent a reasonable response to the grounds of his or her concern, he or she may report the matter in writing to the Civil Service Commissioners.

13 Civil servants should not seek to frustrate the policies, decisions or actions of Government by declining to take, or abstaining from, action which flows from ministerial decisions. Where a matter cannot be resolved by the procedures set out in paragraphs 11 and 12 above, on a basis which the civil servant concerned is able to accept, he or she should either carry out the ministerial instructions or resign from the Civil Service. Civil servants must continue to observe their duties of confidentiality after they have left Crown employment.

<u>1999: The revised Civil Service Code</u>, which takes account of the affect of devolution on the accountability arrangements for those civil servants working in the devolved administrations.

1 The constitutional and practical role of the Civil Service is, with integrity, honesty, impartiality and objectivity, to assist the duly constituted Government of the United Kingdom, the Scottish Executive or the National Assembly for Wales constituted in accordance with the Scotland and Government of Wales Acts 1998, whatever their political complexion, in formulating their policies, carrying out decisions and in administering public services for which they are responsible.

2 Civil servants are servants of the Crown. Constitutionally, all the Administrations form part of the Crown and, subject to the provisions of this Code, civil servants owe their loyalty to the Administrations in which they serve.

3 This Code should be seen in the context of the duties and responsibilities of Ministers (set out elsewhere) which include:

accountability to Parliament or, for Assembly Secretaries, to the National Assembly;

the duty to give Parliament or the Assembly and the public as full information as possible about their policies, decisions and actions, and not to deceive or knowingly mislead them;

the duty not to use public resources for party political purposes, to uphold the political impartiality of the Civil Service, and not to ask civil servants to act in any way which would conflict with the Civil Service Code;

the duty to give fair consideration and due weight to informed and impartial advice from civil servants, as well as to other considerations and advice, in reaching decisions; and

the duty to comply with the law, including international law and treaty obligations, and to uphold the administration of justice;

together with the duty to familiarise themselves with the content of this Code.

4 Civil servants should serve their Administration in accordance with the principles set out in this Code and recognising:

the accountability of civil servants to the Minister or, as the case may be, to the Assembly Secretaries and the National Assembly as a body or to the office holder in charge of their department;

the duty of all public officers to discharge public functions reasonably and according to the law;

the duty to comply with the law, including international law and treaty obligations, and to uphold the administration of justice; and ethical standards governing particular professions.

5 Civil servants should conduct themselves with integrity, impartiality and honesty. They should give honest and impartial advice to the Minister or, as the case may be, to the Assembly Secretaries and the National Assembly as a body or to the office holder in charge of their department, without fear or favour, and make all information relevant to a decision available to them. They should not deceive or knowingly mislead Ministers, Parliament, the National Assembly or the public.

6 Civil servants should endeavour to deal with the affairs of the public sympathetically, efficiently, promptly and without bias or maladministration.

7 Civil servants should endeavour to ensure the proper, effective and efficient use of public money.

8 Civil servants should not misuse their official position or information acquired in the course of their official duties to further their private interests or those of others. They should not receive benefits of any kind from a third party which might reasonably be seen to compromise their personal judgement or integrity.

9 Civil servants should conduct themselves in such a way as to deserve and retain the confidence of Ministers or Assembly Secretaries and the National Assembly as a body, and to be able to establish the same relationship with those whom they may be required to serve in some future Administration. They should comply with restrictions on their political activities. The conduct of civil servants should be such that Ministers, Assembly Secretaries and the National Assembly as a body, and potential future holders of these positions can be sure that confidence can be freely given, and that the Civil Service will conscientiously fulfill its duties and obligations to, and impartially assist, advise and carry out the policies of the duly constituted Administrations.

10 Civil servants should not without authority disclose official information which has been communicated in confidence within the Administration, or received in confidence from others. Nothing in the Code should be taken as overriding existing statutory or common law obligations to keep confidential, or to disclose, certain information. They should not seek to frustrate or influence the policies, decisions or actions of Ministers, Assembly Secretaries or the National Assembly as a body by the unauthorised, improper or premature disclosure outside the

Administration of any information to which they have had access as civil servants.

11   Where a civil servant believes he or she is being required to act in a way which:

   is illegal, improper, unethical;

   is in breach of constitutional convention or a professional code;

   may involve possible maladministration or

   is otherwise inconsistent with this Code;

he or she should report the matter in accordance with procedures laid down in the appropriate guidance or rules of conduct for their department or Administration. A civil servant should also report to the appropriate authorities evidence of criminal or unlawful activity by others and may also report in accordance with the relevant procedures if he or she becomes aware of other breaches of this Code or is required to act in a way which, for him or her, raises a fundamental issue of conscience.

12   Where a civil servant has reported a matter covered in paragraph 11 in accordance with the relevant procedures and believes that the response does not represent a reasonable response to the grounds of his or her concern, he or she may report the matter in writing to the Civil Service Commissioners.

13   Civil servants should not seek to frustrate the policies, decisions or actions of the Administrations by declining to take, or abstaining from, action which flows from decisions by Ministers, Assembly Secretaries or the National Assembly as a body. Where a matter cannot be resolved by the procedures set out in paragraphs 11 and 12 above, on a basis which the civil servant concerned is able to accept, he or she should either carry out his or her instructions or resign from the Civil Service. Civil servants should continue to observe their duties of confidentiality after they have left Crown employment.

<u>2006: The Civil Service Code</u> – version for all Home civil servants.

Civil Service Values

1 The Civil Service is an integral and key part of the government of the United Kingdom. It supports the Government of the day in developing and implementing its policies, and in delivering public services. Civil servants are accountable to Ministers, who in turn are accountable to Parliament.

2 As a civil servant, you are appointed on merit on the basis of fair and open competition and are expected to carry out your role with dedication and a commitment to the Civil Service and its core values: integrity, honesty, objectivity and impartiality. In this Code:

> 'integrity' is putting the obligations of public service above your own personal interests;
>
> 'honesty' is being truthful and open;
>
> 'objectivity' is basing your advice and decisions on rigorous analysis of the evidence;
>
> 'impartiality' is acting solely according to the merits of the case and serving equally well Governments of different political persuasions;

3 These core values support good government and ensure the achievement of the highest possible standards in all that the Civil Service does. This in turn helps the Civil Service to gain and retain the respect of Ministers, Parliament, the public and its customers.

4 This Code sets out the standards of behaviour expected of you and all other civil servants. These are based on the core values. Individual departments may also have their own separate mission and values statements based on the core values, including the standards of behaviour expected of you when you deal with your colleagues.

<u>Standards of behaviour</u>

<u>Integrity</u>

5 You must:
> fulfil your duties and obligations responsibly;
>
> always act in a way that is professional and that deserves and retains the confidence of all those with whom you have dealings;

make sure public money and other resources are used properly and efficiently;

deal with the public and their affairs fairly, efficiently, promptly, effectively and sensitively, to the best of your ability;

handle information as openly as possible within the legal framework; and

comply with the law and uphold the administration of justice.

6   You must not:

misuse your official position, for example by using information acquired in the course of your official duties to further your private interests or those of others;

accept gifts or hospitality or receive other benefits from anyone which might reasonably be seen to compromise your personal judgement or integrity; or

disclose official information without authority. This duty continues to apply after you leave the Civil Service.

Honesty

7   You must:

set out the facts and relevant issues truthfully, and correct any errors as soon as possible; and

use resources only for the authorised public purposes for which they are provided.

8   You must not:

deceive or knowingly mislead Ministers, Parliament or others; or

be influenced by improper pressures from others or the prospect of personal gain.

Objectivity

9   You must:

provide information and advice, including advice to Ministers, on the basis of the evidence, and accurately present the options and facts;

take decisions on the merits of the case; and

take due account of expert and professional advice.

10   You must not:

ignore inconvenient facts or relevant considerations when providing advice or making decisions; or frustrate the implementation of policies once decisions are taken by declining to take, or abstaining from, action which flows from those decisions.

Impartiality

11   You must:

carry out your responsibilities in a way that is fair, just and equitable and reflects the Civil Service commitment to equality and diversity.

12   You must not:

act in a way that unjustifiably favours or discriminates against particular individuals or interests.

Political Impartiality

13   You must:

serve the Government, whatever its political persuasion, to the best of your ability in a way which maintains political impartiality and is in line with the requirements of this Code, no matter what your own political beliefs are;

act in a way which deserves and retains the confidence of Ministers, while at the same time ensuring that you will be able to establish the same relationship with those whom you may be required to serve in some future Government; and

comply with any restrictions that have been laid down on your political activities.

14   You must not:

act in a way that is determined by party political considerations, or use official resources for party political purposes; or

allow your personal political views to determine any advice you give or your actions.

Rights and responsibilities

15   Your department or agency has a duty to make you aware of this Code and its values. If you believe that you are being required to act in a way which conflicts with this Code, your department or agency must consider your concern, and make sure that you are not penalised for raising it.

16   If you have a concern, you should start by talking to your line manager or someone else in your line management chain. If for any

reason you would find this difficult, you should raise the matter with your department's nominated officers who have been appointed to advise staff on the Code.

17 If you become aware of actions by others which you believe conflict with this Code you should report this to your line manager or someone else in your line management chain; alternatively you may wish to seek advice from your nominated officer. You should report evidence of criminal or unlawful activity to the police or other appropriate authorities.

18 If you have raised a matter covered in paragraphs 15 to 17, in accordance with the relevant procedures, and do not receive what you consider to be a reasonable response, you may report the matter to the Civil Service Commissioners. The Commissioners will also consider taking a complaint directly. If the matter cannot be resolved using the procedures set out above, and you feel you cannot carry out the instructions you have been given, you will have to resign from the Civil Service.

19 This Code is part of the contractual relationship between you and your employer. It sets out the high standards of behaviour expected of you which follow from your position in public and national life as a civil servant. You can take pride in living up to these values.

Appendix H My Open University teaching and consultancy

Mathematics

M351	Numerical Computation	1979 – 1987
M371	Computational Mathematics	1988
TM361	Graphs, networks and design. I was also a consultant to this course.	1982 – 1991
M355	Topics in software engineering	1990
M206	Computing: An Object-oriented Approach	1998 – 2005
	Consultancy contract ETMA Guide	2000
M254	Java Everywhere, critical reader	2004
M358	Relational Database: Theory and Practice, critical reader	2005

MBA and MBA(Technology Management)

B880	Accounting and Finance for Managers Strategic use of IT	1990 – 1993
B800	Foundations of Senior Management Residential School	2000 – 2001
B889	Performance measurement and evaluation	1994 – 1999
B889	Residential School	1996 – 1999
	Consultancy contract 'European and UK Quality Awards : A Study of Their potential Value for Quality Improvement in the OUBS'.	1995 – 1996
B855	The Human Resource Professional, private communication	2005
B856	Shaping Public Policy: Contexts and Processes, critical reader	2006
PT621	Implementation of New Technology	1992
T843	Management Information Systems	1998 – 2000
	Consultancy contract to write two systems courses	2001
T889	Problem solving and improvement: quality and other approaches	2008

Technology

T363	Computer Aided Design I was also a consultant to this course	1987 – 1992
T302	Innovation - Design, Environment and Strategy	1996
T302	Residential School	1996 – 1997

REFERENCES

Further Reading

The Governance of Britain by Sir Harold Wilson. Published by Sphere in 1977. ISBN 0-722-19212-6

The Crossman Diaries: Selections from the Diaries of a Cabinet Minister 1964-1970 by Richard Crossman and edited by Anthony Howard. Published by Magnum Books in 1979. ISBN 0-417-02670-6

The Mighty Micro by Christopher Evans. Published by Victor Gollancz in 1979. ISBN 0-575-02708-8

Be your own P.R. Man by Michael Bland. Published by Littlehampton Book Services in January 1984. ISBN 0-850-38765-5

The Complete Yes Minister. The Diaries of a Cabinet Minister by the Right Hon. James Hacker MP. Edited by Jonathan Lynn and Antony Jay. Published by BBC Books in 1987. ISBN 0-563-20323-4

Yes Prime Minister. The Diaries of the Right Hon. James Hacker MP. Edited by Jonathan Lynn and Antony Jay. Published by BBC Books in 1987. Volume I ISBN 0-563-20469-9. Volume II ISBN 0-563-20584-9

Upwardly Mobile - An Autobiography by Norman Tebbit. Published by Weidenfeld and Nicolson in 1988. ISBN 0-297-79427-2

Whitehall by Peter Hennessy. Published in paperback by Fontana Press in 1990. ISBN 0-00-686180-6

The Enterprise Years - A Businessman in the Cabinet by Lord Young of Graffham. Published by Headline Book Publishing in 1990. ISBN 0-7472-0275-3

A Passion for Excellence by Tom Peters and Nancy Austin. Published by Fontana/Collins in 1990. ISBN 0-00-637062-4

The Competitive Advantage of Nations by Michael E Porter. Published by The MacMillan Press in 1990. ISBN 0-333-51804-7

The Art of the Long View by Peter Schwartz. Published by Doubleday in 1991. ISBN 0-385-26731-2

The First Global Revolution by Alexander King and Bertrand Schneider. Published by Simon & Schuster in 1991. ISBN 0-671-71094-X

The Downing Street Years by Margaret Thatcher. Published by Harper Collins in 1993. ISBN 0-00-638321-1

The Turbulent Years by Kenneth Baker. Published by Faber and Faber in 1993. ISBN 0-571-17077-3

A Day in the Life of Humphrey the Downing Street Cat, by David Brawn. Published by Collins in 1995. ISBN 0-004-71000-2

Industrial Policy in Britain by David Coates. Published by Macmillan in 1996. ISBN 0-333-61529-8

John Major The Autobiography by John Major. Published by Harper Collins in 1999. ISBN 0-00-257004-1

Life in the Jungle – my Autobiography by Michael Heseltine. Published by Hodder and Stoughton in 2000. ISBN 0-340-73915-0

Open Secret The Autobiography of the Former Director-General of MI5 by Stella Rimington. Published by Hutchinson in 2001. ISBN 0 09 179435 8 and 0 09 179360 2

Betty Boothroyd The Autobiography. Published by Arrow Books in 2002. ISBN 0-09-942704-4

Strutting on Thin Air by Chris Benjamin. Self-published in 2009. ISBN 978-09561579-0-4

Official and technical papers

PART ONE: MANAGING MYSELF

Research and Technology Policy

Science and Technology Act 1965. Chapter 4. Published by HMSO.

Standard Industrial Classification Revised version 1968. Published by HMSO. ISBN 0-11-630063-9

A Framework for Government Research and Development. Cmnd 4814 Published in November 1971 by HMSO. ISBN 0-10-148140-3

Industry Act 1972 Chapter 63. Published by HMSO SBN 10-546372-8

Industry Act 1975. Chapter 68. Published in 1976 by HMSO. ISBN 0-10-546875-4

Committee Procedure. Published in 1978 by the Civil Service Department. Ref 141

Review of the Framework for Government Research and Development (Cmnd 5046) Cmnd 7499. Published in March 1979 by HMSO. ISBN 0-10-174990-5

ACARD Report. Improving research links between Higher Education and Industry. Published in June 1983 by HMSO. ISBN 0-11-630784-6

A Study of Commissioned Research Report by Sir Ronald Mason to the Advisory Board for the Research Councils. Published in November 1983 by HMSO. Ref 3415588 Dd 8816931 2m 11/83

Intellectual Property Rights and Innovation. Cmnd 9117. Published in December 1983 by HMSO. Reprinted in 1984. ISBN 0-10-191170-X

PART TWO: MANAGING OTHERS

The Enterprise Initiative

DTI – the department for Enterprise. Cm 278. Published in 1988 by
HMSO. ISBN 0-10-102782-6

The Enterprise Initiative An Introduction. Published in 1990 by the DTI
and printed by HMSO. Ref Dd 8241229 COI J1323NJ 9/90 10970

Open Systems for Manufacturing

Standards, Quality and International Competitiveness. Cmnd 8621.
Published in July 1982 by HMSO. ISBN 0-10-186210-5

Open Systems Planning Next Steps Published by the DTI as part of the
Enterprise Initiative Ref OT/NS/070

Open Systems Planning Exploring Key Issues Published by the DTI as
part of the Enterprise Initiative Ref OT/KI/060

Open Systems Management Briefing. Published by the DTI as part of the
Enterprise Initiative. Ref OT/TP/080, OT/MB/070

Open Systems Case Studies. Published by the DTI as part of the
Enterprise Initiative.

Open Systems in Manufacturing. Published by PFour for the DTI. Ref
OSM/SD/081

OSTC Status Report. Published in 1991 by the Open Systems Testing
Consortium.

Manufacturing Message Specification (MMS). Published by the DTI.

Manufacturing Technology

Guidelines for the use of the Initial Graphics Exchange Specification
(IGES). Published in July 1986 by the CADCAM Data Exchange
Technical Centre in Leeds.

The DTI MAP Event Executive Summary. Published on 15 May 1986 by the DTI.

Through MAP to CIM. Published in 1986 by the DTI.

Manufacturing in the 1990s. Report 776. Published in Summer 1989 by SRI International.

The Manufacturing Services Imperative. Report 778. Published in Fall 1989 by SRI International

Product Data Exchange. Published in 1990 by Findlay Publications for the DTI.

Employment Effects of New Technology Manufacturing by Ian Chris, Jim Northcott and Annette Walling. Published in 1990 by the Policy Studies Institute. ISBN 0-85374-495-5

ACOST Report Advanced Manufacturing Technology. Published in 1991 by HMSO. ISBN 0-11-430052-6

The Management of Technology in UK Manufacturing Companies. Published in May 1991 by the Fellowship of Engineering. ISBN 1-871-63410-5

Advanced Manufacturing Technology. Published in March 1991 by the DTI. Ref DTI/Pub 332/5K/3/9

What are anthropocentric Production Systems? Why are they a strategic issue for Europe? Report EUR 13968 EN Published in 1992 by the Commission of the European Communities ISBN 92-826-3810-3

Computer Integrated Manufacturing. A Survey of Worldwide R&D. Published in April 1993 by the DTI. Ref DTI/Pub 1094/1K/4/93

Manufacturing into the Late 1990s. Published in July 1993 by HMSO for the DTI. ISBN 0-11-515336-5

Alvey and Advanced IT

A Programme for Advanced Information Technology. The Report of the Alvey Committee. First published in 1982 by HMSO. Third impression 1984 ISBN 0-11-513653-3

Information Technology – A Plan for Concerted Action. The Report of the IT'86 Committee. Published in 1986 by HMSO. ISBN 0-11-513966-4

Alvey Achievements. Published in June 1987 by the DTI. Ref DTI/Pub 002/19K/06/87

House of Commons Trade and Industry Committee. Information Technology Minutes of Evidence on Wednesday 10 February 1988. Published in 1988 by HMSO. ISBN 0-10-277788-8

House of Commons Committee of Public Accounts Session 1987-1988. Minutes of Evidence on Wednesday 4 May 1988. The Alvey Programme for Advanced Information Technology. Published in 1988 by HMSO. ISBN 0-10-289888-X

House of Commons Trade and Industry Committee. Information Technology First Report Volume 1. Published in 1988 by HMSO. ISBN 0-10-271489-4

House of Commons Trade and Industry Committee. Information Technology First Report Volume II Minutes of Evidence and Appendices. Published in 1988 by HMSO. ISBN 0-10-272989-1

Information Technology. Cm 646. Published in March 1989 by HMSO. ISBN 0-10-106462-4

Advanced Information Technologies. A Technology Transfer Programme. Published in April 1990 by the DTI. Ref DTI/Pub 184/5K/04/90

Advanced Information Technologies. A Business Opportunity. Published in April 1990 by the DTI.

Evaluation of the Alvey Programme for Advanced Information Technology. A Report by SPRU and PREST. Published in 1991 by HMSO for the DTI. ISBN 0-11-515281-4

Evaluation of the Alvey Programme for Advanced Information Technology. Summary and Conclusions by SPRU and PREST. Published in 1991 by HMSO for the DTI and SERC. ISBN 0-11-515281-4

The Diffusion of Information Technology by N Hanna, K Guy and E Arnold. Published in June 1995 by The World Bank. ISBN 0-8213-3216-3

<u>Software, Software Quality and Safety Critical Systems</u>

ACARD Report. Software A vital key to UK competitiveness. Published in 1986 by HMSO. ISBN 0-11-630829-X

IT Advisory Panel/ACARD Report on Learning to Live with IT. Published in 1986 by HMSO. ISBN 0-11-630831-1

Software Development Fashioning the Baroque by Darrel Ince. Published in 1988 by Oxford University Press ISBN 0-19-853758-1

LINK programmes for collaborative research. Published in 1988 by COI for the LINK Secretariat. Ref Dd 8940161 INDY J0454RP

What is Quality by Alec Dorling of NCC Limited. Published in 1988 by the NCC.

IT-STARTS Developing Systems Together. Published in 1989 by NCC for the DTI.

Getting to Grips with Quality Published in January 1989 by COI for the DTI. Ref Dd 8171409 INDY J0661NJ

Usability Now! IT and the User Working Together. Published in July 1990 by the DTI.

SafeIT: A Government Consultation Document on the Safety of Computer-controlled Systems. Vol 1 and Vol 2 published in May 1990 for the DTI.

The TickIT Scheme. Making a better job of software. Published in February 1993 by IT World for the DTI.

Expert Systems: A Management Guide by Dr Mike Turner. Published in 1985 by PA Computers and Telecommunications.

Multimedia Industry Advisory Group Report. Published in December 1995 by the DTI.

PART THREE: LEADERSHIP AND MANAGEMENT

Education and Training Policy

The Development of Higher Education into the 1990's. Cmnd 9524.
Published in 1985 by the Department of Education and Science ISBN
0101952406

Higher Education: Meeting the Challenge Cm 114. Published in April
1987 by HMSO for the Department of Education and Science.

1990s The Skills Decade. Published in 1990 by the Employment
Department Group. Ref PP3 8701/1090/24

National Institute of Economic and Social Research. 48th Annual Report.
Published in 1990.

Britain's Real Skills Shortage and what to do about it by John Cassels.
Published in 1990 by the Policy Studies Institute. ISBN 0-85374-478-5

Investors in People. An initial Briefing Pack for TECs and LECs.
Published in November 1990 by the Employment Department.

Investors in People Your Handbook. Published in 1994 by TQM
International Ltd. ISBN 1-899566-05-8

R&D and Technology Transfer

Review of DTI Industrial Support. Joint report by Treasury and DTI.
Published August 1985

Implementing New Technologies edited by E Rhodes and D Wield.
Published by Basil Blackwell for the Open University in 1985. ISBN 0-
631-14381-5

Working Together. Sharing the Risk. Published in July 1989 by COI for
the DTI. Ref Dd8171769 INDY J0790NJ

ACOST Report Developments in Biotechnology. Published in 1990 by
HMSO. ISBN 0-11-430045-3

Research in the UK, France and West Germany: A comparison. Published in July 1990 by SERC. ISBN 1-870-66981-9 (Vol 1)

The Research and Technology Initiative. Guide to collaborative research. Published by DTI in 1990. Ref DTI/Pub300/10K/11/90

Report to the Secretary of State on a Review of the operation of DTI support schemes for industrial research and development and technology transfer (The Innovation Review) by the Central Unit. Printed on 25 January 1991

The National Network of Regional Technology Centres. Published in June 1991 by the DTI. Ref DTI/Pub 360/130K/6/91

The First UK R&D Scoreboard. Published in June 1991 by the Independent newspaper and then by Company Reporting Ltd.

A Review of the Technology Transfer and Awareness Mechanisms used by the DTI. Assessment Paper 18. Published in July 1992 by the DTI Assessment Unit.

Science and Technology in a Policy Context edited by van Raan, de Bruin, Moed, Nederhof and Tijssen. Published in 1992 by DSWO Press, Leiden University. ISBN 90-6695-073-0

Advanced Technology Programmes (ATP) Collaborative Industrial Research in Key Technologies. Published in June 1992 by the DTI. Ref DTI/Pub 937/2K/6/92

UK R&D Scoreboard 1992. Published in June 1992 by Company Reporting Ltd of Edinburgh.

Managing the R&D Pipeline by David Connell of the Technology Partnership Ltd. Paper given at the 12th annual international conference of the Strategic Management Society in October 1992.

The Carrier Technology Programme. Published in September 1992 by the DTI. Ref DTI/Pub 957/10K/9/92

UK R&D Scoreboard 1993. Published in June 1993 by Company Reporting Ltd of Edinburgh.

UK R&D Scoreboard 1994. Published in June 1994 by Company Reporting Ltd of Edinburgh.

UK R&D Scoreboard 1995. Published in June 1995 by Company Reporting Ltd of Edinburgh. ISSN 1358-6351

General Purpose Technologies, Industrial Competence and Economic Growth by Gunnar Eliasson of KTH Stockholm. Paper prepared October 1995.

UK R&D Scoreboard 1996. Published in June 1996 by Company Reporting Ltd of Edinburgh. URN 96/31 ISSN 1358-6351

The Role of the European Commission in Funding Research and Technological Development. AIRTO Paper 96/1.

Innovation

Innovation Policies – An International Perspective, edited by Gerry Sweeney who was then Chairman of the 6CP. Published by Frances Pinter (Publishers) Ltd in 1985. ISBN 0-86187-574-5

Review of DTI Industrial Support. Joint Report by the Treasury and the DTI. Published in August 1985.

Academics and Entrepreneurs by Richard Stankiewicz. Published in 1986 by Frances Pinter. ISBN 0-86187-582-6

Innovation, Entrepreneurs and Regional Development by G P Sweeney. Published in 1987 by Frances Pinter. ISBN 0-86187-647-4

Innovation and Industrial Strength by Joan Cox and Herbert Kriegbaum. Published in 1989 by the Policy Studies Institute. ISBN 0-85374-458-0

The Innovation Review. A Report to the Secretary of State by the Central Unit of the DTI. Published on 25 January 1991.

Innovation: Support for Technology Audits. Guidelines for Applicants. Published in 1991 by the DTI.

Innovation: Support for Industrial Units. Guidelines for Applicants. Published in 1991 by the DTI.

The First UK Innovation Lecture by Akio Morita. Published in February 1992 by the DTI. Ref DTI/Pub 901/30K/2/92

Technology Audits. A Guide to best practice for HEIs. Published in April 1992 by the DTI.

Innovation Technology and Change. Published in October 1992 and printed by the COI. Ref 10/92 O/N INDY J1843AR 30M

Getting the message across. Innovation Plans Handbook. Published in January 1993 by HMSO for the DTI. Ref INDY J1865RP.O/N 13828/A

'Innovate or liquidate' the CBI/DTI Report. Published on 27 January 1993.

Innovation Awards 1993. Published by the DTI and the British Business Press.

Realising our potential – A Strategy for Science, Engineering and Technology Cm 2250. Published on 26 May 1993 by the Office of Science and Technology

DTI to spend more on industrial innovation. DTI Press Notice P/93/283. Published on 26 May 1993.

Innovation The Report. Published in 1993 by the DTI and CBI.

The UK Innovation lecture 1993 by Sir Paul Girolami. Published in August 1993 by the DTI and COI. Ref INDYJ1871NE 20M

The UK Innovation lecture 1994 by Dr Lars Ramqvist. Published in February 1994 by the DTI. Ref DTI/Pub 1231/10K/2.94/NJ

The UK Innovation lecture 1995 by Dr Peter Williams. Published in February 1995 by the DTI. Ref DTI/Pub 1495/10K/2.95/NJ URN 95/550

The Power of Innovation by Min Basadur. Published in 1995 by Pitman Publishing. ISBN 0-273-61362-6

CBI/NatWest Innovation trends survey Issue 6 1995. Copyright NatWest/CBI 1995 ISBN 0-85201-500-3

The DTI's Support for Innovation. House of Commons papers 1994-95. Published in August 1995 by HMSO. ISBN 978-0100202351

The UK Innovation lecture 1996 by Dr William E Coyne. Published in March 1996 by the DTI. Ref URN 96/619

CBI/NatWest Innovation trends survey 1997. Published in 1997.

Selective Finance for Investment in England (SFI). Published in 2004. DTI/Pub 7266/6k/03/04/NP. URN 04/867.

Developing a Longer Term Strategy

The European Challenge 1992 The benefits of a Single Market by Paolo Cecchini. Published in 1988 by Wildwood Press. ISBN 0-7945-0613-0

Innovation and Short-Termism Conference. London 25 June 1990. Proceedings published by the DTI and Financial Times Conferences.

Promoting Innovation and Long Termism. Action programme of the Innovation Advisory Board, which advised the DTI. Published in October 1990.

European Competitiveness in the 21st century by Mike Cooley. Published by the Commission of the European Communities for the FAST programme, probably in 1990. (Text refers to results published in 1989)

R&D Short-Termism? Enhancing the R&D Performance of the UK team. Published in 1991 by Sciteb and the CBI. ISBN 1-873-24401-0

Britain in 2010 by Jim Northcott. Published in paperback by PSI Publishing in 1991. ISBN 0-85374-493-9

DTI Information Technology Futures. Published in December 1991 by Butler Cox.

Pressures and trends in British Space R&D. Private note by Christine Hewitt in October 1992.

Global Scenarios 1992-2020. Published in April 1993 by Shell Group Planning. Ref PL 93 S 04

Made in Europe. A Four Nations Best Practice Study. Published in November 1994 by IBM/London Business School. ISBN 0-902598-02-3

Open Futures. The OU's strategic priorities 2004-2008. Published in May 2004 by the Open University.

Emerging Technologies and Technology Foresight

Industrial Technology Trends and Issues. White Paper published in 1988 by MITI, Japan.

Research Foresight by Ben R Martin and John Irvine. Published by Pinter Publishers in 1989. ISBN 0-86187-510-9

Key Technologies. Turbulent Changes in Industry as a Result of Innovative Dynamics by Heinrich Revermann and Philipp Sonntag. Published in 1989. ISBN 3-8007-1516-3

Emerging Technologies: A Survey of Technical and Economic Opportunities. Published in 1990 by the US Department of Commerce.

Critical Technologies Plan, 1990. Published by the US Department of Defense and printed at the US Government Printing Office.

Commerce ACTS: Advanced Civilian Technology Strategy. Published in November 1993 by the US Department of Commerce.

Research Foresight and the Exploitation of the Science Base. Published in March 1993 by HMSO for the Cabinet Office. ISBN 0-11-430082-8

ACOST Working Group on Emerging and Generic Technologies. Report produced on 28 July 1993.

Europe: Funding for the Fourth Framework Programme for Research and Technological Development (1994-1998) Published in 1994 by the Office of Science and Technology.

Les 100 technologies clés pour l'industrie française à l'horizon 2000. Published in Paris, France for the Ministère de l'Industrie in July 1995. ISSN 0767-5380

Foresight. Consultation on the next round of the Foresight programme. Published in March 1998 by the DTI. Ref DTI/Pub 3284/50K/3/98/NP. URN 98/628

Managing the budget for the NMS

Measuring up to the Competition Cm 728. Published in 1989 by HMSO.

National Measurement System: introduction for users and contractors. Published in 1992 by the DTI.

Measurement and Technology Support Budget: information and guidance for contractors. Published in 1992 by the DTI.

House of Commons Committee of Public Accounts. The termination of the PFI contract for the National Physical Laboratory. Fifteenth Report of Session 2006-07. HC 359. Published on 13 March 2007.

Small firms Use of Technology

Small Firms Merit Award for Research and Technology (SMART). Published in 1990 by the DTI. Ref DTI/Pub 263/20K/6/90

The SMART Scheme Evaluation Report by the Assessment Unit of the DTI. Published in January 1991 by the DTI.

Identifying and Exploiting New Market Opportunities. Published in July 1993 by the DTI and COI. Ref INDYJ060854NJ

Business Link. A supplement to the prospectus. Published in August 1993 by the DTI. Ref DTI/Pub 1137/10K/8 93

Small Firms in Britain 1994. Published in 1994 by HMSO for the DTI. ISBN 0-11-51575-6

Science Connections. A Guide to Leading Organisations Promoting Science, Engineering and Technology. Published in March 1994 by the Office of Science and Technology. ISBN 0-7115-0267-6

The SPUR and SMART Awards. Rewarding innovation and excellence in research and technology. Published in May 1994 by the DTI. Ref DTI/Pub/1295/5.94/NP

An Evaluation of Support for Products under Research (SPUR) by the Assessment Unit of the DTI. Published in June 1994 by DTI URN 94/514

An Evaluation of the Small Firms Merit Award for Research and Technology (SMART) by the Assessment Unit of the DTI. Published in November 1994 by the DTI URN 94/644

Analysis of Experience in the Use of Verifiable Objectives. Report EUR 15634 EN. Published in 1994 by the European Commission. ISBN 92-826-8175-0

DTI Management and Technology Services Division wallet with leaflets. Published in 1995 by the DTI

Competitiveness. Helping smaller firms. Published in May 1995 by the DTI. Ref URN 95/663 DTI/Pub 1576/10K/5.95NP

Les Centres de Ressources Technologiques pour l'innovation dans les PME. Published in February 1995 in Paris, France by the Ministère de l'Enseignement supérieur et de la recherche

Joining Forces. A strategic issue for Business. Published in April 1995 by TWI. Ref TTS.296.04/95

Management advice for Industry

Managing into the 90s. Published in October 1989 by the DTI and COI. Ref 10/89 Dd 8221674 INDY J0978NE

Managing in the 90s. Total Quality Management and Effective Leadership Published in October 1991 by DTI. Ref DTI/Pub 1257/20K/3.94AR

Managing in the 90s. Best Practice Benchmarking. Published in January 1992 and reprinted in November 1994 by the DTI URN 94/917

Managing in the 90s. Product Data Management. Published in April 1994 by the DTI. Ref DTI/Pub 1294/3K/4/94

Winning in the 90s. The DTI strategy road show. Maidstone May 1994.

Inside UK Enterprise. 1994 Edition. Published by the DTI

Managing in the 90s. Business planning – a quick guide. Published in August 1994 by the DTI.

Managing in the 90s. Making information work for you. Published in December 1994 by the DTI. Ref DTI/Pub 1473/10K/12/94 URN 95/508

Tomorrow's Best Practice. Published in December 1994 by the Foundation for Manufacturing and Industry, DTI, and the IBM Consulting Group. ISBN 1-85979-008-9

Managing for Success. A self-assessment workbook. Published in 1995 by the DTI as part of Managing in the 90s.

Today's support for Tomorrow's winners. A briefing pack prepared by DTI's MTS Division. Published in 1995 by the DTI URN 95/909

Manufacturing winners. Published in June 1995 by the DTI.

Service in Britain. How do we measure up? Published in July 1995 by Severn Trent plc. ISBN 0-95-262-324-2

The Learning Organization: Making it Happen, Making it Work. PRISM Third Quarter 1995. Published by Arthur D Little

Quality and Striving for Excellence

Total Quality Management and Effective Leadership. Published in October 1991 by the DTI. Reprinted in 1995. Ref DTI/Pub 1555/20K/5.95 AR

The Quality Gurus. Published in October 1991 by the DTI

BS 5750/ISO 9000/EN 29000: 1987 A positive contribution to better business. Published in January 1992 by the DTI

The European Quality Award 1992 Rank Xerox. The Submission document, published by Rank Xerox in 1992.

Quality Circles. Published in March 1992 by the DTI.

The case for costing quality. Published in March 1992 by the DTI. Ref DTI/Pub 1156/5K/12.94 AR URN 94/638

Lean Enterprise Benchmarking Project Conference on 17 November 1992. Conference papers published by Andersen Consulting.

Presentation of first UK Quality Awards in UK Quality December 1994 Published by the British Quality Foundation.

How Rover Group became World Class. Case study in UK Quality magazine. March 1995

Small Business Total Quality by Neil Huxtable of Peratec. Published in 1995 by Chapworth and Hall. ISBN 0-412-60270-9

The European Way to Excellence by T W Hardjono, S ten Have and W D ten Have. Produced and designed by European Quality Productions Ltd on behalf of EFQM and the European Commission. ISBN 1-901305-007

Kaizen The Right Approach to Continuous Improvement. By Ken C E Lewis. Published in 1995 by IFS International. ISBN 1-85907-021-3

Purchasers and BS EN ISO 9000. Published in 1995 by HMSO for the DTI. Ref URN 95/763

Assessing Business Excellence by Les Porter and Steve Tanner. Published in 1996 by Butterwort-Heinemann. ISBN 0-7506-2479-5

Towards Business Excellence. Published in 1998 by the British Quality Foundation.

The Competitiveness White Papers

Competitiveness Helping Business to win. Published in May 1994 by HMSO Cm 2563 ISBN 0-10-125632-9

Competitiveness Helping Business to win. A Summary. Published in May 1994 by the DTI. Ref DTI/Pubs 1303/130K/5.94.NJ

Competitiveness How the best UK companies are Winning. Joint CBI/DTI report. Published in 1994 by the DTI.

Competitiveness Forging Ahead. Published in May 1995 by HMSO Cm 2867 ISBN 0-10-128672-4

Competitiveness Forging Ahead. A Summary. Published in May 1995 by the DTI. Ref DTI/Pub 1575/20K/5.95NP

Competitiveness Creating the enterprise centre of Europe. Published in June 1996 by HMSO. Cm 3300 ISBN 0-10-133002-2

Competing in the Global Economy – The Innovation Challenge. DTI Economics Paper No. 7. Published in November 2003. DTI/Pub 7104/0.5k/01/04/RP URN 03/1394

Annual Reviews and Expenditure Plans

Trade and Industry 1992 The Government's Expenditure Plans 1992-93 to 1994-95. Published in February 1992 by HMSO. Cm 1904 ISBN 0-10-119042-5

Annual Review of Government Funded R&D 1992. Published by HMSO. ISBN 0-11-430083-3

Trade and Industry 1993 The Government's Expenditure Plans 1993-94 to 1995-96. Published in February 1993 by HMSO. Cm 2204 ISBN 0-10-122042-1

Annual Review of Government Funded R&D 1993. Published by HMSO. ISBN 0-11-430062-6

MINIS 1994: The Overview. Published by the DTI to be read in conjunction with Cm 2504 (below)

Trade and Industry 1994 The Government's Expenditure Plans 1994-95 to 1996-97. Published in March 1994 by HMSO. Cm 2504 ISBN 0-10-125042-8

Trade and Industry 1995 The Government's Expenditure Plans 1995-96 to 1997-98. Published in March 1995 by HMSO. Cm 2804 ISBN 0-10-128042-4

DTI 1995 Annual Report. Published in March 1996 by the DTI. Ref URN 96/117 DTI/Pub 1822/10K/3/96/NP

The Civil Service Yearbook 1995. Published by HMSO. ISBN 0-11-701990-9

The Civil Service Yearbook 1996. Published by HMSO. ISBN 0-11-430136-0

Management in the Civil Service

Development of Quality of Service Standards. Published in 1992 by the Cabinet Office. Executive Summary, Main Report and Case Studies, Approaches, Techniques and Definitions. ISBN 0-7115-0244-7.

Results Through People. Published in March 1993 by the DTI. Ref DTI/Pub 10741/5.5K/3/93.

A Guide to Working with Ministers. Published in March 1994 by the DTI for staff. Ref DTI/Pub 864/5K/3/94

DTI – The Way We Work. Published in June 1994 by the DTI. Ref DTI/Pub 1308/11K/6.94/NP

Briefing Notes on Current DTI Issues. Published in June 1994 by the DTI Information and Library Services.

An Introduction to Investors in People. A Civil Service perspective. Published by the Cabinet Office. ISBN 0-7115-0278-1 (undated, presumed 1994)

Results through Quality. Published in March 1995 by the DTI for staff. Ref DTI/Pub 1522/5.5K/3/95

DTI Services for business. Published by the DTI in February 1995. Ref DTI/Pub 1503/25K/2/95

DTI Guide for Business. Published in March 1995. Ref DTI/PUB 1501/50K/2/95

Taking Forward Investors in People in the Civil Service. Published in December 1995 by the Cabinet Office. Ref Dd8439294 12/95 77569

Leading for Quality Ideas for Action. Published in 1994 by the Cabinet Office. ISBN 0-7115-0274-9

Quality in Policy Areas. Published in 1996 by the DTI. Ref DTI/Pub 1714/0.75K/1.96NP URN 96/503

Measuring Quality Improvements. Published in 1996 by the Cabinet Office. ISBN 0-7115-0309-5

Job Evaluation for DTI Jobs in the Senior Civil Service 'Majic" Published in March 1996 by the DTI.

The Civil Service: Continuity and Change Cm 2627. Published in July 1994 by HMSO. ISBN 0-10-126272-8

Fifth Report from the House of Commons Treasury and Civil Service Committee. The Role of the Civil Service. HC(1993-94). Published in November 1994.

The Civil Service: Taking Forward Continuity and Change Cm 2748. Published in January 1995 by HMSO. ISBN 0-10-127482-3

The Public Sector MBA Programme. Published in 1995 by Cranfield University, Manchester Business School and the Civil Service College.

Key Contacts Department of Trade and Industry. Published in August 1996 by the DTI. Ref DTI/PUB 2385/50K/8/96/NIE URN 96/47

Guidance on Guidance An index to useful documents. Published in February 1996 by the Office of Public Service.

Politico's Guide to How to be a Civil Servant by Martin Stanley. Revised
Second Edition published in September 2000 by Politico's Publishing.
ISBN 1842750976

Internet References

National Physical Laboratory
www.npl.co.uk

Department for Business, Enterprise & Regulatory Reform
www.berr.gov.uk
Department for Business Innovation and Skills
www.bis.gov.uk

Jacques Vert
www.jacques-vert.co.uk

Liberty of London
www.liberty.co.uk

John Cleese
www.johncleesetraining.com

Oxford University Bodleian Library
www.bodley.ox.ac.uk

United Oxford and Cambridge University Club
www.oxfordandcambridgeclub.co.uk

SPATS programme
www.nationalschool.gov.uk/programmes/programme.asp?id=18261

ADAS
www.adas.co.uk

PERA
www.pera.com

Grob gliding company
www.grob-aerospace.net/index.php?id=527

Teaching Company Scheme and Knowledge Transfer Partnerships
www.ktponline.org.uk/strategy/history.aspx

Teaching Company Scheme in Hong Kong
www.itf.gov.hk/eng/TCS.asp

Oxford University Computing Laboratory and Professor Leslie Fox
www.comlab.ox.ac.uk/endre.suli/fox/

Esprit projects CIM-OSA and CNMA from the Cordis database
cordis.europa.eu/search/index.cfm?dbname=proj

National Centre for Information Technology (NCC)
www.ncc.co.uk

Ian Cook Piling
www.cookpiling.co.uk

Shetland boats
www.shetlandboats.co.uk

David Piper Boats
www.piperowners.co.uk/piperowners_history.htm

Kewill Systems plc
www.kewill.com

British Midland accident at Kegworth
en.wikipedia.org/wiki/Kegworth_air_disaster

Six Countries Programme
www.6cp.net

Iittala Glass, Finland
www.iittala.com

Business Futures Network
businessfutures.com

Technology Foresight
www.foresight.gov.uk/
cordis.europa.eu/foresight/home.html

MITI White Paper: Trends and Future Tasks in Industrial Technology
Made available by the US Defense Technical Information Center
http://handle.dtic.mil/100.2/ADA347562

The National Measurement System
www.dti.gov.uk/innovation/nms/index.html

TWI – The Welding Institute
www.twi.co.uk

The Civil Service Code
www.civilservice.gov.uk/iam/codes/cscode/index.asp

Office of Public Sector Information and Crown Copyright
www.opsi.gov.uk/advice/
www.opsi.gov.uk/click-use/index.htm

How to be a Civil Servant
www.civilservant.org.uk

British Quality Foundation
www.quality-foundation.co.uk

Winemaking
www.pcurtis.com/homewine.htm

Concorde and the Supersonic Dream
www.pbs.org/wgbh/nova/concorde/

LIST OF ABBREVIATIONS AND ACRONYMS

5YFL Five Year Forward Look at DTI
6CP Six Countries Programme

ACARD Advisory Council for Applied Research and Development
ACOST Advisory Council on Science and Technology
ADAS Agricultural Development Advisory Service
AERE Atomic Energy Research Establishment, at Harwell
AIRTO Association of Independent Research and Technology
  Organisations
AMT Advanced Manufacturing Technology
AMTRI AMT Research Institute
A/S Assistant Secretary
ATP Advanced Technology Programme

BCS British Computer Society
BERR Department for Business Enterprise and Regulatory Reform
BFN Business Futures Network
BIS Department for Business Innovation and Skills
BPR Buckingham Palace Road
BPR Business Process Re-engineering
BQF British Quality Foundation
BRITE Basic Research in Industrial Technologies
BSI British Standards Institution

CAD Computer Aided Design
CADCAM CAD and Computer Aided Manufacturing
CADCentre CAD Centre near Cambridge
CADDETC CADCAM Data Exchange Technical Centre, at Leeds
CAPM Computer Aided Production Management
CAST Chief Advisor on Science and Technology
CATRA Cutlery and Allied Trades Research Association
CBI Confederation of British Industry
CEng Chartered Engineer
CERN Conseil Européen pour la Recherche Nucléaire Laboratory (in
  Geneva)
CEST Centre for Exploitation of Science and Technology

CHI CHI Research Inc of the USA
CIM Computer Integrated Manufacture
CIMAC A demonstration following CIMAP and sited at the NEL
CIMAP The DTI MAP Event held at Birmingham in 1986
CIM-OSA ESPRIT CIM Open Systems Architecture project
CNMA ESPRIT Communications Network for Manufacturing
  Applications project
ComCentre UK Centre for Communications Standards
CoSIRA Council For Small Industries in Rural Areas in Great Britain.
CREST EC Committee for Research and Evaluation of Science and
  Technology
CSE Centre for Software Engineering
CSG Chief Scientist Group of the Department of the Environment
CSR Centre for Software Reliability

DASL NPL's Data Approximation Subroutine Library
DES Department of Education and Science
DIUS Department for Innovation, Universities and Skills
DOD Department of Defence, in the USA
DOE Department of the Environment
DOI Department of Industry
DPhil Doctor of Philosophy, at Oxford University
DTI Department of Trade and Industry
DWP Divisional Work Programme

EC European Commission
ED Employment Department
EDS Electronic Data Systems
EEC European Economic Community
EFQM European Foundation for Quality Management
EII Economic Importance Indicator
EMUG European MAP User Group
ENE '88i International Enterprise Networking Event held in Baltimore
  USA in 1988
EO Executive Officer
EQA European Quality Award
ESPRIT European Strategic Programme for Research in Information
  Technologies

FAST Forecasting and Assessment in Science and Technology
FBCS Fellow of the British Computer Society
FIRA Furniture Industry Research Association
FRS Fellow of the Royal Society
FTSE100 Financial Times Stock Exchange – main 100 companies

GDP Gross Domestic Product
GO-EM Government Office for the East Midlands
GO-ER Government Office for the Eastern Region
GO-L Government Office for London
GO-M Government Office for Merseyside
GO-NE Government Office for the North East
GO-NW Government Office for the North West
GO-SE Government Office for the South East
GO-WM Government Office for the West Midlands
GO-YH Government Office for Yorkshire and Humberside
GP General Practitioner

HEI Higher Education Institution
HEO Higher Executive Officer
HMSO Her Majesty's Stationery Office
HPTO Higher Professional and Technical Officer
HQ Headquarters
HSO Higher Scientific Officer

IAB Innovation Advisory Board
IAB ATC IAB Action Team on Communications
ICSE Inter-Departmental Committee on Software Engineering
ICSESRS ICSE Task Group on Safety Related Software
IEC International Electrotechnical Commission
IED Information Engineering Directorate
IEE Institution of Electrical Engineers
IGDS Integrated Graduate Development Scheme
IGES Initial Graphics Exchange Specification
IKBS Intelligent Knowledge-based Systems
ILAN Industrial Local Area Network
IMA Institute of Mathematics and its Applications
IMechE Institution of Mechanical Engineers
IPC Innovation Policy Committee
IPCS Institution of Professional Civil Servants
IProdE Institution of Production Engineers
IT Information Technology
ITAB IT Advisory Board
ITS Innovation and Technology Support budget

JFIT Joint Framework in IT of the DTI and SERC

KTP Knowledge Transfer Partnership

LEC Local Enterprise Company
LGC Laboratory of the Government Chemist
LTSG Long Term Studies Group
LTSG Long Term Steering Group
LTSU Longer Term Studies Unit

MAFF Ministry of Agriculture, Fisheries and Food
MAP Microelectronics Applications Programme
MAP Manufacturing Automation Protocol
MAS Manufacturing Advisory Service
MBA Master of Business Administration
MCDA Multi-Criteria Decision Analysis
MEE Mechanical and Electrical Engineering Division
MINIS Management Information System for Ministers
MISP Microelectronics Industry Support Programme
MIT Manufacturing and Information Technologies Division
MITI The Japanese Ministry for International Trade and Industry
MMI Man Machine Interface
MMT Mechanical Engineering and Manufacturing Technology Division
MOD Ministry of Defence
MP Member of Parliament
MRPII Materials Requirements Planning software
MSc Master of Science
MTIRA Machine Tool Industry Research Association
MTM Manufacturing Technology and Materials Division
MTS Management and Technology Services Division

NACCB National Accreditation Council for Certification Bodies
NAG Numerical Algorithms Group
NAMAS National Measurement Accreditation Service
NAO National Audit Office
NBS National Bureau of Standards in the USA
NCC National Centre for IT at Manchester
NEDC National Economic Development Council
NEDO National Economic Development Office
NEL National Engineering Laboratory at East Kilbride
NERC Natural Environment Research Council
NHS National Health Service
NMI National Maritime Institute
NMS National Measurement System
NMSPU National Measurement System Policy Unit
NPL National Physical Laboratory

OECD Organisation for Economic Co-operation and Development
OSI Open Systems Interconnection

OST Office of Science and Technology of the Cabinet Office
OU Open University

PDES Product Data Exchange Specification
PERA Production Engineering Research Association
PES Public Expenditure Survey
PFI Private Finance Initiative
PhD Doctor of Philosophy
PIRA Research Association for the paper and packaging industry
PPDS Product and Process Development Scheme
PPTO Principal Professional and Technical Officer
PQ Parliamentary Question
PRA Paint Research Association
PREST Programme of Policy Research in Engineering, Science and
  Technology at the University of Manchester
PS Policy Score
PSI Policy Studies Institute
PSO Principal Scientific Officer

QDE Quality, Design and Education Division

R&D Research and Development
RAL Rutherford Appleton Laboratory
ROAME Rationale, Objectives, Appraisal, Monitoring, Evaluation
ROP Realising our Potential – A strategy for Science, Engineering and
  Technology
RTD Research and Technology Development
RTO Research and Technology Organisations
RTP Research and Technology Requirements and Perspectives Division
RTP Research and Technology Perspectives Division
RTP Research and Technology Policy Division
RTS Research and Technology Requirements and Space Division

S&T Science and Technology
SAST Strategic Analysis in Science and Technology
SEO Senior Executive Officer
SERC Science and Engineering Research Council
SET Science, Engineering and Technology
SFDC Shop Floor Data Collection
SfI Support for Innovation scheme
SFI Selective Finance for Investment in England
SFTES Small Firms Technical Enquiry Service
SMART Small Firms Merit Award for Research and Technology
SME Small and Medium Enterprises
SME Society of Manufacturing Engineers (in the USA)

SO Scientific Officer
SOGAME Ad Hoc Senior Officials Group on Advanced Manufacturing
  Equipment
SOGITS Senior Officials Group for IT Standardisation
SPATS Senior Professional Administrative Training Scheme
SPEAR Supporting Programme for Evaluation of Applied Research
SPRU Science Policy Research Unit at the University of Sussex at
  Brighton
SPS Strategic Planning Society
SPSO Senior Principal Scientific Officer
SPTO Senior Professional and Technical Officer
SPUR Support for Products Under Research
SQMAC Standards, Quality and Measurement Advisory Committee
SRAMA Spring Research and Manufacturers' Association
SSO Senior Scientific Officer
STARTS Software Tools for Application to large Real-Time Systems
STEP Short Term Experience Postings scheme
STIP Systems Technology and Integration Programme
SWOT Strength Weakness Opportunity and Threat analysis

TCS Teaching Company Scheme
TEC Training and Enterprise Council
TEED Training and Enterprise Division of the Department of
  Employment
TNC The Networking Centre
TNO Technical Policy Division of the Netherlands
TOP Technical Office Protocol
TQM Total Quality Management

UNECE United Nations Economic Commission for Europe
UOCUC United Oxford and Cambridge University Club

VDE Society of German Electrotechnicians
VDI Society of German Engineers
VLSI Very Large Scale Integration or 'chip' technology

WSL Warren Spring Laboratory at Stevenage